METAL DEVO

PASTOR BOB BEEMAN
with Thomas Nørgård

SANCTUARY

PUBLISHING

METAL DEVO

ISBN-13: 978-1986559027 Paperback
ISBN-10: 1986559025 Paperback

Cover and Interior design by Steve Kuhn, www.stevekuhndesign.com

WE ARE METAL.
WE ARE FAMILY.

It's been the joy of my life to be on the forefront of the Christian Metal scene for over three decades. This is my family. It's YOUR family!

As a "father" in this movement, I have been involved with the bands, festivals, teaching, speaking, podcasting, and writing. My focus has always been to provide you with the tools you need to get to know Jesus Christ personally and to grow in that relationship. My travels have taken me around the world many times. I have met you at concerts, festivals, weekend retreats, pubs, and coffee shops. In the United States, Sweden, Mexico, Switzerland, China, Italy, Israel, Portugal, Denmark and around the world the main question is the same: "How can I know Jesus Christ more fully and intensely?" That was the motivation behind this daily devotional.

Make this book a daily event. Your "appointment with God" will help you find a greater intimacy with the God who made you, and give you some life-tools in your walk with the Lord. I am excited to take this journey with you!

Pastor Bob Beeman

SPECIAL THANKS

I am forever grateful to the people who have helped put METAL DEVO together. I love you all very much!

Thomas Nørgård (Denmark)
Thanks for spending 3 months writing with me!
This was our second book. Your dedication to detail,
your knowledge of the Word, and your love for Heavy
Metal has made you the perfect writing partner!

Proofreading and Composition Support
Christopher Dorman (Colorado USA)
Rafael de Carvalho da Cunha Sequeira (Portugal)

Manuscript Construction:
Daniel Berg (Sweden)
Julie Allart (France)

Layout:
Steve Kuhn Design (Oregon USA)

Front Cover Photo:
Michael Bolli (Switzerland)

Back Cover Artwork:
Tony Sobota (Tennessee USA)

Metal Bible Coordination:
Carl Johannes Jonsson (Sweden)

WHAT IS TRUTH?

P ontius Pilate, the Roman governor of Judea, posed this question to Jesus of Nazareth over 2,000 years ago. Pilate was skeptical, sarcastic really, of Christ's claim His mission was to testify to the truth, and that all who are interested in truth listen to Him. Pilate, like most people, thought truth to be relative, subjective, elusive...ultimately unknowable. What you think is truth another might see as a lie, right? Yet, if we dare be honest with ourselves, we all secretly hunger for truth– truth in life, truth in love, truth in our governments, truth in our worldview, truth in understanding our purpose and our destiny. This hunger for truth can make us so desperate that, if we aren't careful, we fall for a lie. Doubt me?

Have you ever seen the MTV show "Catfished?" This show is a series of (mostly) super sad stories of people being tricked in on-line relationships to think a relationship exists when it really doesn't...tricked by someone pretending to be someone/something they aren't, pretending to have feelings for their victim that they don't. Isn't it sad (and more than a little ironic) that something so painful can happen in an "information age?" I mean, it is so easy to log on, go to Google and find out SOMETHING about EVERYTHING, right? Yet, folks are "catfished" all the time—led to believe a lie. Have you ever stopped and asked yourself WHY so many seem so vulnerable to being tricked like this? There are probably lots of reasons, but for me I think there are two primary reasons: a legitimate hunger for real, meaningful relationship (or "true" relationship) in an age of superficial ones, as well as a desire for meaning, a sense that our lives are important, that we can make a difference.

Now, I just said that we live in an age of superficial relationships. Disagree with me? Well, how many "friends" do you have on Facebook or followers on Instagram you've never met? Of your Facebook/Instagram friends that you personally KNOW, how many of them would you miss if you never heard from them again? For your closest friends, how many of them are you completely, totally, unreservedly honest with? Are there *any*? Do you actually have *anyone* in your life you would call a close friend— and when I say a "close friend" I mean someone that, if you needed $20 and they didn't have it would go sell a pint of their blood to give you the money? I can't tell you how often I've been contacted by someone who has dozens...maybe hundreds of "friends," and feels totally isolated, alone. Maybe this describes you. For folks suffering like this a real connection with a real person is all they hunger for. But isn't that something we all need? Don't all of us want relationships that will survive crisis, disagreements, and total, brutal honesty? What kind of a difference would it make in your life to have a real, personal connection with a real person? Someone who doesn't know *about* you but really, deeply knows YOU— and actively pursues a relationship with you anyway?

As important as relationship is to us, though, I wonder if the hunger for meaning isn't even more important. Think about this, ok? Have you ever dared to ask yourself "why am I here?" If not, why not? Could it be because you're afraid of the answer? What if you search for meaning and conclude that your life is meaningless...that there is no great purpose for you being alive at all—that, in the end, your life has no value to anyone but yourself? So, if we are honest with ourselves, we are all desperate for meaning and at the same time terrified of asking the question because we can't face the possibility our lives are meaningless. The result? A life void of purpose, of meaning...a life filled with constantly looking past what is in front of us while we search for that ever elusive "something" that will make everything else make sense. We wander from job to job, relationship to relationship, all in an effort to answer the question "why am I here" yet the answer eludes us. Why?

Because we are looking in the wrong place!

This hunger for truth, for real relationship, and for meaning can't be resolved by looking at ourselves. To do so is to like looking for a needle in a haystack. It is, as that old song says, like looking for love in all the wrong places. Until we go to the source of Truth—God Himself—we will never find answers to these most perplexing of problems.

That's right...the answer is God. Whether we like it or not, or care to admit it, we are creatures who were made by a Creator, and until we figure that relationship out, nothing in life—NOTHING—will make any sense.

But where can we go to get good, trustworthy, reliable information about God? How can we avoid being "catfished" into believing in a god that doesn't actually exist? Can't we just Google it? Oh, I'm sure you can ask all kinds of questions on Google about God. Unfortunately, you'll get hundreds/thousands of answers, and be no closer to Truth, or having real relationship or knowing what your purpose in life really is.

To get accurate information about anyone you really need to meet them, hang out with them, and see them at their best and their worst. Well, we can't really do that with God. Yet, He has left us the Bible, His written Word, in which He reveals to all who search for Him who He truly is *and* who we really are. I mean, how can one have real relationship with another without knowing themselves? Yet, as amazing as the Bible is, God did not stop there. He wanted us to have as complete a picture of Him as is possible, as much as our finite minds could handle, so He sent His Son, Jesus Christ, to live on this earth and make it clear to all who want to know who God is just how much He loves us.

If you read the Bible, you will learn that humanity is broken. We are all selfish people who, more than anything else, want what we want when we want it. No matter how old we get, until we have a right relationship with God, we are all like two year olds—throwing a tantrum because we wanted chocolate and were given an apple. The Bible calls this "sin." This sin separates us from God, and until we see how desperately we need God, we will never know real love nor will we ever understand why we are here.

In the Bible you will find that this God made you on purpose and that to know that purpose and live it out requires a relationship with Him. But how can we who are so sinful have a relationship with God? How can we get past our sin, our selfishness, to get to God?

Jesus Christ is the answer our souls crave. In His death on the cross He paid the price for your sin to restore your relationship with your Creator. Yep, the only thing keeping you from a relationship with God is your sin, and through a personal relationship with Jesus of Nazareth your bondage to sin will be forever broken, you will know forgiveness, your relationship with your Creator will be permanently restored, and you will know finally and forever why you are here.

Eternal Love and real purpose—what we so desperately crave—can only be found through a relationship with Jesus Christ.

So, what keeps us from a relationship with Christ? Our unwillingness to admit the obvious: that we are sinners in need of a savior and that we owe a debt to God we can never pay on our own. There is no way we could ever build a stairway to heaven and get to God on our own. Sin has created a gulf that no amount of good deeds could ever bridge; only in the sacrifice of Christ can we who are sinners be forgiven and our relationship with God restored.

Jesus is the only way to relationship with God, and the only way to this relationship is to surrender your life to Christ. Yes, if you want to be FREE from the bondage of sin you must confess your sin and surrender to Christ! The only real freedom we can experience is through Christ! Why? Because in Christ what enslaves us—sin—is vanquished, and in its place a love that surpasses all other human experience is known.

The Metal Devos are designed to enhance your understanding of the Bible, and to encourage and strengthen you as you seek Him. Please use these devotionals as a companion to your Bible reading.

God has promised to reward all who earnestly seek Him, and if you are searching for Truth, for relationship, for meaning and purpose through the Bible as assisted by the Metal Devos, I am confident you will find what your soul longs for.

I pray your searching leads you home to your God and to the salvation that can only be found through His Son, Jesus Christ.

Soli deo Gloria!
Pastor Christopher Dorman
Sanctuary International

DAY 1

*Hope is the power of being cheerful in circumstances
that we know to be desperate.*

G K CHESTERTON

*And endurance develops strength of character, and
character strengthens our confident hope of salvation.*

ROMANS 5:4

H ave you noticed that when you feel hope, life seems to get a lot better? When going through pain, you know it will disappear one day, but when you feel happy, you feel as if your happiness will increase a thousand fold and last forever. As we grow in our relationship with Christ, we also grow in hope. We get a stronger focus on the Kingdom of God and care more about the things that are on God's heart. As a result, we have even more hope since we're focused on the coming of his Kingdom.

His hope can be present in your life every day, if you choose to allow it. Belonging to Christ means always having his hope, because nothing can separate us from him. Our destiny is eternal glory. What can destroy this hope? What could happen in your life that could ruin it? Nothing! No matter how badly our lives go, we'll still have the hope of eternity to live for. Should we lose our lives, then the hope simply becomes reality for us!

Hope is therefore a constant factor in our lives here on earth. And the hope we live by is an amazing testimony for the people around us. When they see the hope we have within us, they'll realize the awesome power it gives us to endure the difficulties of life.

THINK ABOUT IT!

Is your life filled with hope?

DAY 2

I was in a very crazy spot in my life. Some people can call it rock bottom, but everything happened the way it was supposed to happen, in the sense that it made everything very real to me.
JOSH SCOGIN (NORMA JEAN, THE CHARIOT, 68)

Dear brothers and sisters, when troubles of any kind come your way, consider it an opportunity for great joy. For you know that when your faith is tested, your endurance has a chance to grow. So let it grow, for when your endurance is fully developed, you will be perfect and complete, needing nothing.
JAMES 1:2-4

There are times when life sucks. Really sucks. I have been at that place more than once. The feelings of hopelessness, despair, and confusion run wild. The joy of living seems to be replaced with heartache. And yet in the middle of all of this, James is telling us to "… consider it an opportunity for great joy." Seriously? That's the last thing I'm feeling. James, however, is talking about the end of the trial, not the beginning or the middle of it. He wants us to see the whole picture. "… when your faith is tested, your endurance has a chance to grow. So let it grow." Whoa! Easy for you to say! I don't usually want to endure; I simply want God to fix the problem so I can feel better.

But, that's the point! God wants me to fully develop. It's like carrying a baby around for the first 5 years of his life. If you don't force him to walk, he will never learn! And walking is important! "…when your endurance is fully developed, you will be perfect and complete, needing nothing." I certainly want that. It isn't easy to go through difficult times. But when we do, it's great to keep the end result in perspective!

THINK ABOUT IT!

Is it difficult for you to put things into perspective when you go through trials?

DAY 3

We would never be able to know God if he didn't reveal himself to us. God has revealed himself through nature, scripture, mind, and by putting his law in our hearts. He's so far above us that we could never reach any knowledge about him on our own. Sin has distorted our image of him and damaged the natural law inside of us. Only through his revelation are we able to know him.

It's so amazing that God has actually made a way for us to know him. He speaks to us in the same way an adult would explain things to a child. Creating understanding for a child involves getting down on their level, using simple language, and telling stories. The child may think he or she has the whole thing figured out, but the adult knows better. It's even sillier when an adult thinks he understands everything about God. Even after God came down to our level we still needed the Holy Spirit to lead us to truth.

Some of the wisest people throughout history have come to the conclusion that they know close to nothing. The wisest theologians have understood that, while trying to deal with the difficult questions of life, they were like children thinking they could understand everything worth knowing. 1 Corinthians 13:12 says, "Now we see things imperfectly, like puzzling reflections in a mirror, but then we will see everything with perfect clarity. All that I know now is partial and incomplete, but then I will know everything completely, just as God now knows me completely."

THINK ABOUT IT!

*Are you aware that you still have a lot to learn? Have you
purposely put yourself on the learning road to adventure?*

DAY 4

Now from my heart flows a living river, so gifted me by the tongues
of fire. I feel the gift so freely placed, now flowing through my veins.
Desperately I search for the answers, to the riddles I have so long
pondered. I will seek You, I will find You, I will seek You, I will know You.
LYRICS FROM "EN HAKKORE" BY THE BURIAL [IN THE TAKING OF FLESH]

Anyone who believes in me may come and drink! For the scriptures
declare, "Rivers of living water will flow from his heart."
JOHN 7:38

When the Spirit of truth comes, he will guide you into all truth.
JOHN 16:13

How would you define "A Christian?" A basic definition would be "one who follows the teachings of Jesus Christ." But that would only be part of the story! When you ask Jesus into your heart, an amazing and quite supernatural thing takes place. His very Spirit takes up residence inside of you. God adopts you, you become His child, and He becomes your father. Spiritually speaking, Jesus' blood, the same blood that was shed on the cross for you, begins to flow through your veins. Like Father, like Son/Daughter.

But it doesn't stop there either. John 16 tells us that his Spirit now "…guides you into all truth." You have the very author of the Bible living inside of you, guiding you into the truth of his Word, and to life itself. Did you realize that? Many Christians live an ordinary life not understanding that they can allow the Holy Spirit to guide them. But it involves something important on your part. You need to allow him to do it! When you actually say "YES" to God moving in your heart, amazing things begin to happen!

THINK ABOUT IT!

Have you said "yes!" to the Holy Spirit working in your life?

DAY 5

*I knew about Him from an early age, but I had my own things
on my mind and not the things or thoughts of God.*
NICKO MCBRAIN (IRON MAIDEN)

*This is real love—not that we loved God, but that he loved
us and sent his Son as a sacrifice to take away our sins.*
1 JOHN 4:10

S o many of us have grown up in Christian or religious homes. Maybe your grandmother took you to church on Easter. Maybe a neighbor invited you to Sunday School at their church. Whatever your experience has been, I think all of us have had some sense that there may be a higher being out there that we need to connect with. You may be like Nicko and knew "about" Him at an early age, but never bothered to really connect with Him.

What makes Christianity different from other religions is that God is reaching down to us! From an early age, you may have had this sense that he is there…somewhere…trying to get your attention. Many have called God "The Hound Of Heaven." The English Anglican cleric John Stott said, "[My faith is] due to Jesus Christ himself, who pursued me relentlessly even when I was running away from him in order to go my own way. And if it were not for the gracious pursuit of the hound of heaven I would today be on the scrap-heap of wasted and discarded lives." It's interesting how many metal songs have religious overtones of some kind. Black metal has been known for its more occult infatuation. But we are all looking for something or someone larger than we are. It can be confusing! It's awesome to know that God is actually pursuing us!

THINK ABOUT IT!

Does The Hound of Heaven have your attention?

DAY 6

The real test of a saint is not one's willingness to preach the gospel, but one's willingness to do something like washing the disciples' feet—that is, being willing to do those things that seem unimportant in human estimation but count as everything to God.

OSWALD CHAMBERS

But among you it will be different. Whoever wants to be a leader among you must be your servant, and whoever wants to be first among you must become your slave. For even the Son of Man came not to be served but to serve others and to give his life as a ransom for many.

MATTHEW 20:26-28

T he Lord has big plans for you!" I have had people tell me that most of my life. And I have heard others receive the same encouragement. Some of those people are still struggling to do anything. They work at a job they hate, have a horrible relationship with their family, and hate life generally. What about those big plans from God? Did they miss something? YES! Besides having a calling to to "big things" for God, we also need to have the courage to get started! None of us start from the top. I am a farm boy from a very small town in rural Montana. The odds of doing anything significant were stacked against me. But I had to take the first step. And then the next one

The small and seemingly unimportant beginnings are a great test to reveal our true character and heart for the Lord. If we're serving him with the small things, then he will be faithful with the bigger things. Nothing is too small for us to do. Instead of lifting ourselves up, we have the opportunity to lift up each other. Even though Christ was worthy to sit on the throne of Heaven without ever serving anybody, he chose otherwise. He became a servant to us. It is his inspiring example that compels us to follow our passions and God's "big plans" for us!

THINK ABOUT IT!

Are you ready to follow God's "Big Plans" for you?

DAY 7

Englishmen learn Christ's law best in English. Moses heard
God's law in his own tongue; so did Christ's apostles.
JOHN WYCLIFFE

When I was with the Jews, I lived like a Jew to bring the Jews to
Christ....When I am with the Gentiles who do not follow the Jewish
law, I too live apart from that law so I can bring them to Christ....
When I am with those who are weak, I share their weakness, for
I want to bring the weak to Christ. Yes, I try to find common
ground with everyone, doing everything I can to save some.
1 CORINTHIANS 9:20-22

Historically, people have been afraid to take the Gospel into certain places. During the time of Wycliffe it was a very controversial thing to translate the Bible, as it's still controversial in some places of the world to play heavy metal with Christian lyrics. Though we absolutely need to preach the Gospel correctly, we don't have to worry about it breaking. The Gospel cannot be torn apart no matter where we take it.

When bringing the Gospel into new territory, we must neither ignore the tradition nor follow it completely. G.K. Chesterton has a good balance: "Whenever you remove any fence, always pause long enough to ask yourself, 'Why was it put there in the first place?'" When Martin Luther started the Reformation, he understood that you couldn't change everything at once, otherwise it would shatter. The Reformers weren't finished. They wanted us to continue, but still with one eye on the rich tradition of the church. We, the Christian metal-family, will bring the Gospel into every metal genre!

THINK ABOUT IT!

Do you enjoy the riches of Christianity's tradition, while
preaching a Gospel that speaks to today's culture?

DAY 8

*We learned to be completely dependent on God's grace
on the road. Often we didn't know how we'd get from
one town to the next, but somehow we always did.*
MICHAEL BLOODGOOD (BLOODGOOD)

*So don't worry about these things, saying, "What will we eat? What will
we drink? What will we wear?" These things dominate the thoughts of
unbelievers, but your heavenly Father already knows all your needs.*
MATTHEW 6:31-32

The year was 1987. We decided to have the very first Christian Metal Festival. Bands like Barren Cross, Guardian, Neon Cross, Deliverance, Bloodgood, and Holy Soldier headlined the fest. I remember Bloodgood pulling up in their old motorhome. It looked like it had been through a war. Not only did it carry the band, but their wives as well. They were just returning from a U.S. tour. They were exhausted. They told of countless churches ripping them off, and so many crooked promoters. But they were excited to say that God had provided for them in spite of the hardships.

Even though they were exhausted, their performance on stage that night was stellar! If you have the opportunity to check it out on YouTube, you will be blessed! I'd love to say that things have changed. But there are still a lot of bands struggling on the road to bring the Gospel message. For many, like Bloodgood, it remains a labor of love. I am thankful for all of these bands, especially the early ones who paved the way for the Christian Metal scene today!

THINK ABOUT IT!

How has the ministry of Christian metal affected you?

DAY 9

I believe that the Bible is God's inspired Word, his instruction
book for Christian living, and the history of his love for all of us.
ROB ROCK

All scripture is inspired by God and is useful to teach us what is
true and to make us realize what is wrong in our lives. It corrects
us when we are wrong and teaches us to do what is right.
2 TIMOTHY 3:16

How can I actually hear God?" Great question! Maybe you are asking the same thing. Did you know that God has been speaking for a few thousand years? In the Bible, from Genesis to Revelation, God spoke to great men and women of faith about his purpose, his desires, and his love for humanity. The Bible is a history book. It is a love story. It is an owner's manual for successful living. It is your personal link to the voice of God!

Many times when I sit down to read the Bible, I feel God's words jump off the page and into my heart. There are times when I wake up in the morning with a difficult question in my mind that he answers through a passage in the Bible during the day. It is amazing to me how many times he has used the Bible to communicate to me the deepest questions of my heart. It's not a coincidence. Why? Because the Bible is inspired by God for ALL generations. Past. Present. Future. It is as relevant now as it was when it was written. How exciting to know that the same words that have moved nations throughout history are the same words that move our hearts today!

THINK ABOUT IT!

Are you reading the Bible? Begin reading a few minutes a
day. Meditate on what you read during the day. You'll be
amazed at how much God speaks to you through his Word!

DAY 10

He who is not angry when there is just cause for anger is immoral.
Why? Because anger looks to the good of justice. And if you can
live amid injustice without anger, you are immoral as well as unjust.

THOMAS AQUINAS

You must not bow down to them or worship them, for
I, the Lord your God, am a jealous God who will not
tolerate your affection for any other gods.

EXODUS 20:5

The Bible describes God as being jealous and angry. While these emotions may seem strange for an almighty and all-powerful God to possess, they reflect how enormous his love for us is. He doesn't want us to serve anything or anyone else. Why? Because only with him will we be truly free and have everlasting joy and intimacy. In this way, his jealousy is an act of his love for us! Some have a hard time thinking about God as being jealous. But if someone tried to flirt with a man's wife, and that man didn't get jealous, wouldn't you wonder if he really loved his wife?

What about anger? Doesn't the Bible tell us not to be angry? God's emotions are completely in line with his righteousness. His anger isn't egoistic, but rather, unselfish. He gets angry when something is hurting the people he loves.

We must reflect the emotions of God. We too should feel anger when faced with the reality of prostitution, child labor, and hunger. Those are godly feelings. It's not just the things that we do that are sinful. It's sinful not to react. It's sinful not to love!

THINK ABOUT IT!

Do you know God as jealous and angry? Is your
emotional life in line with his godly emotions?

DAY 11

*Above all the grace and the gifts that Christ gives
to his beloved is that of overcoming self.*

FRANCIS OF ASSISI

*My old self has been crucified with Christ. It is no longer I who
live, but Christ lives in me. So I live in this earthly body by trusting
in the Son of God, who loved me and gave himself for me.*

GALATIANS 2:20

Brian Head Welch from Korn did an album and wrote a book with the title "Save me from myself." That's a great way of putting it. Jesus really saved us from ourselves by giving us a clean slate. But he continues to save us from ourselves by letting the messy things in our lives die and helping us grow in freedom.

It's a fulfilling experience to have God transform you. First of all, it just feels good! We find ourselves growing in patience, self-control, and love. But, honestly, it has its downside emotionally as well. We get to see ourselves more clearly. We get confronted with the horrors of realizing how imperfect we actually are. We see our selfishness in acts we may have considered to be good, but upon closer examination we find they were also self-serving.

Lord, save me from myself! Realize those things that need some work, see the Holy Spirit's help to fix them, and move on. Allow the Holy Spirit to work in you and produce his fruit instead. Realize how badly you need a savior and how much Jesus has forgiven you. Pray that, with Jesus' help, you will overcome yourself!

THINK ABOUT IT!

Do you have Christ where your ego used to be?

DAY 12

I t can be very difficult to explain Christianity as a worldview, especially to someone outside of the faith. Answering others questions is really important. But there's a limit to how much they'll understand until they experience it themselves. Christianity has the capacity to give good reasons for a non-believer to believe, but there are things that can only be viewed from the inside.

When a person stops simply thinking about the Christian worldview and starts experiencing it, that changes everything for them. God is no longer just a philosophical idea, but he becomes personal. You begin to feel him. To experience him. The Bible becomes more than something you consider critically as a historical document. It begins to encourage you and speak into your life. Instead of only considering the logic of the Trinity, you hear the Father, feel the Son, and see the fruit of the Spirit.

That's why it can be difficult persuading friends about the truth of Christianity. You can help them walk a certain distance, but they'll only come all the way by experiencing it from the inside. The testimony of your life is therefore a powerful thing! If they see the difference in your life, then you've already made a powerful case for the Christian faith.

THINK ABOUT IT!

Have you invited someone from the outside, inside?

DAY 13

"No one else holds or has held the place in the heart of the world which Jesus holds. Other gods have been as devoutly worshipped; no other man has been so devoutly loved."

JOHN KNOX

Jesus replied, "You must love the Lord your God with all your heart, all your soul, and all your mind."

MATTHEW 22:37

If you desire to know the heart of God, this would be a great place to begin! Jesus was asked, "What is the greatest commandment?" His answer surprised them! "LOVE!" This is the very core of God's being, and it should be the same for us. The Bible says it very radically and clearly: "But anyone who does not love does not know God, for God is love" (1 John 4:8).

You have the opportunity to love God with everything you've got. All your heart. He asks you to have an emotional connection with him. All your soul. The very core of your being. Let love be your very identity. All your mind: Trust the Lord. Seek answers to the questions of faith that you find difficult. Reflect on his being and search for understanding. Have the mind of Christ.

What makes Christianity so radically different from every other religion is that you don't have to perform it. God has already done everything for you. It isn't based on fear or actions, but love. And once you accept this amazing reality, you cannot help but loving him back. It's impossible to understand the cross and not love the person hanging on it.

THINK ABOUT IT!

Do you love God with all your guts, heart, soul, and mind?

DAY 14

*I clearly see the invitation to return back to Megadeth as God's timing,
not mine. I view it as a way to finally clear the past once and for all, to
mend fences and show the world that even a messy situation like
a rock and roll band's demise can be made right through Christ.*

DAVID ELLEFSON (MEGADETH)

*For God in all his fullness was pleased to live in Christ, and through him
God reconciled everything to himself. He made peace with everything
in heaven and on earth by means of Christ's blood on the cross. This
includes you who were once far away from God. You were his enemies,
separated from him by your evil thoughts and actions. Yet now he has
reconciled you to himself through the death of Christ in his physical
body. As a result, he has brought you into his own presence, and you
are holy and blameless as you stand before him without a single fault.*

COLOSSIANS 1:19-22

Our lives get messy. All of us have situations from our past that
we'd rather not think about. We'd love to have some "do-
overs!" Even though MEGADETH is a household name in
the metal community, David realizes the band's history is less than perfect. How exciting that he has an opportunity to make some things "right
through Christ!"

None of us are trapped. Christ died on the cross to redeem us. And,
with his redemption, we can mend the past and reconcile what was lost.
How does that happen? Colossians here tells us that, as a result of Christ's
death on the cross, "he has brought you into his own presence, and you are
holy and blameless as you stand before him without a single fault." Imagine what that looks like when you model your new position in Christ to
those who have watched you fail. Imagine the HOPE that comes from
simply seeing someone transformed by the power of Jesus Christ!

THINK ABOUT IT!

How many people from your past need to see your "do-over"?

DAY 15

*If you believe what you like in the gospels, and reject what you
don't like, it is not the gospel you believe, but yourself.*
SAINT AUGUSTINE

*There is a path before each person that
seems right, but it ends in death.*
PROVERBS 14:12

I believe in the kind of god that" I can't tell you how many times I have
had this conversation with people. I ask them if they believe in God,
and they describe the kind of god they believe in. It's a game people play. You simply pick out the qualities of a god you would feel comfortable with, and then worship it! Wouldn't it make a lot more sense to
actually figure out who God is in the first place?

What if you did that with your mate? You choose the attributes that
you like about them, and then you simply ignore all of those things you
don't feel comfortable with. There are two problems with this kind of
thinking: First, you don't see the person for whom they really are. And
second, the relationship would be short lived. Besides, the more you
learn about God's attributes, the more awesome he becomes!

THINK ABOUT IT!

Are you guilty of defining God the way you think he should be?

DAY 16

The Bible, to me, is like water. When I drink water, it cleanses my
body; when I read God's Word, it cleanses my heart, mind, and soul.
MICHAEL SWEET (STRYPER)

Let us go right into the presence of God with sincere
hearts fully trusting him. For our guilty consciences have
been sprinkled with Christ's blood to make us clean, and
our bodies have been washed with pure water.
HEBREWS 10:22

A few years ago I bought a special water-filtration bottle. The selling point of this special bottle was its ability to filter even the most filthy water. I remember the first time I used it. I went down to the lake to fill it up. The water was a bit muddy, with turtles and a lot of "sea creatures" skimming the water. When I thought about actually drinking this water, the prospect was less than appealing. But the bottle actually worked! The water tasted fresh and clean. It was amazing!

This is really the process God offers to us. Like that filtration bottle, he washed us with pure water. As Michael Sweet says, "It cleanses my heart, mind and soul." When I come to him with all kinds of impurity, he cleanses me! And then he goes one step further. He sprinkles me with Christ's blood to clean my guilty conscience. You may never forget your past (sometimes it's a reminder not to go down that path again!), but the guilt from your past was nailed to the cross!

THINK ABOUT IT!

Are you trusting God to cleanse you and
relieve your guilty conscience?

DAY 17

You've gotta love people right where they're at.
REGINALD QUINCY "FIELDY" ARVIZU (KORN)

Love your neighbor as yourself.
LEVITICUS 19:18

S ome people are easy to love. Your best friend who stuck by you through difficult times. That person who saved your life. But then, there're also those people who rub you the wrong way. This is where it gets more difficult. When Jesus was asked what the greatest commandment was, he answered, "LOVE!" Love God. Love your neighbor. Love yourself. Perhaps then, NOT to love may also be our greatest sin?

It's important to pray for those people who irritate us. Praying for them actually changes our attitude towards them. Loving someone unconditionally is also the best way to share your faith. Maybe you've been been hurt by someone you love. Those are very difficult emotions to process. You may need some time and healing to start trusting again. Loving unconditionally takes courage.

Unconditional love begins with our relationship with God. As humans, we simply don't have endless love to give. When we start realizing how much God loves us, it changes everything. Now, when you love people that might not love you back, you can rest assured you are already eternally loved! He will never stop loving you. He will be the one starting to love people through you as you grow in your relationship with him. We become a vehicle for his amazing love.

THINK ABOUT IT!

Have you surrendered yourself to him? Have you started letting the Holy Spirit work on the hurt emotions inside of you that keep you from loving unconditionally?

DAY 18

My heart goes out to the people who are grinding, and to the
people that are tired, beaten down, they don't have anything,
they're spiritually broken. I'm right there with them.
BROOK REEVES (IMPENDING DOOM)

The Lord is close to the brokenhearted; he rescues those
whose spirits are crushed. The righteous person faces many
troubles, but the Lord comes to the rescue each time.
PSALM 34:18-19

Sometimes life sucks. I can't think of a better word for it. They say you should try to find something good in any situation, but many times life has you simply scratching your head. Christians sometimes paint a picture of a perfect life once you become a Christian. Seriously? The Bible is full of examples where that didn't happen. So why doesn't God make our lives easy?

That's not the point of our salvation. It isn't just about making our outside circumstances better—it's about changing our hearts and minds to handle them! With the Holy Spirit inside, we have new strength and insight. And, even though times may be difficult, we have a loving Father who desires to be there every step of the way. No longer do we have to feel alone and abandoned. The Bible tells us that Jesus stays "closer than a brother" to us!

THINK ABOUT IT!

Are you able to trust God with your daily circumstances?

DAY 19

Give your life to the Lord. He is the only one who can make your
life complete and fill the emptiness you have on the inside.
BRIAN "HEAD" WELCH (KORN)

My soul thirsts for you; my whole body longs for you in
this parched and weary land where there is no water.
PSALM 63:1

Did you know that the Book of Psalms were actually songs: lyrics originally written to music? David is expressing his deepest desires to the Lord. His passion reminds me of so many heavy metal artists that I know. His words come through in a very powerful yet poetic way. The Psalms have been recorded in so many different musical styles through the years. Maybe there is a metal growler out there who is ready to put these words to music? That would be powerful!

In this Psalm, though, David expresses the deepest longings of his heart. His soul thirsts for God. His whole body longs for the Lord. Just as if he were in a parched land with no water in sight. That is how so many of us felt before we invited Jesus to into our lives. As Brian "Head" Welch says here, "He is the only one who can make your life complete."

THINK ABOUT IT!

Does Jesus continue to make your life complete?

DAY 20

Have you been asking God what He is going to do?
He will never tell you. God does not tell you what He
is going to do; He reveals to you Who He is.

OSWALD CHAMBERS

And we have received God's Spirit (not the world's spirit), so we can
know the wonderful things God has freely given us. When we tell you
these things, we do not use words that come from human wisdom.
Instead, we speak words given to us by the Spirit, using the Spirit's
words to explain spiritual truths. But people who aren't spiritual
can't receive these truths from God's Spirit. It all sounds foolish to
them and they can't understand it, for only those who are spiritual
can understand what the Spirit means. Those who are spiritual can
evaluate all things, but they themselves cannot be evaluated by others.
For, "Who can know the Lord's thoughts? Who knows enough to teach
him?" But we understand these things, for we have the mind of Christ.

1 CORINTHIANS 2:12-16

I receive a lot of messages every day. People ask about the Bible, and about God's nature. Many times they are confused about a situation in their lives and want to know how God feels about it. I understand that. I have been there before. And honestly, I am seldom at that point anymore.

I have been a Christian for many years, and I have developed a relationship with him. We are like an old married couple who complete each other's sentences! Honestly, I don't pretend to know the deep wisdom of God, but I have learned "Who he is" enough to either figure out where he is leading me, or to simply trust him. I would rather walk blindly with him by my side then to walk with full sight without him!

THINK ABOUT IT!

Is God in the process of revealing who he is to you?

DAY 21

I wanna tell people that God can make us
be our best at what we wanna do.
PETE SANDOVAL (MORBID ANGEL)

We do this by keeping our eyes on Jesus, the
champion who initiates and perfects our faith.
HEBREWS 12:2

Trust in the Lord with all your heart; do not depend
on your own understanding. Seek his will in all you
do, and he will show you which path to take.
PROVERBS 3:5-6

God INITIATES and PERFECTS our faith. Before you start on a journey, there are two things you need to know: First, where do you have a desire to go? And second, how do you get there? Did you know that God is instrumental in both aspects? He first gives you the desires that you feel. When you say, "Lord, I have a great desire to…"—God says, "Yes, I know. I put that desire there in the first place." So if he has placed that desire in your heart, doesn't it make sense that he has already figured out how to take you there? It is an exciting road that we're on as we follow Christ's leading. Once we identify our God-given desire to travel a certain road, we can be sure that he knows which path to take!

THINK ABOUT IT!

How is God initiating and perfecting your faith?

DAY 22

When Accept released our first couple of albums, we became famous very fast. As a result, I started living a life mostly dedicated to myself. Even though we were traveling all around the world playing for thousands of fans every day, my life started to become unfulfilling. Every show was the greatest high, but soon the rest of the day just became routine.

PETER BALTES (ACCEPT)

And what do you benefit if you gain the whole world but lose your own soul?

MARK 8:36

Are you a musician? Then you totally understand this scenario: The lights go dim. The spotlights come up. Your intro begins to play as thousands of screaming fans chant your name as you take the stage. As the intro leads into the actual lyrics of the song, thousands of devoted fans begin to sing along to every word. They love you. They want to be just like you. There's no high like it! Again, that is the dream of every musician. We all want to be loved and adored for our music. If we can just get to that pinnacle, we will be happy for the rest of our lives. Really? How many happy rock stars do you know?

Peter knows this feeling. He has experienced those thousands of fans cheering him on. But, after the music stopped, the rest of his life felt empty. We always have this idea that our lives would be better if we could just achieve popularity or success. But no one ever profits from gaining the world. It is our connection with God and our relationship with him that truly matters. Everything else will always become empty and meaningless. Make sure you seek the One who will actually fulfill your deepest longings.

THINK ABOUT IT!

Is it your goal to gain the world, or to please God?

DAY 23

...but I can use what I do have. I have a platform. I have a voice.
MATTIE MONTGOMERY (FOR TODAY)

*Instead, we speak words given to us by the Spirit, using
the Spirit's words to explain spiritual truths.*
1 CORINTHIANS 2:13

You have a voice. Wait…what? Are you telling me that I can sing? No. Sorry. If you are like me, you're stuck simply appreciating others' talent. I love listening to Mattie. He obviously has a great growling voice. That's why he also has a huge scene and group of listeners to sing to! But you also have a voice. A platform. A place where you can use your voice. It may be smaller and look completely different than Mattie's, but it's *your* voice. You're able to reach people that Mattie can't. None of us can touch everybody, but there will be people you'll encounter that others won't be able to reach.

Many of us will never have a big platform. But a small platform is just as important. In chatting with people one-on-one, you have opportunities that a stage doesn't give you. You get to explain things that maybe are difficult to understand the first time. And you get the chance to live your life in front of people. That is really the best testimony. You get to love people! Using your voice in a kind way on social media is fine. But getting a chance to speak truth into someone's life—face-to-face—really is something else!

THINK ABOUT IT!

*What is your platform? Colleagues? Classmates? Friends?
Is your voice accompanied by actions as well?*

DAY 24

It's important to recognize that there will be dark times but there is always that light at the end of the tunnel. Music saved my life and Jesus saved my soul.
JOSH SCOGIN (NORMA JEAN, THE CHARIOT, 68)

Music is one of the fairest and most glorious gifts of God, to which Satan is a bitter enemy, for it removes from the heart the weight of sorrow, and the fascination of evil thoughts.
MARTIN LUTHER

Praise the Lord! Praise God in his sanctuary; praise him in his mighty heaven! Praise him for his mighty works; praise his unequaled greatness! Praise him with a blast of the ram's horn; praise him with the lyre and harp! Praise him with the tambourine and dancing; praise him with strings and flutes! Praise him with a clash of cymbals; praise him with loud clanging cymbals. Let everything that breathes sing praises to the Lord! Praise the Lord!
PSALM 150

Music has always been a very important part of my life. I enjoy everything from Jazz to Classical, from Swing to Death Metal. There are days when I'm in the mood to listen to Johnny Cash, and other days when I listen to the most brutal black metal. There are songs from my past that bring back specific memories. I can even recall what I was wearing and what I was doing the first time I heard a specific song played on the radio. The older you get, the more you will become aware of the importance of music in your life.

Josh Scogin says, "Music saved my life and Jesus saved my soul." I understand exactly what he is talking about. I don't know what I would have done without music as an outlet and a way to express my deepest feelings. So many times I have listened to music to uplift my spirit! It's because music is so powerful that it's important to be careful that its' messages are uplifting and in keeping with your personal belief system. Those songs that you listen to today may become one of the greatest encouragements to you in the future!

THINK ABOUT IT!
What difference does music play in your life?

DAY 25

Dear Sir: Regarding your article 'What's Wrong with the World?' I am. Yours truly, G K Chesterton

G K CHESTERTON

This is a trustworthy saying, and everyone should accept it: "Christ Jesus came into the world to save sinners"—and I am the worst of them all.

1 TIMOTHY 1:15

What's wrong with the world? To answer this question, we love to point fingers at our political systems and social structures. The Apostle Paul and G.K. Chesterton both show us a key insight to understanding the real reason for the problems of the world: ME! YOU! The reason we never experience a perfect fellowship is because we're a part of it. The reason a political system never works completely is because of people. It's our fault. Before we understand that, we'll not be successful in trying to fix it.

When Mel Gibson made the movie The Passion of the Christ he used himself in the role of hammering a nail through Jesus' hand. He explained that it was his fault Christ had to die. Again, a key insight to understanding the world and the cross. When facing the horrors of the world, we must look in the mirror. When facing the cross of Christ we must look at ourselves honestly. Until we understand this, we'll continue to feel superior to others and look down on people.

Christ would have given his life, even if you were the only one who'd receive his sacrifice. He would have died for you to live. His death on the cross was extremely intimate and personal. The cross is the starting point for understanding our situation and doing something about it. Only because of the cross can we become a new creation who can help bring healing to a sick and dying world. Why? Because Christ in us is greater than anything we may encounter!

THINK ABOUT IT!

How do you view yourself in relation to the problems of the world and the death of Christ?

DAY 26

All high and lofty things are brought low before The Lord.
LYRICS FROM "EN HAKKORE"
BY THE BURIAL [IN THE TAKING OF FLESH]

Human pride will be brought down, and human arrogance will be humbled. Only the LORD will be exalted on that day of judgment.
ISAIAH 2:11

Pride goes before destruction, and haughtiness before a fall.
PROVERBS 16:18

You can always tell what is important to someone by watching them for a while. How they dress, the music they listen to, the things they do in their spare time, the friends they surround themselves with, and the topic of their conversations—all of this tells a lot about the person. Luke 6:45 says, "What you say flows from what is in your heart." Some people live their whole lives being prideful of their possessions and status, never realizing that it is only temporary.

None of us will take a single thing with us when we leave this earth. Our wealth, our status, and even our collection of Metal CD's will mean nothing to us when we die. The only thing that remains is who we are in Christ! It is the only thing that truly defines us for eternity. The Apostle Paul says he has learned to take pride in his relationship with God. On that Judgment day, we who are Christians will hear, "Well done, my good and faithful servant" (Matthew 25:23).

THINK ABOUT IT!

What do people see when they watch you for a while?

DAY 27

Heaven is reality itself. All that is fully real is heavenly. For all that can be shaken will be shaken and only the unshakeable remains.

C.S. LEWIS

And I saw the holy city, the new Jerusalem, coming down from God out of heaven like a bride beautifully dressed for her husband.

REVELATION 21:2

D o you ever take a break from life to reflect upon eternity? It's easy to get so caught up in our current situations that we completely forget the bigger picture. We're just traveling through this earth on our way home, inviting people to tag along. The Bible says our real citizenship is in Heaven. Philippians 3:20 says, "But we are citizens of heaven, where the Lord Jesus Christ lives. And we are eagerly waiting for him to return as our Savior."

Imagine a society where nobody steals, lies, or breaks the law. There is no need for police, judges, or prisons. No one talks behind your back. There are no murders, no accidents, no sickness, and no pain. Imagine a perfect fellowship where everyone cares for each other, feels good about each other, and wants the best for each other. It's difficult to imagine, isn't it? The world around us is very different. Even if we could imagine it, we still wouldn't be able to comprehend the awesome glory of the Kingdom of God.

Intense worship. Playing blast-beats. Shredding distortion guitar. And the best part is spending eternity with God and living in perfect relationship with our Maker. That's the part that will satisfy our deepest, innermost needs. Reflecting on what awaits us makes any situation in life more joyful.

THINK ABOUT IT!

Are you living with this perspective in your daily life?

DAY 28

Can't get away. I swear I'm gonna break. I'm paralyzed I need you now
LYRICS FROM "PARALYZED"
BY LOVE AND DEATH [BETWEEN HERE & LOST]

"Anyone who listens to my teaching and follows it is wise,
like a person who builds a house on solid rock.

MATTHEW 7:24

Where do you go when you're feeling mental pressure and in pain? Is God is the one you run to when you're in desperate need? When we find ourselves in times like these, temptations are everywhere. Pornography, drugs, and alcohol are suddenly way more tempting. We want to get a quick fix and make ourselves feel better. We want a little bit of pleasure to give us a break from the pain and emptiness we feel. This is where our character is put to the test. How we navigate in small situations will reflect how we navigate in larger ones.

An example of this would be beer. Even though I don't use alcohol at all, I don't believe there is anything wrong with having a beer. But if having a beer becomes your go-to-move every time you've had a bad day, then alcohol will be the thing you go to during extreme pain or difficulties. The same applies to God. Do you seek him on bad days as well? Otherwise, you're not going to seek his strength in your most desperate hours.

God is the one foundation you can rely on in the worst of times. Other things will fail you and maybe even make you an addict and a slave to them. Build up your character in the small problems so you'll be ready for for big ones.

THINK ABOUT IT!

Do you seek simple pleasures that will only last for
a short time and in the long run bring you further
down? Or do you seek the One that will fulfill your
deepest need in eternity and strengthen you now?

DAY 29

The only freedom I found, is radical love
LYRICS FROM "CLUTCHES"
BY SLEEPING GIANT [FINISHED PEOPLE]

"Look at you now!" they yelled at him. "You said you were going to destroy the Temple and rebuild it in three days. Well then, if you are the Son of God, save yourself and come down from the cross!"
MATTHEW 27:40

The cross is the most powerful event in human history. It changes our understanding of everything: life, death, time, and our Creator. As a result of the cross, we now have a new understanding of what love really means. God wanted a meaningful relationship with each one of us, so he sent Jesus to die on the cross for our sins. It's through this pivotal event in history that our lives are profoundly changed.

Our relationships take on new meaning. We view marriage differently. We view friendships differently. We even find the capacity to love people who are difficult to love. We accept the challenge to be vulnerable. We begin to allow his love to flow through us. Unconditionally.

THINK ABOUT IT!

Are you prioritizing love above comfort and happiness?

DAY 30

You have overcome the world. A new way for humanity
LYRICS FROM "UNVEILING THE OBSCURE"
BY EXTOL [EXTOL]

Jesus told her, "I am the resurrection and the life. Anyone who believes in me will live, even after dying."
JOHN 11:25

We have a very strong focus on the cross in western Christian tradition. We focus on Jesus' pain and suffering, and his death. And, of course, there's nothing wrong with that. But in the eastern (orthodox) Christian tradition they have a very strong focus on the resurrection. And here we have a great opportunity to learn from each other. We're both right!

The cross was not the end of Jesus' story. He rose from the dead! He defeated death! The gospel of John has a special focus on this. Jesus is portrayed as the victor. We get to share his victory. If you're a Christian, hold your head high. You're a champion! You'll always be a winner! Reading through the gospel of John is a great way to see this.

The great thing is this: you'll never lose this victory. "And I am convinced that nothing can ever separate us from God's love. Neither death nor life, neither angels nor demons, neither our fears for today nor our worries about tomorrow—not even the powers of hell can separate us from God's love." (Rom 8:38).

THINK ABOUT IT!

Maybe you feel like life is beating you down today. You may be pressured by battles in your mind or struggles with your flesh. You may need to remind yourself that you are a winner! Jesus' awesome victory is yours!

DAY 31

*I don't think of us as "spiritual giants" or anything like that. But
I can tell you that, in spite of all the many mistakes we made
collectively, at the core we were truly about serving the
Lord. And we were—and are—excited about ministry.*
REX CARROLL (WHITECROSS)

*I don't mean to say that I have already achieved these things or
that I have already reached perfection. But I press on to possess
that perfection for which Christ Jesus first possessed me. No,
dear brothers and sisters, I have not achieved it, but I focus on
this one thing: Forgetting the past and looking forward to what
lies ahead, I press on to reach the end of the race and receive the
heavenly prize for which God, through Christ Jesus, is calling us.*
PHILIPPIANS 3:12-14

I get that sick feeling in the pit of my stomach when I remember some of the mistakes I have made in ministry. During the last 45 years it seems like I have done everything wrong at least once. I once heard a definition for success that has meant a lot to me as I sort through my shortcomings: "Success is getting up when you have fallen down for the last time." It doesn't matter how many times you have failed. Many people fail. Most millionaires have declared bankruptcy at least once before they were successful. It simply means that we don't stay down—we keep getting up—until we are able to get up for the last time.

Galatians 5:7-8 says, "You were running the race so well. Who has held you back from following the truth? It certainly isn't God, for he is the one who called you to freedom." How does the Apostle Paul encourage us when we have fallen, and step out of the race? GET BACK IN THE RACE! Don't waste your time feeling discouraged or disqualified. Run. Move. Remember that Christ is your source, and he will give you the wisdom and energy you need to get up "for the last time!"

THINK ABOUT IT!

Have you fallen, and find it difficult to get back up?

DAY 32

Corrie ten Boom was a famous holocaust survivor, and a beacon of the faith. Her story was told in the bestselling book, "The Hiding Place" which came out in 1971, followed by the movie by the same title a few years later. In the early 70's, I had the honor of escorting her from the hotel where she was staying to the conference center where she was speaking across the street.

As I went to the elevator to navigate to her room, there were a lot of people with drinks in their hands laughing and talking loudly in the lobby. As I escorted Corrie out of the elevator, everyone stopped what they were doing. These people who had been making a lot of noise and partying loudly, were silent as Corrie walked through the crowd. They didn't know who she was. But they recognized the "light" that defined her. I will never forget that moment, although it was a long time ago. My prayer is that my life will one day reflect my faith so strongly that people will see the "light" in my life and recognize Jesus in me. Just like they did with Corrie.

THINK ABOUT IT!

Is your faith reflected in your countenance?

DAY 33

Sometimes I post the needs of our homeless ministry on Facebook. One time in particular I asked for people to help financially with mylar sleeping bags to keep our homeless friends from the freezing cold. For many of them, it was life or death! Many people commented, and told me how sad it was that these dear people were on the streets. Even more "shared" it to their Facebook page and asked others to help. But at the end of the day, no one had actually helped financially.

It inspired me to do a short video depicting the problem. I made small posters with the Facebook "like" symbol, and filmed myself handing the posters out to the homeless. They were a bit confused, and asked what they were supposed to do with these? Exactly! Just being aware of a problem and "posting" about it doesn't make the difference. That is what makes this verse so important. Don't just listen to the problem and talk about it: do something about it!

THINK ABOUT IT!
Are you a "talker" or a "doer?"

DAY 34

Every facet of the human condition and spiritual journey is covered in this book. Times change, but the basic fabric of humanity does not.
MATT SMITH (THEOCRACY)

And because I preach this Good News, I am suffering and have been chained like a criminal. But the word of God cannot be chained.
2 TIMOTHY 2:9

Good News! That is what this great message of Jesus Christ is called. Many throughout history have suffered for it, fought for it, and proclaimed it. And here we are a few thousand years later, and it is still the best selling book in all of history. Why? It's a personal love letter, written just for you. It is an owner's manual on how to live your life. It is a book of history, sharing stories of people just like you and me. People with difficulties. People who often fail. People who are sometimes confused. And people who have found the same victory in connecting to the God who made them!

Matt Smith talked about a spiritual journey. That is the exciting part about our life with Christ. It is a journey. We are learning every day, through good times and difficult times. We are being trained in righteousness as we live out the Word of God. And one day, this journey ends in Heaven, where we will be reunited face to face with the Author and Perfecter of our faith!

THINK ABOUT IT!

How have the examples of the characters in the Bible influenced your life?

DAY 35

*And I feel like so many people, they can actually accept Christ
and push people away by being a little too self-righteous*
REGINALD QUINCY "FIELDY" ARVIZU (KORN)

*Then Jesus told this story to some who had great
confidence in their own righteousness.*
LUKE 18:9

elf-righteousness is ugly. Nasty. Sinful. It can turn good deeds into blasphemy against Christ. Charles Spurgeon explains it this way: "The greatest enemy to human souls is the self-righteous spirit, which makes men look to themselves for salvation." When we think our good deeds balance our bad deeds, then we're truly ignorant about how messed up we really are. If we think we can be make up for our sins by giving money and helping others, we fail to see how sin has corrupted us.

Remember, if we could redeem ourselves there would be no reason for Christ to die on the cross. We need to nail our self-righteousness to the cross as well. We must ask for forgiveness for being silly enough to think we could ever come close to earning our forgiveness. It's actually a sin we cannot get rid of ourselves. If we could, we'd probably end up feeling proud about it! The Holy Spirit lives deep inside of us. He is deeper than our emotions. Deeper than our sin. And deeper than our self-righteousness. Only he can do it!

THINK ABOUT IT!

*Is self-righteousness keeping you from fully enjoying the
beauty and depth of what Christ has done for you?*

DAY 36

The gospel is not a doctrine of the tongue, but of life.
It cannot be grasped by reason and memory only, but
it is fully understood when it possesses the whole soul
and penetrates to the inner recesses of the heart.

JOHN CALVIN

Dear brothers and sisters, I want you to understand that the gospel
message I preach is not based on mere human reasoning.

GALATIANS 1:11

Did you grow up in a church? If you are like me, you have heard someone preach the Gospel message thousands of times! Your reaction when you hear it, can tell you a lot. If your heart leaps every time you hear it, then the truth of the Gospel has penetrated your heart. If you react with boredom and think to yourself, "Couldn't he speak about something else," then you need to consider if you've really understood it.

The gospel is so much more than just head knowledge. Its power penetrates every aspect of our life. Its reality amazes our minds and fills our hearts with emotions. It's incredible that one as wonderful as Jesus would carry the sins of the whole world for messed up people like us! The exalted and most high God reached down to earth to pick us up. It's the most incredible act in human history.

THINK ABOUT IT!

How do you react when hearing the Gospel?

DAY 37

The essence of life poured out in every being…
Shaped in the likeness of the Triune.
LYRICS FROM "A GIFT BEYOND HUMAN REACH" BY EXTOL

Put on your new nature, created to be like
God—truly righteous and holy.
GALATIANS 4:24

What does God look like? Man has been asking that question for thousands of years! Some would answer that you see God in the creation. Paul tells us that nature itself speaks of the glory of God. Others would say that you see God in the miracle of birth. If you were to describe God's essence, there is only one word that would fit: Agapé. It's a Greek word that means "God's unconditional love." No conditions. No strings attached. The kind of love we cannot fully comprehend. And it's because of this great love that we are "truly righteous and holy."

When God created you, this is what he had in mind. Why did he create you in his image? Simple. He has a desire to connect with you. His divine plan is to have a loving relationship with you. He initiated it. You simply respond! When you do, the connection is made, and he accepts you as a son or daughter. Again no strings attached!

THINK ABOUT IT!

Have you accepted God's free gift of eternal life
and unconditional relationship with him?

DAY 38

Our faith is not about what we look like, how we are dressed,
what kind of music we enjoy, what kind of style we have. It
is about our heart, the inside of us, not the outside!
SIMON "PILGRIM" ROSÉN
(CRIMSON MOONLIGHT)

But the Lord said to Samuel, "Don't judge by his appearance
or height, for I have rejected him. The Lord doesn't see
things the way you see them. People judge by outward
appearance, but the Lord looks at the heart.
1 SAMUEL 16:7

I wish I had a dollar for every time I have used the above scripture over the years. I have always been a bit out-of-the-box. I have had every hair style imaginable: from my huge afro during the hippie days, to my poofy metal hair in the 80's. Along with my piercings, tattoos, and clothing well, it has always been a bit controversial. And honestly, I've enjoyed that part. I have never had a heart to minister to the "normal" people of the world. My heart gets excited to connect with people on the edge—just like me!

"Pastor Bob, how do you justify your dress and looks before God?" I have been asked that question hundreds of times. My answer? "You'll have to ask God. He made me this way." Some people do very well looking like everyone else—and listening to pop music. But some of us don't. Who is more spiritual and more enlightened? Neither! We are simply different. I like to think that we all compliment each other. We all have something to add to this great mix of people we call "Christians." Because, as Pilgrim says above, "It is about our heart, the inside of us, not the outside!"

THINK ABOUT IT!

Are you guilty of judging people according to what they look like?

DAY 39

I think that if God forgives us we must also forgive ourselves. Otherwise, it is almost like setting up ourselves as a higher tribunal than him.

C.S. LEWIS

You have come to Jesus, the one who mediates the new covenant between God and people, and to the sprinkled blood, which speaks of forgiveness instead of crying out for vengeance like the blood of Abel.

HEBREWS 12:24

Forgiving others is difficult. Forgiving yourself? That's even more difficult! Maybe you're beating yourself up for something you did a long time ago. Perhaps your patience with a habitual sin is at its limit. Jesus' forgiveness is so radical that we often want to add to the process. We think we need to really repent strongly so we can feel the pain of what we did. We try to add good works to feel less guilty. Yet, this is not biblical.

The Bible says: "No one is righteous—not even one" (Rom 3:10). And "When we display our righteous deeds, they are nothing but filthy rags" (Isaiah 64:6). See, we cannot add anything to what Jesus did. We need to understand that Jesus did it all. Completely. 100%!

THINK ABOUT IT!

If you're beating yourself up for something Jesus has forgiven you for, then you need to forgive yourself as well. Learn from your mistakes, and move on. It's time to stop feeling guilty. The Lord has forgiven you. Have you forgiven yourself?

DAY 40

*Faith never knows where it is being led, but it
loves and knows the One who is leading.*

OSWALD CHAMBERS

*It was by faith that Noah built a large boat to save his family from
the flood. He obeyed God, who warned him about things that had
never happened before. By his faith Noah condemned the rest of
the world, and he received the righteousness that comes by faith.*

HEBREWS 11:7

Can you imagine God promising you a child when you are 100 years old? That really took a lot of faith for Abraham and his wife Sarah! It was a unique miracle since God had many things to teach Abraham and his wife Sarah through this experience. And, as a result, we are part of his descendants! Or, even more, how about Noah and his ark? Since nothing like that even existed God had to also show him how to build it. They didn't possess the technology to build something that large that was sea worthy. It would almost be like God telling you to build a spaceship!

Faith. When you develop a relationship with God, you learn by experience that you can trust him. For Abraham and Noah, their faith was a result of their relationship with God. When God called the Apostle Paul, he took him into the desert for 3 years to spend time with him and establish a relationship. It was because of the strength of this relationship that Paul ways able to say, "That is why I am suffering here in prison. But I am not ashamed of it, for I know the one in whom I trust, and I am sure that he is able to guard what I have entrusted to him until the day of his return" (2 Timothy 1:12).

THINK ABOUT IT!

*Are you establishing the kind of relationship with
God that will allow you to walk by faith?*

DAY 41

*"If the highest aim of a captain were to preserve
his ship, he would keep it in port forever."*
THOMAS AQUINAS

*He gave five bags of silver to one, two bags of silver to
another, and one bag of silver to the last—dividing it in
proportion to their abilities. He then left on his trip.*
MATTHEW 25:15

Maybe you know this story. The guys with five and two used what they'd gotten to earn more for the master, returned it to him, and got entrusted with more. The guy with one bag buried it, returned it to the master and was called "wicked and lazy."

What are you good at? What talents has the Lord entrusted you with? Use what God has given you to increase the Kingdom of God, and you will be rewarded. There are many reasons why you might not be using your gifts. You may feel that you don't have much to offer. That isn't true! In fact, if you feel this way, you're very ready for being used! It proves you are not struggling with pride, and are able to allow the Holy Spirit to work through you. Maybe you're afraid of making mistakes. Making mistakes is inevitable. It proves that you're actually trying. Learn from your mistakes and move on.

God made you and entrusted you with gifts. Make sure you put them to use. Whether you feel like you've received five, two, or one, use it and double the value. You'll receive a grand reward in Heaven.

THINK ABOUT IT!
What is holding you back from using your gifts for the glory of God?

DAY 42

I thought that the devil would protect me and that he would give me the desires of my heart. I was even willing to give up my own soul for this.
MARK ALLEN (EX-VOTO)

For you are the children of your father the devil, and you love to do the evil things he does. He was a murderer from the beginning. He has always hated the truth, because there is no truth in him. When he lies, it is consistent with his character; for he is a liar and the father of lies.
JOHN 8:44

Satan's lies can be a real trap. Even though he was defeated when Jesus died on the cross, he is still the father of lies. In fact, this verse describes his character as "liar." It's important that you know that, and that you remember it! It is one of the reasons why I have written this book, together with the Metal Bible.

The more you read about God in the Bible the more you know who he is. Then, when Satan tries to lie to you, you recognize his deception. Mark Allen thought Satan would take care of him. He was even willing to sell his soul for the devil! But the Bible says, "And you will know the truth, and the truth will set you free." John 8:32. How great to know that while Satan is the father of lies, God is the Father of Truth!

THINK ABOUT IT!

Because God is The Father of Truth, you can always trust him!

DAY 43

"A man with God is always in the majority."

JOHN KNOX

All the believers devoted themselves to the apostles'
teaching, and to fellowship, and to sharing in meals
(including the Lord's Supper), and to prayer.

ACTS 2:42

Are you the only Christian at your workplace or school? It's easy to feel alone. A lack of fellowship can add to your social pressure. Though it's important to have people around you to share the faith with, remember: you're not alone! You're not even in the minority.

When we pray, we pray with the rest of the Christians in the world. When we celebrate communion, we remember Christ's death with all the Christians before us throughout history. When we go through pain, we remember that there are brothers and sisters in Christ who are presently going through the same. We have fellowship with all Christians before us throughout history: all the martyrs, all the radicals, all of the Church. Even the Christians of the future. Therefore, you'll always be in the majority. You share a rich faith with Christians who have gone before you, and those who will live after you.

There are brothers and sister praying for you and your country both now and in the past. Even Jesus is praying for you: "I am praying not only for these disciples but also for all who will ever believe in me through their message. I pray that they will all be one, just as you and I are one—as you are in me, Father, and I am in you. And may they be in us so that the world will believe you sent me." (John 17:20-21).

THINK ABOUT IT!

Do you realize how enormous the Christian fellowship is?

DAY 44

"Complete abstinence is easier than perfect moderation."
AUGUSTINE

A person without self-control is like a city with broken-down walls.
PROVERBS 25:28

I f you truly loved me, you would have sex with me!" "Sometimes I just need to unwind and get wasted." Lame excuses. Moderation takes balance and experience. Most of the pleasures of life are things we need to balance. Enjoying good food without overeating, enjoying alcohol without getting drunk, enjoying sexuality in the right context, and so on. This involves being totally honest with yourself. If your tendency is to overdo, then abstinence will be the far easier choice.

Greek philosophy talks about searching for the good life by trying to figure out the middle road. Others who have tried to deal with questions of existential character have thought about balance as well. The Bible, for example, calls us to be both stewards and generous with our money. Ten percent isn't enough. When it comes to keeping your job, working for the Kingdom, and spending time with your family, it is difficult to find balance. It takes years to moderate.

Sensitivity towards the Holy Spirit is, once again, the most important key. But here, friends are also important. Our close friends are good at seeing the things we cannot see ourselves. Meeting people from other countries and learning about history and culture helps us get some perspective on ourselves. Be humble enough to learn. View how others live and use it to balance yourself.

THINK ABOUT IT!
Which areas do you need balance in?

DAY 45

*Show us how to die. How to give our lives. Living
sacrifice. How do we get there.*
LYRICS FROM "BRUISES"
BY LOVE AND DEATH [BETWEEN HERE AND LOST]

*And so, dear brothers and sisters, I plead with you to give your
bodies to God because of all he has done for you. Let them be
a living and holy sacrifice This is truly the way to worship him.*
ROMAND 12:1

Being a living sacrifice means many things. There's obviously a sexual undertone to it. Honoring God with your body means not being controlled by lust or pornography. It means to manage your sexuality in a moral and healthy way, whether you're married or not. It also means being humble. You can't take credit for the Holy Spirit's work in you. He's the one that can make you the person you never thought you could be. Being a living sacrifice could also mean being ready to sacrifice your life for the Kingdom. Many who have gone before us have experienced those kinds of choices!

"Don't copy the behavior and customs of this world, but let God transform you into a new person by changing the way you think" (Romans 12:2). We must receive the "mind of Christ" to be successful. But there's also a shared aspect to being a living sacrifice. We're all different body-parts of the body of Christ. We're not better than our brothers and sisters. Nor are we any worse. God has a plan for you. This means that nobody can do what God has planned for you better than you! Our diversity is an amazing thing.

It also comes with responsibility. For as your body now is a living sacrifice to God, you need to also be ready to make sacrifices. Help those around you to do what they are not able to do. And allow others to help you in ways you are not able to help yourself.

THINK ABOUT IT!
*In which areas do you still need to make your
body a living sacrifice for God?*

DAY 46

I'm not the richest guy in the world; money is tight.
BROOK REEVES (IMPENDING DOOM)

*Those who love money will never have enough. How
meaningless to think that wealth brings true happiness.*
ECCLESIASTES 5:10

Money won't buy happiness. It's a cliché! But it's also very true. We've heard it so many times that we forget the truth in it. Have you seen those exposés of people who win the lottery? Family and friends who haven't spoken to them for years suddenly want to be friends again. Their moral values change. Their greed explodes. Statistically, many of them end up spending all their lottery money very quickly, and then return to their old lives. That is difficult for many of them since they have tasted an extremely different lifestyle!

"I would handle things a lot differently. I would invest the money, and put most of it in the bank," you say. Really? We think we'd manage the money a lot better. We would be more charitable. But honestly, most of us wouldn't be able to handle it either. How do we establish the kind of character that would handle a situation like this correctly? The Bible tells us we have to prove ourselves before we can be entrusted with larger responsibilities. Here's the key: Are you giving to those in need around you even though you don't have a lot of money? If not, rest assured that you wouldn't be able to handle more money either.

THINK ABOUT IT!

The best way to learn how to give is by simply beginning to do it. There are opportunities to help those in need every day. Many of us, especially in the West, have no idea how rich we really are. Compared to the worldwide average, we are extremely wealthy.

DAY 47

...a young man who was martyred for his faith. I put myself in his shoes and had to face the questions: Would I make the same decision?
MATTIE MONTGOMERY (FOR TODAY)

*We know what real love is because Jesus gave up his life for us.
So we also ought to give up our lives for our brothers and sisters.*
1 JOHN 3:16

Can you imagine what it was like to be martyred for Christ? The early church really understood what this was about. During the early days, people even sold themselves into slavery to save their families. Under extreme persecution, many of them would not renounce their faith, even when facing death. Even though many of them were killed, this was an important part of what helped the church grow over a very short period of time.

Would you renounce your faith to save your life? We'd like to say that we'd stand strong. But we really wouldn't know for sure unless it actually happened. A better question would be: "Is our relationship with Jesus the most important thing in our lives? If we had to choose between our life and Jesus, what would we do?" Matthew 25:40 says, "When you did it to one of the least of these my brothers and sisters, you were doing it to me!" Would you give your life for another person? These questions are difficult, but they reveal our priorities.

The amazing thing in life is this: Death is dead! If we should lose our lives because of Jesus, we have already won eternal life. So really, there's nothing to fear. As Christians, we have already gone from death to life! It may seem a bit simplistic, but that's only because we haven't truly understood it yet. Most of us won't have to give our lives for the cause of Christ. But if we did, we can be assured of where we are going!

THINK ABOUT IT!
Who or what would you die for?

DAY 48

*The light just went on and I realized that I was actually
living in this world of darkness, and this life of darkness.*
PETE SANDOVAL (FORMER MORBID ANGEL)

*The light shines in the darkness, and the
darkness can never extinguish it.*
JOHN 1:5

Anger. Frustration. Hate. Depression. In certain periods of life these can feel like your controlling emotions. Life doesn't feel worth living. Your emotions seem out of control, to the point where it bothers you to be around happy people!

When we experience darkness over a long period of time, we tend to let our emotions dictate our theology. You may even begin to question your salvation and your relationship with God altogether.

In these times the teachings of Christianity become very important. No matter how much hate is in your life—towards others or yourself—God loves you! No matter how depressed you feel, God cares for you. No matter how much anger and frustration you have toward God, he wants to be with you forever. These basic foundations of our faith are solid. They are promises from God. Every emotion in your body may scream against it today, but you can still be certain about these simple truths. God loves you. Jesus saved you. The Holy Spirit lives inside of you!

THINK ABOUT IT!

Do you cling to God's promises despite your emotions?

DAY 49

"Brothers, listen! We are here to proclaim that through this man Jesus there is forgiveness for your sins."
ACTS 13:38

et's face it. For some reason it seems difficult to understand just how forgiven we really are! When we think about all of the sins we have committed in our lives, it gives us a sick feeling in our stomach. We feel like we have to make up for the things we've done wrong. The only problem is this: there's no way we could ever redeem ourselves. If we could, it wouldn't have been necessary for Jesus to die on the cross. And when we think about those things that cannot possibly be forgiven, we have to remember that Jesus' death on the cross was the perfect sacrifice!

Our messed up record gets exchanged for his perfect record. Our sinful deeds gets swapped for his holy deeds. Instead of punishment we get eternal glory. Instead of death we receive life in abundance. The old is gone—the new has come! Jesus' sacrifice was perfect. There's nothing you can add to it that will help your case. You've already won. Are you still defining yourself by your mistakes? Don't! God defines you according to Jesus' perfect and flawless record. He created you! Shouldn't he also be the one defining you?

THINK ABOUT IT!

Simply remind yourself today that you're completely and utterly forgiven!

DAY 50

Jesus says, "Come as you are." He wants to clean you up.
REGINALD QUINCY "FIELDY" ARVIZU (KORN)

*The Spirit and the bride say, "Come." Let anyone who
hears this say, "Come." Let anyone who is thirsty come. Let
anyone who desires drink freely from the water of life.*
REVELATION 22:17

Jesus is calling filthy people. He is calling disgusting people. He is calling lost people. It's a relief to know that he isn't requiring us to become perfect to come to him. Actually, he doesn't even require that we make any attempt at perfection. He simply says, "Come!" Why? Because it isn't something we can do anyway! You have no choice.

Jesus' death on the cross made a bold statement about our ability to become perfect. If there was even a glimmer of hope that we could attain perfection, Jesus would have aborted his mission. That is the point. He tells us to come to him, and he will clean us up! Maybe you have been a Christian for some time, and still feel this way? Good! The Christian life isn't about being successfully disciplined. It's all about surrendering to the work of the Holy Spirit inside of you. He will help you to become what you never could have been through your own efforts!

THINK ABOUT IT!

*Have you learned to surrender to the work of the
Holy Spirit inside of you, rather than trying to
discipline yourself to be perfect on your own?*

DAY 51

Embrace life and live it to the full!
JAYSON SHERLOCK
(MORTIFICATION, PAREMAECIUM, HORDE)

My purpose is to give them a rich and satisfying life.
JOHN 10:10

What is stopping you? What is holding you back? Is there some thing that keeps you from following your passions? Do you dare to dream big? It is so easy to talk ourselves out of doing things. We let people and situations dictate our lives, and stifle our heart's desires. We need to be better at letting things go. God asks us to forgive the person that hurt us. We need to focus on opportunities instead of letting our problems get in the way.

Christ calls us to freedom. Galatians 5:1 says, "So Christ has truly set us free. Now make sure that you stay free, and don't get tied up again in slavery to the law." In standing firm in our freedom, we break free of the things that restrain us. We need to forgive where we have been hurt. We need to realize that we are forgiven for the horrible things we have done. Get back up when you have experienced defeat. Break the yoke of bondage in your life. Remember, Christ paid a huge price for your freedom!

Have you hesitated in following your dreams? Do you live in freedom? God is always dreaming bigger than you are. And he wants you to experience true freedom. Stand firm in your freedom and lay those things that bind you behind you!

THINK ABOUT IT!

What passions are you trying to ignore in your life?

DAY 52

When the Spirit of truth comes, he will guide you into all truth. He will not speak on his own but will tell you what he has heard. He will tell you about the future. He will bring me glory by telling you whatever he receives from me.
JOHN 16:13-14

J esus promised us that he wouldn't leave us as orphans when he left. His spirit would "guide us into all truth." What an exciting guarantee! No longer would mankind have to struggle to know God in an intimate way, but we understand these things, for we have the mind of Christ (1 Corinthians 2:16). Now, the very mind of Christ has taken possession of our being! Right now. Inside of you. The Holy Spirit is speaking to you. Guiding you.

Are you listening? What an exciting thing to know that the God of this universe desires such intimacy with YOU! He is always talking. Our difficulty is actually listening. The more you learn to recognize his voice, the more intimate he becomes. Nicko was able to listen to God's voice through the Holy Spirt and respond. And, once you respond, he continues to guide us the rest of our lives!

THINK ABOUT IT!
Are you listening? Have you learned to hear the Holy Spirit inside of you?

DAY 53

A knife in the hands of a murderer can kill life, but a knife in the hands of a doctor can save life. Now is the knife evil itself? No, it depends on how you use it. The power is in our hands to decide what we want to use music for.
SIMON "PILGRIM" ROSÉN (CRIMSON MOONLIGHT)

Then a herald shouted out, "People of all races and nations and languages, listen to the king's command! When you hear the sound of the horn, flute, zither, lyre, harp, pipes, and other musical instruments, bow to the ground to worship King Nebuchadnezzar's gold statue. Anyone who refuses to obey will immediately be thrown into a blazing furnace." Daniel 3:4-6

The Jews in the time of King Nebuchadnezzar (not a good choice if you are picking out a name for your new baby!) realized their choice of worship had to come from their hearts, and the worship of a false god was wrong. We may not have to make those kinds of life-and-death decisions about our music today, but we still need to decide how we will use the great power that music has in our lives.

I am often asked, "Is it okay if I listen to Metal music that talks about Satan and sex, as long as I don't believe what they are singing about?" No, it's not okay. It wasn't okay when the Jews were asked to sing about and worship something they didn't believe in, and it really isn't okay for us either. Music is such a huge force in our lives. The power of music is stronger than you realize. Advertisers spend millions promoting a "jingle" for their companies. They know that if they can get that jingle stuck in your head, that you may buy their product. If that strategy didn't work, they wouldn't spend the money. Choose music that reflects your lifestyle and your beliefs. There is plenty of great music out there!

THINK ABOUT IT!

Are you selective in the music you listen to? Do you understand the effect the lyrics will have on you?

DAY 54

*It costs to be a true disciple of Jesus in these times, and I think
that is the way it should be. We've been too lax of late, and I think
we are entering times that will challenge and test all believers.*
MICHAEL BLOODGOOD (BLOODGOOD)

*You should know this, Timothy, that in the last days there will be very
difficult times. For people will love only themselves and their money.
They will be boastful and proud, scoffing at God, disobedient to their
parents, and ungrateful. They will consider nothing sacred. They will
be unloving and unforgiving; they will slander others and have no self-
control. They will be cruel and hate what is good. They will betray their
friends, be reckless, be puffed up with pride, and love pleasure rather
than God. They will act religious, but they will reject the power that
could make them godly. Stay away from people like that! You have been
taught the holy scriptures from childhood, and they have given you the
wisdom to receive the salvation that comes by trusting in Christ Jesus.*
2 TIMOTHY 3:1-5, 15

These verses define these "last days." When we think of the last days, we think in terms of decades. But this term is used for all the years past the death and resurrection of Jesus Christ. These last 2,000 years have been "the last days." If you have any interest in history at all, you will see that these traits have always been part of society outside and within the church. They are the traits that our flesh gravitates toward.

This is exactly what Jesus came to save us from! Paul's advice to Timothy here is paramount! "Stay away from people like that!" Why? Our tendencies are to become like the people we hang out with. We struggle with these things anyway. We really need to help each other stay strong. How? Paul goes on: "You have been taught the holy scriptures" Paul knew the wisdom that came from the scriptures would be enough to keep Timothy on the right path. His foundation would be enough if he eliminated the temptation!

THINK ABOUT IT!

How are you influenced by the people around you?

DAY 55

God can show us how to live the way he has intended us to live.
PETE SANDOVAL (MORBID ANGEL)

*I have discovered this principle of life—that when I want to do what
is right, I inevitably do what is wrong. I love God's law with all my
heart. But there is another power within me that is at war with my
mind...Who will free me from this life that is dominated by sin and
death? Thank God! The answer is in Jesus Christ our Lord...*
ROMANS 7:21-25

I t's impossible to "get it right" every minute of every day. We end up
bombing out in our walk with the Lord continuously. As the Apostle
Paul says in this verse, when I want to do right, I eventually do what is
wrong. So, just because I cannot "get it right" does this mean it's a death
sentence for my spiritual walk with God?

No! This is actually where it gets exciting! When you love God's
law with all your heart, you become open to his leading. You may mess
up from time to time, but God is dedicated to showing you where you
messed up and how to correct it. The more you walk down this road with
God, the more you will learn the pitfalls and correct them. As in any relationship, you don't start out being great at it. There's a lot to learn. But
that's okay. He's patient with you. He knows it's a process. He lovingly
says, "This is the way. Walk in it!" (Isaiah 30:21).

THINK ABOUT IT!
Do you get discouraged when you don't "get it right?"

DAY 56

*I think it's okay to live in the world and enjoy the activities and
fun things God has placed here for us to partake in, as long
as our convictions aren't compromised in the process.*
DAVID ELLEFSON (MEGADETH)

*For the world offers only a craving for physical pleasure, a
craving for everything we see, and pride in our achievements and
possessions. These are not from the Father, but are from this world.
And this world is fading away, along with everything that people
crave. But anyone who does what pleases God will live forever.*
1 JOHN 2:16-17

What we enjoy and what we crave are two different things. Physical pleasure, achievements, possessions, all of these can be a blessing from God if we keep them in the proper perspective. After all, God created these for us to experience. But, when we live to please God and not our flesh, these become merely things we enjoy temporarily.

Our real pleasure lies in serving God—and doing what pleases him! When these pursuits become our cravings, and when they become our prime motivation, we have lost our perspective. I live on a lake. In my front yard are ducks, geese, deer, turtles, squirrels, and all sorts of wildlife! Enjoying the view and feeding the animals never gets old. I really enjoy it! Every day feels like a celebration of his wonderful blessings to me!

THINK ABOUT IT!

What things do you crave, and what things do you enjoy?

DAY 57

*People sometimes think that because I'm in a Christian
band and I tour and I talk about Jesus on stage all
the time that I don't have problems. I do.*
BROOK REEVES (IMPENDING DOOM)

Problems troubled the people of every land.
2 CHRONICLES 15:5

Who are your idols? Come on. We all have them! Who is that person you really look up to? Do you have a realistic perception of them? We see certain people in the media who look like they have everything under control. But, the media doesn't portray the truth about their lives. Even non-famous people on social media make their lives seem like they are close to perfect. Social media has become the "highlight reel" of our lives.

Choose your role-models with care. Look up to the people who have the courage to be transparent and real about their lives and struggles. It's good to have people to look up to. During the great Reformation, the Protestants took such a big step away from the reverence of the saints that we often fail to see the value of the church-fathers as role-models today. We have posters and shirts of our favorite bands and musicians today, but if we were to do the same with some of the amazing Christians throughout history we would think of it as worship of past saints of the church.

Posting an inspiring quote from someone you admire is a great idea! Musicians can be great role-models. But throughout history there have been some truly incredible Christians who haven't strayed from their convictions in the face of extreme resistance. THEY kept doing what God put on their hearts, even when the world was against them.

THINK ABOUT IT!
Who are your role models?

DAY 58

*"I have held many things in my hands, and I have lost them all;
but whatever I have placed in God's hands, that I still possess."*
MARTIN LUTHER

*Store your treasures in heaven, where moths and rust
cannot destroy, and thieves do not break in and steal.*
MATTHEW 6:20

Where are your priorities? This verse is really a test. Have we understood that everything we collect here on earth will disappear one day? When we analyze our priorities, we clearly don't get it. Most people spend their whole lives paying for their house and cars. And there certainly is nothing wrong with owning that stuff. The problem is when it turns in to a slippery slope. The new car has to be better than the last one. The house keeps getting bigger. And slowly we develop a need for more and more luxuries that, quite honestly, we have no need for.

THINK ABOUT IT!

*It is a good idea to pause once in a while and reflect on
your lifestyle. Have you acquired new stuff since last year?
Do you have clothes in your closet you don't use? Someone
else is in great need of them. Downsizing is an awesome
way to live. You become more thankful for the stuff you
have, and at the same time, you have less to worry about.*

DAY 59

*To all three belong the same eternity, the same
unchangeableness, the same majesty, the same power.*
AUGUSTINE

But anyone who does not love does not know God, for God is love.
1 JOHN 4:8

The Trinity is difficult to understand for most people. It's often debated philosophically. And even though we might not be able to grasp the mystery of the Trinity it's still one of the most wonderful doctrines that helps us better know the nature of our God.

Some present the Trinity as three Gods equal one God, or three persons equals one person. If this was correct, the critics would be right and the doctrine of the Trinity would be philosophically inconsistent. There is only one God and one divine nature. There are, however, three persons existing eternally in this one nature. This is still a mystery, but it's not a self-contradiction philosophically. In fact, there would be some major problems if God consisted of only one person. He wouldn't be love. Love is something that you do in relationship with others. If God had been completely alone at any point, there would be no one to love. He wouldn't BE love. He wouldn't be a social God of fellowship either. This is a huge problem for the Jewish and Muslim understanding of God!

Even though the Triune God may seem to be difficult to understand, it turns out to be one of the most wonderful things in our relationship with him. It may be a mystery, but it assures us that his nature is love and relationship oriented. God-Father, God-Son, and God-Spirit have already existed in a perfect, loving relationship, and you are invited to be a part of it!

THINK ABOUT IT!
Do you reflect on the awesome nature of God?

DAY 60

*Man is corrupt. Man is imperfect. The bottom line is that man
has, let's say, destroyed just about everything he's touched
since the dawn of time. There are a lot of men in this world that
have absolutely distorted and corrupted the Word of God.*
ERIC CLAYTON (SAVIOR MACHINE)

*When the Spirit of truth comes, he will guide you into all
truth. He will not speak on his own but will tell you what
he has heard. He will tell you about the future.*
JOHN 16:13

How do you know what to believe in the Bible? Everyone has their own opinions, and every church seems to have a different idea of what it means!" I have heard this excuse for not reading the Bible hundreds of times. And honestly, it isn't a very good one. This prediction from the the Gospel of John above has rung true for the last 2,000 years! There have been many people who have distorted the Word of God. I have to admit I've been one of them over the years. It is always a temptation to try to make the Bible fit into our understanding of theology and life. But that isn't how it works.

Let me give you the best piece of advice that I can possibly give you concerning your personal Bible reading: Lose your agendas! If you begin your reading with preconceived ideas of what it is going to say, you will twist it to fit. Remember, it isn't about you trying to manipulate the Bible. It is about the Holy Spirit inside of you teaching you; he will "guide you into all truth." Pray, "Lord, help me to see your truth and not my agenda. Guide me to understand those things that my own mind cannot understand."

THINK ABOUT IT!

*Have you allowed the Holy Spirit to give
you insight into the Word of God?*

DAY 61

*If through a broken heart God can bring His purposes to pass
in the world, then thank Him for breaking your heart.*
OSWALD CHAMBERS

*The Lord is close to the brokenhearted; he
rescues those whose spirits are crushed.*
PSALM 34:18

*God saved you by his grace when you believed. And you can't take
credit for this; it is a gift from God. Salvation is not a reward for the
good things we have done, so none of us can boast about it.*
GALATIANS 2:8-9

We still have this idea that, the better we become as a person, the more God will like us. The truth? God doesn't accept you on the basis of your accomplishments. It is Christ's finished work on the cross that he sees. We really need to stop depending on our abilities and start relying on Him! It begins with salvation and holds true for every aspect of our lives. Proverbs 3:5 says, "Trust in the Lord with all your heart; do not depend on your own understanding. Seek his will in all you do, and he will show you which path to take."

When we fail, our hearts are broken. The world around us instructs us to take control and try again. That isn't bad advice, but it isn't complete advice. When you're broken, allow him to rescue you and lift you up. It has never been about your strength to succeed. It's about his grace and power in your life. For many of us, it is only after our hearts are broken that we begin to pay attention to God's leading in our lives!

THINK ABOUT IT!
Have you allowed God to rescue your brokenness?

DAY 62

Don't throw away another day
LYRICS FROM "I W8 4 YOU"
BY LOVE AND DEATH [BETWEEN HERE AND LOST]

Make the most of every opportunity in these evil days. Don't act thoughtlessly, but understand what the Lord wants you to do.
GALATIANS 5:16-17

What occupies your time every day? What are your daily and weekly habits? Its been said if you don't control your day, your day will control you! Watching television, checking your cell phone every 15 minutes, playing mindless video games—all of these things can become addictive. Don't let technology and entertainment take control over your priorities.

We're way more affected by society than we realize. Social pressure has the power to overrule our convictions. Studies show that social media can change your actions despite your opinions. Know what you believe. Stand firm in it. Use some discipline. Make sure you are always gleaning truth in your life.

Our priorities need to reflect the things that will last: relationships, love, service to our communities, etc. Don't waste your life! When you look back at it from when you are 40, 60, and 80 years old, you need to feel good about your life.

THINK ABOUT IT!

Find a good balance between working, relaxing, and your spiritual life. It's okay to enjoy watching television, but don't let it take too much of your time. Use the exciting opportunities of social media for meaningful relationships, but don't be a slave to your computer and your phone. Face-to-face relationships are always better! Keep your eyes on the things that will last forever and bring you eternal satisfaction in the end. Don't let a day go by without seeking the Lord. Are you balanced in your priorities?

DAY 63

"It was mind-boggling, the deeper I got into it and one day it hit me like a shot. I'm reading the living word of a living God."
BLACKIE LAWLESS (W.A.S.P.)

Therefore, we never stop thanking God that when you received his message from us, you didn't think of our words as mere human ideas. You accepted what we said as the very word of God--which, of course, it is. And this word continues to work in you who believe.
1 THESSALONIANS 2:13

Some of us have been brought up in the Christian faith. We have been taught from childhood that the Bible is the Word of God. But, there comes a time in all of our lives when we wonder if that is actually true? Blackie explains this very well: "So I start reading and I start discovering and you have 66 books written by 40 different authors spread over three different continents, in three different languages, over a 2,000-year period. Most of the authors did not know each other, had no knowledge of each other but yet I see consistently that they're not just answering each other's questions, they're finishing each other's sentences."

It's important for you to start experiencing the Word of God for yourself. One of the cool things about reading the Bible is this: the more you get to know it, the more you will enjoy it! This doesn't mean you should force yourself to read several chapters every single day. Sometimes we jump in and overwhelm ourselves! Simply read it with your heart. Ask yourself while reading how it affects your life. Many people enjoy just reading a few verses a day. However you begin, make sure it is something that becomes life to you. Let it transform your thinking. The Bible has changed millions of lives throughout history and it can do the same for you!

THINK ABOUT IT!

Have you actually realized what you're reading?

DAY 64

Grasping at knowledge and still lacking the truth.
LYRICS FROM "ITCHING EARS" BY THE BURIAL [IN THE TAKING OF FLESH]

That night God appeared to Solomon and said, 'What do you want? Ask, and I will give it to you!' Solomon replied to God, '…Give me the wisdom and knowledge to lead [the people] properly, for who could possibly govern this great people of yours?' God said to Solomon, 'Because your greatest desire is to help your people, and you did not ask for wealth, riches, fame, or even the death of your enemies or a long life, but rather you asked for wisdom and knowledge to properly govern my people, I will certainly give you the wisdom and knowledge you requested.'
2 CHRONICLES 1:7-12

What would you ask God for, if he asked you the same question that he asked Solomon? Would you have asked for a new guitar? A new car? Or even a bigger house? Would you ask to be the smartest person in the world? Solomon was already a wise man when he had this conversation with God. His answer shows his wisdom. But he knew it wasn't enough.

Notice how he asks for knowledge AND wisdom. What is the difference? Knowledge is knowing HOW to speak well. Wisdom is knowing WHEN to speak, and when to be quiet. As you can see, they work together. Some people spend their whole lives learning about their faith, but never acquiring the wisdom to use it. This is no longer a conversation you need to have with God. You have received the knowledge of God through his Word, the Bible. And you have received the wisdom of God through the Holy Spirit who lives inside of you. You have everything you need to live a godly life!

THINK ABOUT IT!

Were you aware that God has already given you knowledge and wisdom?

DAY 65

*Father in heaven (…) Bring unto this darkened
earth the Kingdom in which you reside.*
LYRICS FROM "VALLEY OF MASS CRUCIFIXION"
BY BROKEN FLESH [BROKEN FLESH]

*For the Kingdom of God is not a matter of what we eat or drink, but
of living a life of goodness and peace and joy in the Holy Spirit.*
ROMANS 14:17

The Kingdom of God begins with Jesus. But there's a futuristic aspect to it as well. We live in a time where God's Kingdom is breaking through. This is very exciting! God wants you to be a part of building his Kingdom. We're part of destroying the evil powers. "For the Kingdom…is living by God's power" (1 Corinthians 4:20). God uses his power through us. We're Kingdom-builders!

When we have healthy church relationships, we're building the Kingdom of God. When we learn how to live in peace and communion with each other, we're building the Kingdom of God. Feeding the homeless and bringing care and restoration to the addicted is building the Kingdom. Gods Kingdom is holistic. It restores everything that is broken. Proclaiming the gospel by growling it from a stage is also building the Kingdom. We must proclaim the victory of Jesus Christ until he returns.

What an honor it is to be a part of building the Kingdom! Surrender to the Lord today and let the Holy Spirit work in you. Ask him how you can be a part of building the Kingdom. We spend our whole lives working on stuff that'll disappear with time. Why not spend your time on the things that'll last forever?

THINK ABOUT IT!

*Are you letting God's strength flow through you
today? And are you using it to build up others?*

DAY 66

My revenge boils inside though I try to oppress it but I cannot deny my newborn freedom. Forgiving is not forgetting. A broken heart mended, no more crying in vain. Regrets, suffer, ignorance, all feelings are dead.
LYRICS FROM "UNCHAINED" BY ANTESTOR [OMEN]

Do not seek revenge or bear a grudge against a fellow Israelite, but love your neighbor as yourself. I am the Lord.
LEVITICUS 19:18

Get rid of all bitterness, rage, anger, harsh words, and slander, as well as all types of evil behavior. Instead, be kind to each other, tenderhearted, forgiving one another, just as God through Christ has forgiven you.
GALATIANS 4:31-32

As Antestor says in this song, "Forgiving is not forgetting." We always feel as if we are not truly forgiving someone if we remember the offense. No, you'll continue to be human. In fact, The Book of Proverbs tells us not to trust someone who has proven to be untrustworthy. You have to remember the offense so you can make good judgements about those who are not trustworthy in the future. But forgiveness is another thing.

"Love your neighbor as you love yourself" is a tall order. He wants you to agapé them, and love them with his love. Unconditionally. When you can truly do that, you have repeated in practice what Jesus did on the cross. Our love is limited, and God knows that. It's the reason that "LOVE" is listed as the first fruit of the Holy Spirit, who's living inside of you. And as he loves through you, his love allows you to forgive.

THINK ABOUT IT!

Have you let him change you so that you may love and forgive?

DAY 67

I sometimes have this feeling that I am not measuring up as a Christian. I convince myself that God is angry and withholding his love for me due to my performance. I imagine him writing on a large chalk board in heaven, and making yet another check mark in the "bad" column next to my name. Of course, nothing could be further from the truth!

The Bible tells us that God keeps no records of our wrongdoing. That is what Michael Sweet is talking about here. God continues to remind us in his Word that his love is undying—full of grace and mercy. When he looks at me he says, "There's Bob. I really love that guy. I love him so much that I sent my only son to die for him. When I look in his eyes I see Jesus!" Amazing! It's only because of Jesus' death on the cross that I am made righteous before God. Why is he pleased with me? Because I do everything perfectly? Hardly! He is pleased because Jesus has made me righteous in his sight. Those of us who are Christians have his Holy Spirit inside of us, and he recognizes Him every time he sees us!

THINK ABOUT IT!

*When was the last time you beat yourself up for your
shortcomings? Did you also remind yourself that you
are deeply loved, forgiven, and saved by his grace?*

DAY 68

*Since you cannot do good to all, you are to pay special
attention to those who, by the accidents of time, or place, or
circumstances, are brought into closer connection with you.*

SAINT AUGUSTINE

Share each other's burdens, and in this way obey the law of Christ.

GALATIANS 6:2

J amie attended the festival because one of his favorite bands would be playing. Before he left home, his friends warned him to stay away from me. "He will try to convert you," they told him. So throughout the festival, he managed to avoid me. As I boarded the plane to return home, I noticed a look of horror come across the face of the person sitting next to me. It was Jamie.

God moved heaven and earth and circumstances just to put him there in that seat. We had a great talk, and continued to stay in touch. Today, he is one of my closest friends, and a podcaster on our SIM network. I have begun to pay attention to the people around me. It amazes me how many divine appointments there are every day if we'll just be aware of them!

THINK ABOUT IT!

In what areas of your life is God trying to get your attention?

DAY 69

*My soul will praise the Lord, and everything
within me extol His holy name.*
LYRICS FROM "EXTOL" BY EXTOL

*A Psalm of David. Let all that I am praise the LORD;
with my whole heart, I will praise his holy name.*
PSALM 103:1

The Book of Psalms in the Old Testament is actually a collection of songs. Most of them were written by David. David was a musician. He understood the power of music. He used it to express to God how he felt. In Palm 150, he even talks about making a lot of noise with loud instruments to God. Sound familiar?

We actually have a lot in common with David. He understood the enjoyment of music. He not only sang it, but he wrote it. He understood how important it was to create music from the depth of his heart. Passionate. Inspired. Like so many metal songs these days, he poured his whole heart into his music and presented a powerful message. Take some time and read through this collection of songs called Psalms in the Bible. You might have more in common with David than you think!

THINK ABOUT IT!

Have you read through the Psalms? There are 150 of them. If you read five every day, you will complete them in a month's time.

DAY 70

I struggle, I fight, I fall, I bleed, but my soul is free!
LYRICS FROM "CANVAS" BY SACRIFICIUM

*When peace, like a river, attendeth my way, when
sorrows like sea billows roll; whatever my lot, thou hast
taught me to say, It is well, it is well with my soul.*

*Though Satan should buffet, though trials should come, let
this blest assurance control, that Christ has regarded my
helpless estate, and hath shed his own blood for my soul.*

*My sin, oh, the bliss of this glorious thought! My sin, not in
part but the whole, is nailed to the cross, and I bear it no
more, praise the Lord, praise the Lord, O my soul!*

*And, Lord, haste the day when my faith shall be sight, the
clouds be rolled back as a scroll; the trump shall resound, and
the Lord shall descend, even so, it is well with my soul.*

This song has always been my favorite. The author, Horatio G. Spafford (1828-1888), was a successful business man from Chicago. Several days after the death of his son, he lost his fortune in the great Chicago fire of 1871. Since they had been through so much, he decided to take a vacation with his family. He sent his wife and 4 daughters ahead on a ship to Europe and planned to follow them in a few days. The ship was struck at sea by another vessel and sank within minutes. Spafford received a telegram from his wife that read: "Saved. Alone." His children were lost at sea. It was after all of this heartbreak that he penned this song. It is well with my soul.

THINK ABOUT IT!

*No matter what happens to us, God is always
our refuge in the time of storms.*

DAY 71

*And then he told them, "Go into all the world and
preach the Good News to everyone."*
MARK 16:15

We get a bit too content in our Christian "bubbles." We shelter our families and friends from the world around us, but in doing so, we shut the world out from our influence. Are you waiting for a special calling to go to the non-Christian world to share the Good News? Get moving! You don't need a special calling to move forward. Jesus already told you to "GO!"

How do you share it? Mostly by living among them. Showing them your life. Living your Christian life in front of people. And when they see a difference in you, they will ask you questions. You don't have to stand on a street corner and yell at people. You simply share your life with people. And as you do, issues of spiritual importance will always come up. In that context, it isn't threatening. It's simply naturally sharing with others the very faith that is important to you!

THINK ABOUT IT!

Have you been waiting for a special calling to "go?"

DAY 72

*Only through Jesus taking this lonely, lost, hurting and broken
soul, cleaning me up and setting me in another direction did I finally
find out who I was, where I had been and where I was going.*
MARK ALLEN (EX-VOTO)

*"For I know the plans I have for you," says the Lord. "They are plans
for good and not for disaster, to give you a future and a hope."*
JEREMIAH 29:11

onely. Lost. Hurting. Broken. That pretty much describes most of us. We have a longing in the deepest parts of our being to be "found." We long for someone to help us find direction, and explain to us where we should be going! How exciting to know that God has a plan for you. Yes, YOU! He has a specific plan for your good. His desire is to take that which is broken and mend it. To take your confusion and give you hope. To give you a future beyond what you could have imagined on your own!

There's never a time when God doesn't have a specific plan for you. Even on those days when it seems hopeless and overwhelming, he is there to give you hope! Sometimes we feel very broken. That's the state we're in when we come to Jesus. It is important that we continue, day by day, to seek him for direction. He has a plan!

THINK ABOUT IT!

Are you relying on God's good plans for your life?

DAY 73

While nothing but darkness encloses the sky—Then I begin
to see—A light in the distance that's calling for me.
LYRICS FROM "VISIONS" BY HOPE FOR THE DYING

The gatekeeper opens the gate for him, and the
sheep recognize his voice and come to him. He calls
his own sheep by name and leads them out.
JOHN 10:3

There are many voices that attempt to get our attention. Television commercials. Roadside billboards. Even short ads we are forced to watch on YouTube. Everyone has something to sell or something they would like to persuade you to do. With so many voices around you, how do you listen to your own conscience or to the Holy Spirit inside of you?

Practice. It takes practice. The Bible tells us that we will know the Truth, and the truth will set us free. Free from what? All of those voices for instance. This verse in John tells us that the sheep recognize his voice. Why? Because they have heard it before. It is nothing new to them. They come to him because they recognize him and they trust him. The more you learn about God from his Word, and the more you allow the Holy Spirit to guide you from your innermost being, the more you will hear him when he calls you. With all the voices trying to get your attention, it is more important than ever to be able to hear HIS voice!

THINK ABOUT IT!
Are you learning to recognize God's voice?

DAY 74

*Most of us would prefer, however, to spend our time doing
something that will get immediate results. We don't want to
wait for God to resolve matters in His good time because
His idea of 'good time' is seldom in sync with ours.*

OSWALD CHAMBERS

*Wait patiently for the Lord. Be brave and
courageous. Yes, wait patiently for the Lord.*

PSALM 27:14

*I waited patiently for the Lord to help me, and he turned
to me and heard my cry. He lifted me out of the pit of
despair, out of the mud and the mire. He set my feet on
solid ground and steadied me as I walked along.*

PSALM 40:1-2

I waited patiently for the Lord to help me" I dislike this scripture. It goes against my flesh. I prefer immediate results. It seems the faster my pace, the less patience I have for God's timing. Now don't get me wrong. I have messed up my life plenty of times by running ahead of God's timing. Romans 8:28 says, "And we know that God causes everything to work together for the good of those who love God and are called according to his purpose for them." It's like saying, "God! The snow and wind are coming. I must build a house for protection." So I begin by constructing the roof. But unless I have the foundation for the house and the walls to support it, the roof isn't going to do me very much good!

The same is true with God's timing. He carefully constructs the foundation of the house so that it will support the roof. When the snow and wind comes, the house stands firm. When we run ahead of God and don't allow "for all things to work together," our house doesn't stand. So, "be brave and courageous. Yes, wait patiently for the Lord."

THINK ABOUT IT!

Do you have a difficult time waiting on the Lord?

DAY 75

*[Jesus said] The Father and I are one." Once again the people
picked up stones to kill him. Jesus said, "At my Father's direction
I have done many good works. For which one are you going to
stone me?" They replied, "We're stoning you not for any good
work, but for blasphemy! You, a mere man, claim to be God." Jesus
replied, "…Don't believe me unless I carry out my Father's work. But
if I do his work, believe in the evidence of the miraculous works I
have done, even if you don't believe me. Then you will know and
understand that the Father is in me, and I am in the Father.*
JOHN 10:30-33, 37-38

J esus didn't ask us to believe in him blindly. Of course, Christianity
does involve a certain amount of faith. But Jesus also challenged
the people of his day to judge his claims about his identity on his
works that proved it. They didn't fully understand what he meant until
after he had risen from the dead and ascended into Heaven.

There are no historical records that record that Jesus' death and resurrection did not occur. On the contrary, there were lots of witnesses that saw
it, so people could ask about it. They knew Jesus had risen from the dead.
There were even people who saw him ascend into heaven that still doubted!
The people argued about the meaning of it, not about the event itself. Even
if we remove the four Gospels, historians still have an extremely difficult
time explaining why Christianity grew so fast without the resurrection.
Many didn't realize that Jesus was actually carrying out his Father's work,
just as he said he would. And he told the people of his time to only believe
that he was who he claimed to be based on the outcome of his mission!

THINK ABOUT IT!

Have Jesus' claims changed your life as well?

DAY 76

I can love people better, so my band sees [being a
Chrisitian] as a better thing, not as a threatening thing.
REGINALD QUINCY "FIELDY" ARVIZU" (KORN)

Always be humble and gentle. Be patient with each other, making
allowance for each other's faults because of your love.
GALATIANS 4:2

F alling in love is an incredible thing! Every relationship begins with
infatuation. You see this person bigger than life, and your stomach
does flip flops at the sight of them. We used to call it "puppy love." It's
wonderful to feel that love from the beginning, even if it's a bit immature.

I love this about the Christian faith as well. We begin by responding to this awesome love that God has for us, and then it develops into
maturity. During this process, we are changed by his love. It becomes our
primary motivation. That is the kind of love Reginald Quincy "Fieldy"
Arvizu is talking about here: to be able to love people with a new heart
and with new eyes. This unconditional love is a free gift from God. It
automatically changes us the more we grow in our relationship with God!

THINK ABOUT IT!

How have you noticed your ability to love others
change since you have become a Christian?

DAY 77

There is so much rich history, strong Revelation, vivid imagery, and absolute Truth in the Bible that it is by far the most fascinating and popular book ever produced on the face of the earth.

ROB ROCK

And now, dear brothers and sisters, one final thing. Fix your thoughts on what is true, and honorable, and right, and pure, and lovely, and admirable. Think about things that are excellent and worthy of praise.

PHILIPPIANS 4:8

It has been estimated that over 6 BILLION BIBLES (in whole or in part) have been printed over the years. No other book even comes close. Surprised? Don't be! Even when anti-christian forces try to stop its production, God is sovereign. He'll always protect his Word! When you open the cover, TRUTH emanates! Something very supernatural happens as you begin to read. God's truth begins to brighten the dark corners of your heart and mind.

As Rob Rock says, it contains "strong revelation, vivid imagery, and absolute truth!" No other book can claim that or even come close. From cover to cover, God's love story to us unfolds. His principles for living an abundant life begin to make sense. It's an amazing feeling when God's truth begins to penetrate your heart! But this is nothing new. The Bible has had this effect on countless generations. Lives have been changed, challenged, and encouraged. And that same life-changing power is still changing lives today!

THINK ABOUT IT!

Have you given the Bible a proper place in your life? Have you allowed its life-giving principles to transform your life?

DAY 78

Don't be selfish; don't try to impress others.
PHILIPPIANS 2:3

S ome people spend their whole lives worrying about what others think. This shapes their actions and controls their thoughts. It also means that the real motivation for doing good deeds isn't being noticed. In some of the worst cases it creates anxiety. We attend social gatherings, and the only thing we can concentrate on is our need to impress those around us. We desperately seek the approval of others. But, we're never satisfied.

Not caring what others think does not mean you'll never need friends who encourage you and care for you. We're still human and have emotional and spiritual needs. But we must not build our lives around getting people to like us. Putting our friendships in proper perspective has lifelong implications. That's how true friendships are made!

THINK ABOUT IT!

Be the kind of person who does good deeds even when no one's looking. Don't be motivated by other's approval. Instead, find your value in God. He loves you and has already approved you!

DAY 79

*It is requisite for the relaxation of the mind that we make
use, from time to time, of playful deeds and jokes.*

THOMAS AQUINAS

*But to all who believed him and accepted him, he
gave the right to become children of God.*

JOHN 1:12

Working hard for the Kingdom of God is a great mindset that all of us should have. But there are some who are a bit too focused. They feel like they are personally responsible to save the whole world. And in reality, they are also usually unpleasant to be around. All work and no play make them difficult. Work hard, but take the time to play as well. Be an enjoyable and chill person to be around. It will take you a lot further.

Taking time to have fun reminds us of important aspects about being children of God. Children run towards the swing, and when they fall, they return to their parents and seek comfort. One of the keys to life is to not take oneself too seriously. Jokes give us a break from serious thinking. There's wisdom in humor, since it reminds us that joy is everlasting and pain is temporary.

THINK ABOUT IT!

How do you play?

DAY 80

Don't let anyone think less of you because you are young.
Be an example to all believers in what you say, in the way
you live, in your love, your faith, and your purity.
1 TIMOTHY 4:12

How do you live your passions? That's a great question! When you're young, it's easy to think that you'll get to live out your passions when you get older. Unfortunately, for a lot of people it results in never getting started and just going with the flow. When Christ called his disciples, they were probably just teenagers. Some have estimated them being between 14 and 16 years old. Pretty young, isn't it? It doesn't matter how old you are, or where you are from. God is ready to use you and help you experience his plans for you!

Alice here describes a deep insight to the Christian faith: We're never done learning. Until we reach the Kingdom of God, our understanding will be limited. We're on a journey. We always feel like we are just getting started. But no matter where you're at personally, God is ready to use you!

We do however experience growth. And if you're at a place where you feel like you have some experience to offer, consider mentoring. The Bible speaks about the older teaching the younger. So if you are young or just feel very young in the faith, God is still ready to use you. No matter what age you are or how experienced in the faith you are, consider having both older people in your life that can mentor you and younger people you can guide into a great relationship with God.

THINK ABOUT IT!

Who are you teaching, and who's teaching you?

DAY 81

*"Don't sin by letting anger control you." Don't let
the sun go down while you are still angry.*
GALATIANS 4:26

I hate church!" I have heard that more than once in my 50 years of ministry. So many have had bad experiences. Some have been taught a "prosperity gospel." They were promised healing and riches if they only had faith enough. Others have been raised in a very strict and legalistic church. The strong focus on all the rules and regulations can really confuse our identity in Christ. Many metal heads have had bad experiences with the church, being looked down on for their music and accused of being satanic. A friend of mine was told that his tattoos were portals for the devil, which obviously isn't the case.

It's very difficult returning to the church after such an experience. Some of you may even need to take a break. In that case, it would be good for you to find a small group of people to have fellowship (church) with.

Even though it looks extremely different around the world, metal heads are generally more accepted by the church today. And even though some of you have been deeply hurt by the church, Christ calls us to forgive and join a Christian fellowship once again. For some this will mean re-entering a church building. For others, it may mean having casual church-fellowship at home. Our Christian brothers and sisters were wrong to judge us, but we must let go of our anger and forgive. Christ has forgiven us for so much more!

THINK ABOUT IT!

*Are you on the road to forgiving and being
a part of a church once again?*

DAY 82

Their confidence hangs by a thread.
JOB 8:14

I t's massively important that you find your identity and foundation in Christ. We're created in his image. We're children of the most high King. Grasping this takes more than a lifetime. Often our thoughts and emotions can hold us back from taking chances. Make sure you have people around you that encourage you in your pursuits, and help you to do the things you feel insecure about—both small things and big dreams. And by daring to take small chances you will, with time, be ready to take the larger ones as well.

In the end, it all comes back to our identity in Christ. He gave us the right to become children of God. God created you. He knows you better than you know yourself. He wants to use you, and that's a pretty good reason to have the confidence to get started!

THINK ABOUT IT!

*Do you have the courage to try something
that may seem a bit frightening?*

DAY 83

His final breath heard both in Heaven and in Hell, against
the gates of which He has prevailed. The veil was torn, the
temple destroyed and in the tomb rebuilt again. He
holds the keys, the One found worthy. It is finished.

LYRICS FROM "IN THE TAKING OF FLESH: "DIAKONOS"
BY THE BURIAL [IN THE TAKING OF FLESH]

When Jesus had tasted it, he said, "It is finished!" Then
he bowed his head and gave up his spirit.

JOHN 19:30

At that moment the curtain in the sanctuary of the Temple was torn
in two, from top to bottom. The earth shook, rocks split apart.

MATTHEW 27:51

The greatest words ever spoken by Jesus were "IT IS FINISHED." Your whole relationship with God and your future eternity in Heaven find their foundation in those words. His death on the cross provided a connection between sinful man and a holy God. But he didn't just connect. He decided to move in. In the back of the Temple was the "Holy of Holies." Only the high priest was allowed to enter it, and only when he had been made clean by a series of sacrifices. He went into this room behind the curtain with fear and trembling to atone for the sins of the people. They tied a bell and a rope around his leg—just in case he didn't live through it. It was an awesome thing to come into the perfect holiness of God.

But watch what happens next! At the moment of Jesus' death, God tore that curtain in half, and made a new covenant with man. He decided to place his spirit inside of you. YOU are now the temple of the Holy Spirit. The same awesome spirit that used to reside in the Holy of Holies now lives inside of you!!

THINK ABOUT IT!

Do you realize you are the temple of the Holy Spirit?

DAY 84

I reflect upon the day the stone was rolled aside.
LYRICS FROM "ORISON"
BY HOPE FOR THE DYING [DISSIMULATION]

*But very early on Sunday morning the women went to the tomb,
taking the spices they had prepared. They found that the stone
had been rolled away from the entrance. So they went in, but
they didn't find the body of the Lord Jesus. As they stood there
puzzled, two men suddenly appeared to them then the men
asked, "Why are you looking among the dead for someone
who is alive? He isn't here! He is risen from the dead!"*
LUKE 24:1-6

Can you imagine what it must have been like to live during the
time of Jesus' death and resurrection? Everyone had a difficult
time trying to figure it all out. Even though Jesus gave them
some pretty big hints, he knew they wouldn't quite understand. It's interesting to me how he gave commentary and explanation all along the way.
He even provided two angels at the tomb to let the women know what
was going on. Why? He didn't want them to miss this! It was extremely
important that they realize he was alive. If he had stayed in the tomb, he
would not have completed the mission. He would not be the mediator
between you and God. The stone was rolled away to prove the tomb was
empty. He is alive—and we are forgiven!

THINK ABOUT IT!

*Have you ever reflected on the impact this
great event has on your life?*

DAY 85

If a preacher is not first preaching to himself, better that he falls on the steps of the pulpit and breaks his neck than preaching that sermon.

JOHN CALVIN

Dear brothers and sisters, I want you to understand that the gospel message I preach is not based on mere human reasoning.

GALATIANS 1:11

Maybe these words from Calvin are a bit extreme. Yes. But he makes a good point! We need to be aware of hypocrisy in our own lives. This doesn't just apply to public speakers. It also applies when you are just talking to friends, both Christians and people of other world views. Do we live up to the words that we're speaking?

People can tell when we're fake! They are usually smarter than we give them credit for. Your message won't get through if you don't live it yourself. Test yourself with your own words. Even better, preach it to yourself! Reflect on your own experience. Have an attitude of looking inward whenever you hear a message, wether that message is from others or from your own mouth.

Pointing fingers is easy. Living up to your own words is much more difficult! Our goal is to speak with integrity. When we are able to do this, we'll get a different response from the people we encounter. When they see that we speak from a point of experience and integrity, then it doesn't matter if we screw up the words. They'll see something real, and they'll want to experience it themselves.

THINK ABOUT IT!

Are you a person of integrity?

DAY 86

*But now you are free from the power of sin
and have become slaves of God.*
ROMANS 6:22

WE ARE FREE! When we receive God's grace, we become free. We no longer have to fear death. When we give ourselves to Christ, he gives us eternal life. We're saved! But you weren't free. 1 Corinthians 6:20 says, "for God bought you with a high price." That means that we no longer belong to ourselves, but we belong to God. He purchased us!

So how can we be free and at the same time slaves of God? Because true freedom is only found in a relationship with God. Being free is about distancing ourselves from all the things that bind us. Sin destroys freedom. It creates a need in us that this world cannot satisfy. But true freedom is living the way God intended.

As you mature in your walk with the Lord you will experience more of his mind and love. And this will set you free. It's like learning how to play a guitar. Without lessons or practice, you won't play very well. If you practice, you'll experience more freedom. Your abilities will improve. We're God's property. And honestly, that's the freest and best thing to be!

THINK ABOUT IT!
Do you understand real freedom?

DAY 87

*"When our will wholeheartedly enters into the
prayer of Christ, then we pray correctly."*
DIETRICH BONHOEFFER

We understand these things, for we have the mind of Christ.
1 CORINTHIANS 2:16

God is not a magic genie. It isn't about you deciding what is best for you, and then informing him what to do. Prayers don't get God to change his mind, or persuade him to give something that is out of his will for you. When you pray, you share in a relationship with the Lord. Prayers express what's on our hearts. It expresses where you're at personally, and what concerns you might have. If you think prayer is about simply asking for stuff, then you've missed the whole point. Just as you would share your thoughts and concerns in any other relationship, so it is with God. It's simply sharing your thoughts. Your emotions. Your heart.

When you pray every day for a friend to be saved, you are expressing to God what is on your heart. He isn't playing a game with you, counting how many times you pray until you reach some magic number. When you pray for something consistently, it makes a difference in you! And don't forget to listen. That changes everything! All of us listen differently, and therefore you cannot tell other people how to pray, but praying together can be a huge blessing.

God will put burdens on our hearts. We will connect with his heart and the things he has already started doing. In that way, he'll show us what to pray for and use us to do the things he has planned.

THINK ABOUT IT!

Are you listening to what God puts on your heart?

DAY 88

It felt like all burdens, everything I had been
carrying, were lifted off my shoulders.
PETER BALTES (ACCEPT)

Take my yoke upon you. Let me teach you, because I am humble
and gentle at heart, and you will find rest for your souls. For
my yoke is easy to bear, and the burden I give you is light.
MATTHEW 11:29-30

FREEDOM is a key word in the New Testament. Paul reminds us over and over again that we are "truly free!" Why is so much time spent on this concept? Because it is the amazing result of becoming a Christian. Isn't it sad that so many Christians don't really understand their freedom?

Peter Baltes had been carrying many of the burdens that life gives you. He didn't have any place to leave them! When he became a Christian, he allowed God to lift all of those burdens off of his shoulders. An actual yoke allowed oxen to pull heavy loads. Jesus tells us that his yoke is easy. It isn't a burden. He wants to carry the heavy load with us as we learn to walk with him. Many times we forget about his offer. We allow the burdens of life to become a heavy yoke around our necks and try to carry them by ourselves. We need to remember every day that God desires to walk beside us.1 Peter 5:7 tells us to "give all your worries and cares to God, for he cares about you."

THINK ABOUT IT!

Are you allowing God to carry your burdens with you, or
are you still trying to carry them on your own?

DAY 89

He always comes through for me, in the craziest
ways, in ways I could never even imagine. We need
Jesus, more than ever, in all of our struggles.
BROOK REEVES (IMPENDING DOOM)

I have told you all this so that you may have peace in me.
Here on earth you will have many trials and sorrows. But
take heart, because I have overcome the world.
JOHN 16:23

I f you're old enough to read this, you've surely noticed that inner peace doesn't happen easily. People actually use it as a marketing strategy. "Our company will give you financial peace." Or "You will have peace of mind knowing that your home is protected by our alarm company." Or "You'll have eternal peace knowing that you have pre-paid your cemetery plot before you die." We throw that word around, mostly because everyone is looking for some kind of peace.

Jesus says that peace doesn't come from anything in the world. He actually told us we would have many trials and sorrows. Then he gives us some great news "I have overcome the world!" Past tense. Because of his death on the cross, we have TRUE peace!

THINK ABOUT IT!

When was the last time you gave your trials and sorrow to Jesus?

DAY 90

I Can Not Understand I Do Not Practice What I Will But I Do What I Hate Who Will Rescue Me From This Body Doomed To Death.
LYRICS FROM "HUMAN" BY ANTESTOR [THE DEFEAT OF SATAN]

I have discovered this principle of life—that when I want to do what is right, I inevitably do what is wrong. I love God's law with all my heart. But there is another power within me that is at war with my mind. This power makes me a slave to the sin that is still within me. Oh, what a miserable person I am! Who will free me from this life that is dominated by sin and death? Thank God! The answer is in Jesus Christ our Lord. So you see how it is: In my mind I really want to obey God's law, but because of my sinful nature I am a slave to sin.
ROMANS 7:21-25

I fully understand what Paul is saying here in this verse. I can't count how many times I have said, "Lord, I promise I will never commit this sin again. I am so sorry. From now on, I will do better." I have prayed that prayer for the same habitual sin over and over for 50 years! Have I gotten any better? Not really. Not in some areas. Do these sins keep me from God's grace? No! It is because of his grace that I am still saved and have freedom in Christ.

It was a monumental day when I realized that perfect people were not going to Heaven. I always had this feeling that if I could just be a better person, I had more of a chance for God's love and eternity with him. But that isn't true. SAVED people are going to Heaven. Only those who accept Jesus Christ and his death on the cross as a substitution for their sin are going to Heaven. That's me!

THINK ABOUT IT!

Is that you?

DAY 91

This is a very misunderstood scripture. Many have preached that it instructs us to speak in tongues all the time. Others suggest that you have to be persistent when you want God to do something. The more you repeat it, the better the chance you have of receiving it. Neither are true. Prayer is all about aligning your heart with God's heart. It is about the Holy Spirit guiding you and inspiring you. But mostly, "Pray in the Spirit at all times and on every occasion" is talking about never-ending prayer.

The original Greek here actually means "prayer that doesn't begin and end." We are instructed to ALWAYS be in fellowship with God through prayer. All day. All the time. On every occasion. Stay alert. Bring everything to God in prayer. It is more important that you stay in a constant state of prayer than it is to carve out a specific time for prayer. That has its benefits as well, but constant never-ending prayer is what will change your life!

THINK ABOUT IT!

Are you in continuous prayer?

DAY 92

Seek out people who will stand by you and love you for who you are,
and truly do as Christ calls them to do, which is to be there for you.
ERIC CLAYTON (SAVIOR MACHINE)

So encourage each other and build each other
up, just as you are already doing.
1 THESSALONIANS 5:11

Let us hold tightly without wavering to the hope we affirm, for God
can be trusted to keep his promise. Let us think of ways to motivate
one another to acts of love and good works. And let us not neglect
our meeting together, as some people do, but encourage one
another, especially now that the day of his return is drawing near.
HEBREWS 10:23-25

Every time I do a podcast about discovering your passions in life I get a lot of mail. "How can I discover my passions?" "I have passions, but no one believes in me. I am losing faith in myself as well." These are typical. And, as I ask about their lives and circumstances, I find that most of them don't belong to a Christian fellowship of any kind. Why is that important? Simple. You were not designed to do this alone. The things you do well are not always obvious to you. And when they are, you rarely have anyone who will encourage you to move forward.

The main purpose for the "church" (the body of Christ—Christians—meeting together) is to "…encourage each other and build each other up." When you are not part of a church like this, you will find yourself seriously lacking in this area. All of us need people to believe in us. We need insight and encouragement when we doubt our calling, or when the road ahead becomes difficult. Having people walk beside us as we live out our calling and passions makes all the difference.

THINK ABOUT IT!

Do you have people around you who encourage
you in pursuing your passions?

DAY 93

The Bible is a mirror that helps us to see ourselves as we really are.
MATT SMITH (THEOCRACY)

*"Now we see things imperfectly, like puzzling reflections in a
mirror, but then we will see everything with perfect clarity. All
that I know now is partial and incomplete, but then I will know
everything completely, just as God now knows me completely."*
1 CORINTHIANS 13:12

Did you ever look into a mirror and feel like you have no idea who that person is who is looking back at you? As much as we think we know ourselves, we realize we don't! All of us are on a quest to "find ourselves." We want to really get to know that person in the mirror that, at times, feels so mysterious.

Matt Smith believes the Bible is a mirror that helps us see ourselves. We not only discover the answers to life's challenges, but we also discover who we are. You see, within that reflection on the other side, Jesus is standing behind me. I begin to see myself as he sees me. I begin to see myself in relationship with him. But it doesn't stop there! This verse tells us that we cannot see the whole picture. As good as it seems to be on this earth, it is nothing like what is coming. I am looking forward to seeing everything with perfect clarity!

THINK ABOUT IT!
Who do you see when you look into the mirror?

DAY 94

"Silence in the face of evil is itself evil: God will not hold us guiltless. Not to speak is to speak. Not to act is to act."
DIETRICH BONHOEFFER

He must have a strong belief in the trustworthy message he was taught; then he will be able to encourage others with wholesome teaching and show those who oppose it where they are wrong.
TITUS 1:9

We have a responsibility to use our voices to defend people who are being wronged. Luther, who Bonhoeffer was strongly inspired by, says: "You are not only responsible for what you say, but also for what you do not say." Silence has many lives on its conscience. Right now there are horrible things going on in the world, and by being silent about it, we are accepting it.

The same applies to your close personal friends. If they're on a bad path, you have the responsibility to talk to them about it. This only applies, however, to close friends with whom you have earned the right to speak into their life. Any true friendship must also include responsibility and accountability.

Bonhoeffer chose to go back to Germany and speak up against the Nazis during World War Two. He ended up paying for this with his life. But he did it anyway.

THINK ABOUT IT!

Are you taking a stand for somebody who's being treated unfairly? Are you using your voice to protect? This obviously doesn't mean bashing people on the internet. It must be done with love!

DAY 95

*So, my dear brothers and sisters...now you are united
with the one who was raised from the dead.*
ROMANS 7:4

The many theological debates going on all the time across the globe are at best confusing. Different denominations. Different views. Different priorities. Most of them have trained scholars who have studied theology for many years who can't agree on much of anything! This makes it almost impossible for Christians to figure out truth from error.

Theology can be difficult. It helps to focus on the things we can know for sure. And even though many denominations may disagree about baptism, the Eucharist, the role of tradition etc., we can agree about Jesus! If we have Jesus as the most important thing, we can call each other brothers and sisters despite denominational differences. This doesn't mean that there aren't important questions we need to think about. However, when all things come to an end, Jesus is all we'll need!

THINK ABOUT IT!

*Don't allow differences in doctrine to divide your relationships.
First and foremost, Jesus wants us to love God and to love each
other. He told us this was the most important commandment!
(Matthew 22:36-40). Protestants, Catholics, Pentecostals,
Lutherans, Calvinists—we might as well start getting along
now, since we're destined to spend eternity together!*

DAY 96

There is a populous of what I refer to as "bubble Christians" that sit on the polarized end of things–touting exclusivity above all, blindly brandishing Christian rhetoric, and giving the rest of humanity all the reason in the world to oppose them.

RYAN CLARK (DEMON HUNTER)

So we tell others about Christ, warning everyone and teaching everyone with all the wisdom God has given us. We want to present them to God, perfect in their relationship to Christ.

COLOSSIANS 1:28

Are you a 'bubble Christian?' Do you have non-Christian friends? Have you reached outside of your comfort zone to include those that may not share the same faith that you do?

These people who Ryan refers to as "bubble Christians" only have people around them with the same worldview. This is not the way Christ asked us to live. Unless you're a friend and have earned the right to speak into somebody's life, you will simply seem like yet another Bible thumper. Are you in a Christian bubble? It's time to break out!

There is really nothing to be afraid of. It's all about establishing meaningful relationships and asking people questions about life. We need to realize that it's not "us vs them." We are all people who seek answers to the big questions of life.

THINK ABOUT IT!

Be honest with those around you about the struggles and joys of your life today.

DAY 97

Hate breeding hate
LYRICS FROM "CRIES OF THE DEAD" BY
BROKEN FLESH [BROKEN FLESH]

Do to others as you would like them to do to you.
LUKE 6:31

S ome people are simply negative. You know the type. No matter what someone says they always have something negative to say. They seem to look at the dark side of life and have difficulty seeing anything positive. When you set out on a new project, they are the ones that give you every reason why it cannot be accomplished. Could this person possibly be you?

There are also those people who always speak positively about others. They seem to get along with everybody. Is this person possibly you?

The Bible is very clear on this subject: Love everybody unconditionally! James 1:23 says, "For if you listen to the Word and don't obey, it is like glancing at your face in a mirror." God can love people through us! We have to allow him to do so. God gives us the capacity to love people. His love never runs out. It never has boundaries. And it's not negative!

THINK ABOUT IT!

*Ask God to give you a soft heart. Let his love flow
through you. When was the last time you prayed for
those people around you who annoy you? :-)*

DAY 98

*Sometimes I wake up before dawn, and I love sitting up in the
middle of the bed with all the lights off, pitch-black dark, and
talking to the Father, with no interruptions and nothing that
reminds me that there's anything in life but me and Him.*

CHUCK SWINDOLL

*Before daybreak the next morning, Jesus got up
and went out to an isolated place to pray.*

MARK 1:35

I love Chuck Swindoll. He was actually the one who strongly suggested that I take time in the morning to spend time with God every day. It was during the beginning of Sanctuary, and he knew I would need this time with the Lord to stay on track. That was 30 years ago. And I am still dedicated to spending some quiet time in the mornings with God.

The "first fruits" of the day are amazing. Before you get hit with the cares of the world, get your mind ready. You're going to need God's help. Give him your day, and the situations the day will bring into your life. Ask him to give you Godly perspective. 1 Peter 5:7 says, "Give all your worries and cares to God, for he cares about you." How wonderful to have that sense of God walking beside you, knowing that nothing you encounter for the rest of the day is beyond his reach and outside of his care!

THINK ABOUT IT!

*Have you made it a point to cast all of your cares upon
God and allow him to care for you during each day?*

DAY 99

[Christians who] say stuff like "God Hates Fags" totally dishonor and disrespect God, and they dishonor and disrespect people who are made in God's image.
MATTIE MONTGOMERY (FOR TODAY)

…let the one who has never sinned throw the first stone!
JOHN 8:7

We often quote this verse, and then we keep throwing stones. Let's step back a moment and understand what Jesus is saying here. He told us not to judge. Why? Because ALL of us fall short of God's judgment. Why do we react to the sins of others? We seem to have a problem with people who sin differently than we do. And these days, the "church" has defined many groups of people whom we are told to love but to hate their sin.

I have never been good at mixing love and hate. I don't think it is a very biblical principle, either. I really have to take sin out the equation. Perhaps, what we should say instead is: "Love the sinner, and mourn the sin." Or "You worry about your sin, I'll worry about my sin, and let's concentrate on loving each other unconditionally." After all, both of these statements reflect the heart of God!

THINK ABOUT IT!

Are you guilty of judging other's sins instead of loving them unconditionally?

DAY 100

*When the Lord saw Moses coming to take a closer
look, God called to him from the middle of the bush,
"Moses! Moses!" "Here I am!" Moses replied.*
EXODUS 3:4

Lord, I am ready to do whatever you like. I will just be here on the couch watching television if you need me." Are you waiting around for the Lord to call you into something you'll be doing for the next 40 years? For most of us, it doesn't work that way. God doesn't reveal our whole life for us. If he revealed all of his plans for our lives, we would probably start running away! It would be way too much for our minds to comprehend. Take one step at a time and let him reveal his plan in his time. He knows us better than we know ourselves. He knows what we can handle. Jesus says this himself to the disciples: "There is so much more I want to tell you, but you can't bear it now" (John 16:12).

Don't be inactive until you receive your call. It takes time to learn to listen to God. Start taking responsibility, even though it may not feel like "your life's big calling." Seek the Lord and listen to him. He will build the character in you so that you'll be ready when he calls you into the unknown. God is mighty and will use you. Begin by proving to be trustworthy in the little things, and then you'll be trusted with larger responsibilities. Besides, the things that look small may make a huge difference in someone's life!

THINK ABOUT IT!

*Have you started serving even though you
may not know God's plans?*

DAY 101

I know that God has given me eternal life through His son Jesus Christ.
NICKO MCBRAIN (IRON MAIDEN)

*This truth gives them confidence that they have eternal life, which
God--who does not lie--promised them before the world began.*
TITUS 1:2

I sure hope I go to Heaven when I die." I can't tell you how many people have told me that. Maybe you are one of them? If you are, I have GREAT news for you! You can be sure that you're going to Heaven. If you have received Jesus Christ as your savior, he promises you eternal life. It isn't just a hope…it's a promise. Why? Because his promise isn't based on anything that you have or can accomplish. It is based on his desire for you to spend eternity with him!

When we ask Jesus to come into our hearts, he blesses us with a new life, and eternal life to come. Jesus paid a great price on the cross so that God could make you this wonderful promise. So, my friend, walk with confidence! Don't just simply "hope" that maybe you will be saved at the end of your life. Rather, plan on eternity. God doesn't lie. What he has promised you is your great inheritance through Christ Jesus!

THINK ABOUT IT!

*How will your life change as you begin to
stand on God's promise of eternal life?*

DAY 102

I said to myself, "Come on, let's try pleasure. Let's look for the 'good things' in life." But I found that this, too, was meaningless.
ECCLESIASTES 2:1

The book of Ecclesiastes may seem strange and perhaps a bit controversial. How could a book that speaks about meaninglessness and emptiness be in the Bible? This led some people to think it shouldn't be included in the Holy Bible. The funny thing is that it's amazingly current in its language and examinations. It's ahead of its time both philosophically and existentially. "The Preacher" has often been thought of as being King Solomon, which may not have been the case. Instead, he is a representation of one of the skeptics, who started to arise in Judaism at that time. This we know from other sources. This skeptic still believes in God, but doesn't think he's loving, caring, and active in the life of humans. He searches for meaning with that picture of God in mind. Without the guidance of the Holy Spirit, he concludes: "But as I looked at everything I had worked so hard to accomplish, it was all so meaningless—like chasing the wind. There was nothing really worthwhile anywhere" (Ecclesiastes 2:11).

This is coming from a man who had a lot of women, riches, knowledge, and pleasures. "I had everything a man could desire!" (Ecclesiastes 2:8). When we make the mistake of thinking that we could be satisfied by earthly things apart from God, it will always end in disappointment. Only God can fulfill your innermost longings. Only in him will your heart find peace and everlasting joy.

THINK ABOUT IT!

Are you still looking to be fulfilled by earthly things, or have you found fulfillment in God?

DAY 103

But the reality is that slowly these successes on earth will end sooner or later, so while we're doing all this, we're slowly destroying our lives.
PETE SANDOVAL (MORBID ANGEL)

He has planted eternity in the human heart, but even so, people cannot see the whole scope of God's work from beginning to end.
ECCLESIASTES 3:11

We forget that life here on earth is just a blink of an eye compared to eternity. It is such a small part of our eternal life that it almost seems insignificant. If you are a Christian, your present life isn't insignificant! In reality, you have already entered eternal life! Jesus has cancelled death. We have already gone from death to life! It gets a whole lot easier when we remember what is yet to come. The evil we experience will perish. The love, joy, and laughter will continue in eternity.

To focus on the new heaven and the new earth is not a way to escape the present life. C. S. Lewis wrote: "If you read history you will find that the Christians who did most for the present world were precisely those who thought most of the next." Those who put life into the right perspective have a wisdom that helps them cope with the struggles of the present age. It also means that we don't have to be serious all the time. There is a wisdom to laughter. We are reminded that all the things that makes us cry will only last for a short while.

THINK ABOUT IT!

Spend some time today reflecting on the glory of the Kingdom of God. We can all use some good news throughout the day!

DAY 104

Let the Truth be known throughout the entire world that Jesus Christ is alive and well! Having said that, be filled with joy and carry on!
LES CARLSEN (BLOODGOOD)

That Sunday evening the disciples were meeting behind locked doors because they were afraid of the Jewish leaders. Suddenly, Jesus was standing there among them! 'Peace be with you,' he said. As he spoke, he showed them the wounds in his hands and his side. They were filled with joy when they saw the Lord! Again he said, 'Peace be with you. As the Father has sent me, so I am sending you.'
JOHN 20:19-22

Did you ever get so excited about something that you just had to tell someone about it? The information is just too amazing not to share! I can imagine that is how the disciples felt. They watched Jesus being crucified and witnessed his last breath. Now they're in hiding. Feeling confused. Abandoned. Afraid. And then Jesus appears out of nowhere! His first words to them? "PEACE BE WITH YOU." In other words, "Chill my brothas. Everything's gonna be alright!" Can you imagine how they must have felt?

Joy is the word the Bible uses to describe their elation! But Jesus also knew that this good news about his resurrection was going to burn inside of them. So he released them, and told them to go tell people about it. The news was just too great to keep it to themselves. He said, "As the Father has sent me, so I am sending you." They were on a mission from God! What does that have to do with you? We're on the same mission. It hasn't changed. The more he changes and transforms you, the more you will simply have to tell somebody!

THINK ABOUT IT!
Are you excited to share this great news?

DAY 105

I quit!" Sounds familiar? So many people quit right before something big is about to happen. How unfortunate. When God puts something in your heart to do, there will be results. Just don't get discouraged and don't give up! Begin with your passion. What do you feel passionate about? What makes you excited?

We often feel that when the opportunity comes around, we'll be ready to succeed. We will rise to the occasion. We're ready to go. We've seen it happen over and over again in the movies, right? It doesn't work that way. Instead you'll default to your training. But that doesn't mean that it isn't worth trying. If you have a dream, start today! Don't postpone preparing. There's something in every one of our hearts that we have a passion for and dream about.

THINK ABOUT IT!

What are your passions? Reflect on that today. And don't hesitate to start chasing your dreams. Get started!

DAY 106

*"The greatest disease in the West today is not TB or leprosy;
it is being unwanted, unloved, and uncared for. We can cure
physical diseases with medicine, but the only cure for loneliness,
despair, and hopelessness is love. There are many in the world
who are dying for a piece of bread but there are many more
dying for a little love. The poverty in the West is a different kind
of poverty -- it is not only a poverty of loneliness but also of
spirituality. There's a hunger for love, as there is a hunger for God."*

MOTHER TERESA

*Dear friends, since God loved us that much, we
surely ought to love each other.*

1 JOHN 4:11

After feeding the homeless all of these years, I have learned that it really isn't about food. It's about hugs. Listening. Sharing stories. Becoming a real friend. Sharing God's unconditional love.

I was speaking to a friend about his ministry in a third-world country with the dying. He explained to me that many in his care had never been touched by another human being. They had no one. They lived a solitary life, and died alone. He told me their biggest need was to feel cared for. Since many of them are dying from illnesses with no cure, it makes a huge difference to die in the arms of someone who cares for you as opposed to dying on the side of the road with no one.

Of course, we don't have to live in a third-world country to feel alone and forgotten. There are people all around you every day who are in emotional pain and despair. God asked us to make connections, and love without limit.

THINK ABOUT IT!

*Are you aware of those around you who may need
your unconditional love and compassion today?*

DAY 107

Use wisdom and choose rightly whom you will serve.
MARK ALLEN (EX-VOTO)

No one can serve two masters. For you will hate one and love the other; you will be devoted to one and despise the other. You cannot serve God and be enslaved to money.
MATTHEW 6:24

Who are you serving today? Good question, isn't it? This Scripture is primarily about money, but the principle works for every area of our lives. Each day is filled with choices. Not all of them are clear and easy. Many of them will involve prayer and Godly wisdom. But all of them will involve a choice. Who will you serve?

One of the reasons I've written Metal Devo is to introduce you to God through his Word, the Bible. So many in our Metal movement call themselves Christians, but they have never really opened the Bible. That's like telling someone you are married, but you don't know any details about your spouse! When asked about your mate's personality and their emotional and spiritual attributes, you answer "I have no idea. They just makes me feel good." Not a very good answer! Dig into the Word. Get to know God personally. Then, when these daily choices some up, you will have a much clearer direction.

THINK ABOUT IT!

Who are you serving today?

DAY 108

When you're really being honest and true to yourself, you go
and pursue the passions that the good Lord put in you.
DAVID ELLEFSON (MEGADETH)

Delight yourself in the LORD and he will give
you the desires of your heart.
PSALM 37:4

Many people feel guilty when they pursue their heart's desires. We have somehow gotten the notion that to truly be in God's will, it will most likely involve something we are not going to enjoy! We have this misguided idea that God will surely call us to be a martyr. All of those things that we enjoy like playing music, sports, cooking must be contrary to his perfect will for us. Actually, nothing could be further from the truth!

When the Holy Spirit begins guiding our lives, he puts those very desires in our hearts! This completes us. He gave us our talents and gifts. No one knows better than he does what will make us happy. And this is the best part: not only does he expect you to use the gifts and talents that he has given you, but he begins to give you excellence in those areas as you pursue them! I can't imagine David Ellefson not doing music. It's his life! It's what makes him happy, and it's the very thing God uses to help him connect with others who need encouragement and guidance. In essence, it makes him "all that he can be!"

THINK ABOUT IT!

What are your talents and passions? Are you using them?

DAY 109

"I believe in Christianity as I believe that the sun has risen: not only because I see it, but because by it I see everything else."

C.S. LEWIS

Faith shows the reality of what we hope for; it is the evidence of things we cannot see.

HEBREWS 11:1

Christianity makes sense. It has the ability to make sense of the things we see and experience around us. But it's not just a logical system we can view from a distance. When we step into the picture and view it from the inside, we're amazed at how much there is to see. Things that may have once been confusing now begin to make sense!

There are still many things we cannot prove. Science continues to try to understand God's universe. As Plantinga points out, it's even impossible to prove that one's reader has a mind, but that doesn't keep us from acting as if you do. In fact, we believe many things to be true, even though we cannot prove them strictly scientifically or logically.

The Christian faith looks at science, philosophy, history, theology, etc. It gives a foundation for making sense of all of it. We don't have to be afraid to use our minds. Engaging in different sciences in the world can be very stimulating. Besides, it's extremely satisfying to see the amazing complexity of our Creator's wisdom and power.

THINK ABOUT IT!

Don't be afraid to engage in difficult questions!
Christianity has some truly magnificent answers.

DAY 110

Numbered are the days of man
LYRICS FROM "FOREVER IN FLAMES"
BY BROKEN FLESH [BROKEN FLESH]

*We couldn't go into the streets without danger to our lives. Our
end was near; our days were numbered. We were doomed!*
LAMENTATIONS 4:18

Today is a gift. It may not feel that way. You may have had a really
bad day where it seems everything went wrong. But it's still a gift.
We did nothing to deserve our lives. We can take absolutely no
credit for our own existence. And if the world were to end tomorrow,
there would be absolutely nothing unfair about it. It's all in his hands.

If you're breathing right now, that is grace from God. If you have
blood running through your body, that is a gift from your Creator. Grace
and goodness are all around us! Some people take great pride in having
built up their quality of life by working hard. But that still doesn't mean
they have come close to justifying their own existence. It could all disappear tomorrow.

None of us know how much time we have left. Our days are numbered. The Lord is in control of time, and he's already given us the greatest gift of all: Eternity! So give thanks for the gift of air and water today.
Be thankful for the grace of life. Don't take any credit for it. And start
your day tomorrow by thanking the Lord for waking up.

THINK ABOUT IT!

Are you aware of all the grace God has shown you?

DAY 111

*If I were worthy of such a favor from my God, I would
ask that he grant me this one miracle: that by His
grace He would make of me a good man.*

SAINT ANSGAR

*And God confirmed the message by giving signs and wonders and
various miracles and gifts of the Holy Spirit whenever he chose.*

HEBREWS 2:4

The Vikings were a brutal bunch! Ansgar was the first to build churches in Scandinavia. When no one else had the guts to be a missionary in Denmark because of their brutality, Ansgar was ready to become a martyr for the Lord. He was humble and extremely kind. He measured his food and water and experimented with how little he could eat to have more to give away for the poor. Many miracles happened around him through prayer. But when one of his companions bragged about this, he replied with the quote above.

He understood that he was not worthy of such miracles. It was God working through him. But he understood something even more profound! Some of us have witnessed God healing the sick, blind, or paralyzed. Others have not. Though miracles like that are awesome, it's more exiting to witness God changing our innermost being. The Holy Spirit changing us and producing his fruit in us is the greatest miracle we encounter.

Watching the Holy Spirit produce good fruit inside you is a personal miracle every time! It proves something that a visual miracle will not. He is very real. And he has the power to change your heart!

THINK ABOUT IT!

What do you consider the greatest miracle?

DAY 112

*I have read the Bible cover to cover several times, and
each time it brings new meaning and insight to the mystery,
wonder, and awe of God's power through Jesus Christ*
ROB ROCK

*Jesus looked at them intently and said, "Humanly speaking, it
is impossible. But with God everything is possible."*
MATTHEW 19:26

Sometimes I get stuck. It feels like there are too many difficulties around me, and I am overwhelmed. Did you ever feel that way? It is those times when we can look to heaven and say, "God, I am stuck. But I know with you ALL things are possible!" Rob Rock is talking about *that* kind of power.

There are days when I feel very small and insignificant. I forget the God of this universe has given me everything that I need to get through difficult and troubling times. When I open up the Bible, life seems a little less challenging. I can look my impossible situations in the face and say, "With God everything is possible!" Rob names four things that he receives when he reads the Word: meaning to life's mystery, insight into the mystery, wonder, and the awe of God's power. With those four things as a foundation for my reading experience, life takes on a new direction. I don't feel so insignificant. And I usually get un-stuck!

THINK ABOUT IT!

*What would happen if you opened up the
Bible the next time you get stuck?*

DAY 113

Oh prince of darkness, the Savior commands you.
For your rebellion, you will ascend no more.
LYRICS FROM "DERISION"
BY HOPE FOR THE DYING [DISSIMULATION]

He's never been the answer, there's a better way. We are
here to rock out and to say "To hell with the devil."
LYRICS FROM "TO HELL WITH THE DEVIL" BY STRYPER

He canceled the record of the charges against us and
took it away by nailing it to the cross. In this way, he
disarmed the spiritual rulers and authorities. He shamed
them publicly by his victory over them on the cross.
COLOSSIANS 2:14-15

Heavy Metal music has gotten a reputation for being satanic. And rightly so. Many of the lyrics in the early days were very dark—both spiritually and socially. When Stryper came out with "To Hell With The Devil" (1986) it was exciting—and caught the Metal community by surprise. Since that time Metal cannot be defined by the lyrical content, but simply just by a musical style. But Stryper did more than that. They helped the Metal community define Christianity, and pointed to the truth about Satan who had a stronghold on Heavy Metal's lyrics.

The truth? Satan has been defeated. You cannot give him any more power in your lyrics since Jesus defeated him on the cross. Since that time, literally thousands of Christian metal bands have put great lyrics to a specific style of music and recorded the GOOD NEWS about Jesus Christ. So, honestly, to hell with the devil!

THINK ABOUT IT!

Have you given Christian Metal a chance?

DAY 114

*The more I study the Bible, the more I realize
that humanity has not changed.*
LUKE RENNO (CRIMSON THORN)

*Yes, Adam's one sin brings condemnation for everyone, but
Christ's one act of righteousness brings a right relationship
with God and new life for everyone. Because one person
disobeyed God, many became sinners. But because one
other person obeyed God, many will be made righteous.*
ROMANS 5:18-19

Did you ever watch one of those old movies from the 1950's and 1960's that depict what life would be like in the year 2000? Some of the inventions they could only dream about are actually outdated today! There's one thing that many of them had in common: they believed mankind would be at peace. Knowledge and technology, travel advancements, and improved communication would bring us to a place of peace and understanding.

As Luke Renno says, humanity hasn't changed. We still have one underlying problem: we need God to change our hearts. We will never do it on our own. What the world needs is a heart attack! Instead of attacking the media, or politics, or world systems, we need to attack our own hearts and fix them! Our ONLY HOPE of change is through surrendering to Jesus Christ and his unconditional love through his Holy Spirit. Nothing else works. History has proven that!

THINK ABOUT IT!

*Are you still believing that the world will change
through outward advances and understanding, or
have you begun to realize that it's a heart issue?*

DAY 115

I have always viewed life as an adventure. That doesn't mean that it is always easy or simple. But then, it would be pretty boring if it was! God sets us on a path, and then he asks us to trust him. No problem! The road is straight, level, and clear. The Apostle Paul tells us to actually run on this road. I can see the end ahead. What could possibly go wrong?

Well, that's where it gets a bit tricky. As we walk/run this path of life, there are all kinds of deterrents. No, they aren't actually on the road. They are on the sides of the road. People telling us we aren't good enough. Lying demons causing doubt about the course of the road itself. And people whom we actually love and admire that lose their footing and lay in the middle of the road defeated. Jesus tells us to keep our eyes on him, the AUTHOR and FINISHER of our faith. With our eyes focused on Christ, the lies and accusations from the sides of the road become obvious!

THINK ABOUT IT!

Are you keeping your eyes focused on Jesus instead of your accusers?

DAY 116

*I felt peace in my heart from the moment your
words came from out of the dark.*
LYRICS FROM "SONG OF SOLOMON"
BY WAR OF AGES [RETURN TO LIFE]

*When I discovered your words, I devoured them. They
are my joy and my heart's delight, for I bear your
name, O LORD God of Heaven's Armies.*
JEREMIAH 15:16

I grew up with the Bible. I began attending our little country church when I was 5 days old, sitting in the pew with my parents. I learned the Word as I was learning to talk. My easiest memories of my parents include seeing them sitting and reading the Bible. Still, to this day, my mom begins each day studying the Bible, just as she has for the last 80 years. "So, was it the fact that the church and your parents displayed reading the Bible that gave you the desire to read it," you ask? No! It was the fact that they lived it.

They devoured it. They used its words to encourage and correct me. During difficult family times, the Word became a source of comfort to us all. As I began to dream about the future, my Dad would use scripture to inspire me to see the possibilities of God's opportunities. It is because I have allowed the Bible to take root in my heart that it has become my joy and my heart's delight.

THINK ABOUT IT!

Have you fallen in love with the Bible?

DAY 117

Lay her down, commence to drill. A primo murder, the legal kill.
I am a child about to die. My mother does not hear my cry.
LYRICS FROM "KILLERS OF THE UNBORN" BY
BARREN CROSS [ATOMIC ARENA]

You made all the delicate, inner parts of my body and knit me
together in my mother's womb. Thank you for making me so
wonderfully complex! Your workmanship is marvelous—how well I
know it. You watched me as I was being formed in utter seclusion,
as I was woven together in the dark of the womb. You saw me
before I was born. Every day of my life was recorded in your book.
Every moment was laid out before a single day had passed.
PSALM 139:13-16

When does life begin? According to this verse, it begins as we are knit together in our mother's womb. How exciting! Before you were born, God designed not only your body, but also your purpose. He knew what spiritual gifts you would have. He know what talents you would develop. He also knew the hardships you would encounter, and provided a way for you to travel through them. He formed you and made you in his image. And all he asks is that you respect your eternal life and make him part of it!

When you accept Jesus as your Savior, God begins to activate all of those wonderful things that he built into you from birth. And then, for our mom's out there, he gives the wonderful honor of hosting children. Little ones formed in his image, and woven together in the womb. What a blessing to be part of this amazing and miraculous cycle of life. You are, indeed, wonderfully complex!

THINK ABOUT IT!

Just imagine God had a plan for you before you were even born!

DAY 118

*My personal faith isn't that much of a struggle for
me. I struggle to be obedient. To be obedient to
everything God has called me to do in this world.*

ERIC CLAYTON (SAVIOR MACHINE)

*Because one person disobeyed God, many became sinners. But
because one other person obeyed God, many will be made righteous.*

ROMANS 5:19

Many Christians carry the wrong view of their spiritual inheritance. We see ourselves camped somewhere just outside of the Garden of Eden, kicked out because of sin, and powerless to do anything about it. We view our inheritance from Adam, who blew it and we are all suffering for his mistake. BUT that is not the end of the story! Jesus changed our inheritance. No longer are we stuck with a sin-based inheritance, but we are set free by Christ's death on the cross. Your new inheritance is from Jesus Christ. He calls you a "Saint," not a sinner. He set you free from the guilt and power of sin, and clothed you in Christ's righteousness.

And now, because of your new inheritance, you have a new name and a new purpose in life! So obedience is no longer a struggle of your own will and discipline, but rather surrendering to the Holy Spirit inside of you and allowing him to guide you. You're no longer stuck. You have a new spiritual desire to keep you on track and obedient. But, as Eric Clayton said, "I struggle to be obedient." It is an everyday choice that we make to allow God to guide us by the power and inspiration of his Holy Spirit.

THINK ABOUT IT!

What is your mindset about obeying: discipline or surrender?

DAY 119

*Sing a new song to the Lord, for he has done wonderful deeds. His right hand
has won a mighty victory; his holy arm has shown his saving power! The
Lord has announced his victory and has revealed his righteousness to every
nation! He has remembered his promise to love and be faithful to Israel. The
ends of the earth have seen the victory of our God. Shout to the Lord, all the
earth; break out in praise and sing for joy! Sing your praise to the Lord with
the harp, with the harp and melodious song, with trumpets and the sound of
the ram's horn. Make a joyful symphony before the Lord, the King! Let the sea
and everything in it shout his praise! Let the earth and all living things join in.*
PSALM 98:1-7

How does a Christian native African tribesman worship God with his music? What about a Christian in underground China? And how does it differ between a person who enjoys classical music compared to a metalhead? Although the musical style expressed by all of these people might differ greatly, there's one thing they all have in common: they're expressing their emotions to God from their hearts. Is there a right or wrong way to do that? Not really. I don't believe God hears a musical style or a drum beat. He doesn't say, "I would accept that worship from you if it weren't Country Western music! (Well, at least that is what I would have said if I were God! LOL) God will always listen to the music of your heart, no matter what style you use to express it. People differ greatly in their personal taste in music. What is an extremely intimate expression from one person may sound like a bunch of noise to the other. We need to be careful that we don't judge the musical style and miss the heart behind the music!

THINK ABOUT IT!

*Have you found a musical style that
you enjoy worshipping the Lord with?*

DAY 120

I have so much to do that I shall spend the first three hours in prayer.
MARTIN LUTHER

*The earnest prayer of a righteous person has great
power and produces wonderful results.*
JAMES 5:16

I read this quote by Martin Luther almost 40 years ago. I have never forgotten it. It has reminded me about the importance of taking time out to pray on countless occasions. It's easy to ignore God as our lives become busy. Many times at the end of a difficult and frustrating day, I realize I should have actually spent more time with the Lord earlier to get perspective.

Prayer isn't so much about telling God what to do for you as it is listening and receiving instructions. Psalm 46:10 tells us to "be still and know that I am God." In other words, remember to shut up and listen! Be sensitive to his leading throughout the day. That is what Martin Luther is talking about. Don't get caught up in the day to the extent that you forget to get God's perspective first!

THINK ABOUT IT!

*Are you spending enough time in prayer to
get God's perspective on your day?*

DAY 121

*God, don't let people fall into the hands of an angry
church. Without love, I never would have made it.*
LYRICS FROM "CLUTCHES" BY SLEEPING GIANT [FINISHED PEOPLE]

*Let me clearly state to all of you and to all the people of Israel
that he was healed by the powerful name of Jesus Christ the
Nazarene, the man you crucified but whom God raised from the
dead. For Jesus is the one referred to in the scriptures, where
it says, 'The stone that you builders rejected has now become
the cornerstone.' There is salvation in no one else! God has given
no other name under heaven by which we must be saved.*

ACTS 4:10-12

How would you define "church?" By denomination? By location? By the style of building? None of these would be correct. The Bible defines Church as the body of believers. It has nothing to do with a building or even a denomination. A building may house a true church, but that doesn't mean that it is truly a church by the biblical definition.

Sleeping Giant make a bold statement here in this song. "God, don't let people fall into the hands of an angry church." There are people who parade as a church that are not. Here in Acts the Bible defines church as having a cornerstone which is Jesus Christ. That means that a true body of believers, a "church," must believe and accept Christ's death on the cross, his resurrection, and his unconditional love for us. No other message or doctrine is acceptable.

THINK ABOUT IT!

*Are you part of a true church,
a body of believers in Jesus Christ?*

DAY 122

*Frantic I scream in agony of not being able to reach my goals
wars inside my head. I do my best, I give my all still I'm so
far away trying to keep my hope I stumble and I fall.*

LYRICS FROM "IN SOLITUDE"
BY ANTESTOR [OMEN]

*"For I know the plans I have for you," says the Lord. "They are plans
for good and not for disaster, to give you a future and a hope."*

JEREMIAH 29:11

I t was the first week in January, 1980. As I drove my newly purchased motor home from Montana to California, I had no idea what was in store. Weeks before, I closed the doors to the ministry that had occupied my efforts for the previous few years. Its end was bittersweet. I believed I was following God as I drove to California, not really knowing what to expect. I continued to work promoting Christian rock music—traveling and speaking about music—the good, the bad, and the ugly.

Five years later, I would discover why God sent me to California as we opened the doors to Sanctuary, The Rock and Roll Refuge. Michael Sweet from Stryper was our first worship leader. 17 Christian Metal bands attended that first church service. The rest is history. I have a lot of these stories. God has always had a plan, even when I have not. I could fill this book with the miracles he has provided through the years as his hand has guided my every step. But now that I am a senior citizen, I can look back at many years of God's faithfulness. It is because of his wonderful care and guidance in my life that I can look ahead once again, and know that he promised "to give me a future and a hope!"

THINK ABOUT IT!

*Are you ready to go where God may call you to
go even if it may not make sense to you?*

DAY 123

If I wanted to learn a whole bunch of information about somebody,
I wouldn't necessarily talk to them. I would just look stuff up
about them. But if I actually wanted to get to know somebody,
I would try to talk to them. Begin to talk to God, and listen.
KEVIN YOUNG (DISCIPLE)

When you pray, don't be like the hypocrites who love to pray publicly on
street corners and in the synagogues where everyone can see them. I tell
you the truth, that is all the reward they will ever get. But when you pray, go
away by yourself, shut the door behind you, and pray to your Father in
private. Then your Father, who sees everything, will reward you. When you
pray, don't babble on and on as the Gentiles do. They think their prayers are
answered merely by repeating their words again and again. Don't be like
them, for your Father knows exactly what you need even before you ask him!
MATTHEW 6:5-8

When I was about 6 years old I spent the night at my grandparent's home. They lived right next door to us. As I lay falling asleep, I could hear them praying together in the next room. They prayed for everyone in our family, and then I heard them praying for me. An amazing feeling of security ran through me, and I knew that God would take care of me. Why? Because my grandparents asked him to!

I grew up watching people pray. My parents, to this day, still have nightly devotions and prayer. The little country church that I grew up in was a praying church. From a very young age I had this sense that God would take care of me. It wasn't until my early teens that I learned to listen and seek a deeper relationship with God. I'm still seeking. I'm amazed by the closeness that I feel at times. His presence in my life has been amazing. As Kevin Young says, don't just learn "about" God, get to know him! He is speaking to you. Are you listening?

THINK ABOUT IT!

How can you make you prayer life more relationship-oriented?

DAY 124

I think that a lot of times people with a lot of hate and anger in their lives have gone through a lot of pain, and we find it that a lot of times it starts at home with the parents not caring about them, or their going through a divorce, just all kinds of things.

TED KIRKPATRICK (TOURNIQUET)

In the same way, husbands ought to love their wives as they love their own bodies. For a man who loves his wife actually shows love for himself. No one hates his own body but feeds and cares for it, just as Christ cares for the church.

GALATIANS 5:28-29

As I write this, my parents have been married for 67 years. They are still very happily married and in love. They depend on each other, and always put the other first. Their parental "team" has always been very loving and Godly. They have been the greatest example of Christ in my life. Having said that, I realize that many don't share the same experiences. Perhaps you are a child of divorce. Or maybe you are currently involved in a relationship that isn't working.

If there is one word that sums up the foundation of a Godly relationship, it would be "nurture." It's a great word that means "encouraging growth and development." My father once told me that he felt his most important role as a husband was to always be mindful of my mom's talents and spiritual gifts, and make sure that she is using them. I notice that she always does the same with him. It is that kind of mutual love and respect that make a life-long relationship work. And it is the example of that nurturing that children see and learn from. When we don't see it from our parents, we desperately need to see it in others!

THINK ABOUT IT!

Were your parents nurturing? Do you think you are nurturing those around you?

DAY 125

*The Word of scripture should never stop sounding in your ears
and working in you all day long, just like the words of someone
you love…Do not ask 'How shall I pass this on.' But 'What does
it say to me?' Then ponder this Word long in your heart until
it has gone right into you and taken possession of you.*

DIETRICH BONHOEFFER

*And we all, with unveiled face, beholding the glory of the Lord, are
being transformed into the same image from one degree of glory
to another. For this comes from the Lord who is the Spirit.*

2 CORINTHIANS 3:18

Transformation. It is what we all long for. We struggle with depression, anxiety, anger, lust, worry… the list goes on. We yearn for better control over our thoughts and emotions. We beg and plead with God to take these negative emotions away, yet we fail to realize transformation is a process. It involves four things: the Bible, prayer, true Christian friends, and allowing the Holy Spirit to work from your innermost being.

Using the Bible as your foundation, the Holy Spirit begins to lead you into all truth. Prayer makes it personal, and Christian friends add the necessary encouragement. When the Bible transforms you, it becomes less about verbally passing it on, and more about living its principles in front of people. As Bonhoeffer says, it takes "possession of you!"

THINK ABOUT IT!
Has the Bible taken possession of you?

DAY 126

Time, missed. I guess I've never contemplated all the
time that I have missed. Time, stress. I guess I've
never contemplated all the time waited in stress.
LYRICS FROM "CHEMICALS" BY LOVE AND
DEATH [BETWEEN HERE AND LOST]

As pressure and stress bear down on me, I find joy in your commands.
Your laws are always right; help me to understand them so I may live.
PSALM 119:143-144

Some days my biggest prayer is "Lord, I'm not asking you to move mountains today. I'm just asking you to move me!" We all need to be more involved in building God's Kingdom. But then, there are some who fall in the other ditch. They are very driven. They have difficulty saying "no" to anything. As a result, they usually push themselves to exhaustion.

Studies show that stress over many years takes a toll on the body. It can have enormous consequences for your health. But it could also have consequences in your relationships and your personal self-esteem.

Here's a command from God: REST! (Exodus 20:9-11). When we're too busy, we get overwhelmed and lose focus. We actually connect less with the people we're trying to help. Being well rested will make you more efficient, present in your conversations, and personally balanced. Get enough sleep. Rest one day a week. And don't be so busy that you forget listening to the Holy Spirit throughout the day, who will guide you to the people he wants to change. To be in tune physically, personally, and spiritually requires rest.

THINK ABOUT IT!

Are you stressed out?

DAY 127

I wanna encourage…
PETE SANDOVAL (MORBID ANGEL)

So encourage each other and build each other
up, just as you are already doing.
1 THESSALONIANS 5:11

We all need encouragement. This is a simple and obvious fact about human beings. It's extremely important. You can really help somebody with a simple word of encouragement. Actually, when a person receives consistent encouragement over a long period of time, they can go on to do extraordinary things.

Have you complimented somebody today? Have you told a co-worker you think he/she is doing a good job? It may feel a little awkward in the beginning. Look them in the eyes and tell them that you care about them. This can totally change another person's day, and eventually, their life! Build them up. Raise their confidence. Help them see themselves as valuable and special. In doing so, you are helping them follow their passions. Be the kind of person that makes others feel good about themselves.

THINK ABOUT IT!

Who can you compliment today?

DAY 128

"If, then, you are looking for the way by which you should go, take Christ, because He Himself is the way."

THOMAS AQUINAS

"No, we don't know, Lord," Thomas said. "We have no idea where you are going, so how can we know the way?" Jesus told him, "I am the way, the truth, and the life. No one can come to the Father except through me."

JOHN 14:5-6

Thomas was one of the 12 disciples of Jesus. We remember him as the doubter. Here we see another side to Thomas. He has the courage to ask the difficult questions, while the others hide their confusion. Without Thomas, we wouldn't have this amazing quote from Jesus! He went to Jesus with his concerns, and Jesus answered them as he answers us today.

Are you in doubt about how you should serve the Lord? Go to Jesus. Seek him in prayer and listen. If you seek Jesus every day, it is easier to stay on the right path. By letting him speak to you and understanding more of his mindset, he will guide you.

Our lives consist of different seasons. So if you're not giving all you've got in service for the Kingdom right now, just seek Jesus. He'll make you more mature, balanced, and spiritually ready for whatever comes next. And while you're not quite sure of what to do, you can rest in the fact that you're personally on the right track by spending time with him.

THINK ABOUT IT!

Do you seek Jesus in both busy and relaxed periods of your life?

DAY 129

Life with God is not immunity
from difficulties, but peace in difficulties
C S LEWIS

Always be joyful.
1 THESSALONIANS 5:16

Wait…what? How are we supposed to be joyful all the time? Is the Bible completely out of touch with the difficulties of reality? Honestly, no. And it isn't silent about the struggles of life either. Psalms, Ecclesiastes, the Gospels, and throughout the Bible, we encounter people who are suffering and in desperation crying out to God. So what's up with this verse?

The New Testament shows us a difference between joy and happiness. Happiness is your mood in any given situation. Good music, your favorite food, and great weather make you feel happy. But when these things turn sour, our happiness is quenched. The Bible isn't telling you to be happy all the time. Joy, however, is something deeper and more profound. It focuses on the bigger picture. We always have joy, because we always have the victory of Christ! We have won Heaven. We have an eternity with God. If this has become the truth for you, you will always have joy! Even on the unhappy days when life sucks.

THINK ABOUT IT!

Be joyful today and every day. The bigger picture never changes.
God is still on the throne, and your relationship with him is
still powerful! Have you reminded yourself of this today?

DAY 130

*[Christian] events and church are like vitamins. Nobody could
survive on just vitamins. If that's all you put in your body all
day long, you would die. You need a real meal to survive.*
KEVIN YOUNG (DISCIPLE)

*Yes, everything else is worthless when compared with the infinite
value of knowing Christ Jesus my Lord. For his sake I have discarded
everything else, counting it all as garbage, so that I could gain Christ.*
PHILIPPIANS 3:8

What does the Christian life look like? Church attendance?
Going to Christian concerts and festivals? Hanging out with
Christian friends? All of that is great, but it isn't the core of
your spiritual walk with Jesus. Kevin Young's example of vitamins is a
great one. Unless you eat actual food, you will eventually die. And so it
is in our relationship with God. He didn't call us to simply be one of the
pack. Part of the group. An insignificant smudge in the face of eternity.
He desires to be your Father. He doesn't have any grandchildren. He only
has sons and daughters. Why? His desire is to have an intimate and direct
relationship with you.

The Apostle Paul says, "…I have discarded everything else so that I
could gain Christ." He knew the value of this relationship. Even though
he had seen Jesus in person, he began his career persecuting Christians.
He actually got to know Jesus the very same way that you and I do—
through the power of the Holy Spirit within him through prayer. He had
learned to trust and rely on Jesus for his very life. And the same power
and guidance is available to you today!

THINK ABOUT IT!

*Do you have an intimate relationship with
Jesus? Do you realize the value of it?*

DAY 131

"The morning prayer determines the day."
DIETRICH BONHOEFFER

Listen to my voice in the morning, Lord. Each morning
I bring my requests to you and wait expectantly.
PSALMS 5:3

When was the last time you talked to God? Yesterday? Last week? Last year? Do you suddenly remember in the evening that you have barely even thought about God the whole day? Sometimes we get so busy with our lives that we forget the most important thing: our relationship with our Creator. When the alarm goes off in the morning, we need to understand what's important. Your first appointment of the day should be with him!

It's good to have this simple habit during the morning. Not because God forces you to do it, but because it's good for you and the people around you. A simple morning prayer, a Christian song, a scripture verse, or a page in the METAL DEVO can set the tone for the whole day. Not seeking God in the morning can, unfortunately, do the same. There are days when we just don't feel like it, because of a bad night or feeling a bit stressed out for the day ahead. Those are the days we need it the most.

By surrendering to God and praying to the Holy Spirit to give us peace, patience, gentleness, and self-control, a bad day can be turned around. It helps us be more sensitive to his calling throughout the day. He guides us to people who need our encouragement. Seek the Lord in the morning. When you do, you'll also end up seeking him at noon, afternoon, and in the evening.

THINK ABOUT IT!

Is God on your mind in the morning?

DAY 132

*Then Jesus wept. The people who were standing
nearby said, "See how much he loved him!"*
JOHN 11:35-36

But as he came closer to Jerusalem and saw the city ahead, he began to weep. "How I wish today that you of all people would understand the way to peace. But now it is too late, and peace is hidden from your eyes." Luke 19:41-42

As Jesus comes closer to Jerusalem he starts to weep. The people he loves so dearly don't understand the way of peace. He loves us so deeply that tears express his pain when we prioritize things that end up hurting us. Ryan Clark from Demon Hunter expresses this in a song: "I'm why Jesus wept."

The tears of Christ prove that God isn't cut off from the harshness of life. He understands pain and suffering, because he has experienced it himself. He understands losing a loved one, dealing with mental issues, and experiencing sickness. So in contrast to every other worldview, we have a God who's very close. He understands, because he has tried it and felt it on his own.

When tears are rolling down your face, Jesus is right there with you. He comforts you and sits by your side from beginning to end. How amazing it is to have a God like that! When God may feel difficult to understand, Jesus is easy to understand. He walked on the same earth as you and felt how you felt. And he promises us that he and the Father are one. The Father is extremely emotionally involved in his children. We see that all throughout the Old Testament. He carries us when we can walk no further.

THINK ABOUT IT!

What does "Jesus wept" mean to you?

DAY 133

*I asked God to make the Bible real to me and he did! Years later, I
now see it as the "instruction book" that shows us how to live.*
TED KIRKPATRICK (TOURNIQUET)

*All scripture is inspired by God and is useful to teach us what is
true and to make us realize what is wrong in our lives. It corrects
us when we are wrong and teaches us to do what is right. God
uses it to prepare and equip his people to do every good work.*
2 TIMOTHY 3:16-17

What if someone handed you a book that told you how to live successfully? There'd be no more guess work, no more confusion when life seems to spin out of control. You would have no more emotional questions and doubts about how to live life to the fullest. That would be awesome, right? That is what Ted Kirkpatrick is talking about. Your Bible is your "'instruction book" that actually gives you the answers to life's deepest questions and concerns. Will God make it real to you? Absolutely! You simply need to take him at his Word. Follow Ted's advice and "ask God to make it real to you."

As a Christian, you have the AUTHOR living inside of you! How cool is that? And as you dig deeper into scripture you'll see new depths and mysteries being revealed before your eyes. The cool thing is that it'll take you a lifetime just to feel like you're scratching the surface. It'll only get better the more you understand.

THINK ABOUT IT!
*Have you actually asked the Holy Spirit to guide
you into his truth as you read the Bible?*

DAY 134

No one heals himself by wounding another.

AMBROSE

*"I tell you the truth, all sin and blasphemy can be forgiven,
but anyone who blasphemes the Holy Spirit will never be
forgiven. This is a sin with eternal consequences."*

MARK 3:28-29

These Bible verses have scared a lot of Christians. Some have been terrified that they have committed this "special sin" that would keep them away from salvation forever. What is blasphemy against the Holy Spirit? We find the answer in verse 30: "He told them this because they were saying, 'He's possessed by an evil spirit.'" So the sin is saying that Jesus gets his power from Beelzebul—not God.

In other words: it's not worse to be blasphemous against the Spirit than against the Son or Father. Then the doctrine of the Trinity wouldn't make much sense. But in the Gospels, the Spirit is often described as God in action. He's the one that creates faith in us. He explains the Gospel to us and brings forgiveness. We need him to understand Jesus and the impact of his death on the cross.

So here's the most important thing: if you're in doubt about having committed this sin you can be sure that you haven't! If you had committed this sin, there would be no desire in you whatsoever to receive Jesus. We can only receive him through the Spirit. If you'd committed blasphemy against the Holy Spirit you simply wouldn't care. So don't be afraid. You haven't done it! But consider how dependent Jesus was on the Spirit and be so yourself as well.

THINK ABOUT IT!

*Can you see the importance of allowing
the Holy Spirit to guide your life?*

DAY 135

The loftier the building, the deeper must the foundation be laid.
THOMAS A KEMPIS

Therefore, go and make disciples of all the nations, baptizing them in the name of the Father and the Son and the Holy Spirit. Teach these new disciples to obey all the commands I have given you. And be sure of this: I am with you always, even to the end of the age." Matthew 28:19-20

We met for coffee later in the morning since he had difficulty getting out of bed before noon. "I don't seem to have a calling on my life. I have no idea what God wants me to do!" This was his excuse for not getting involved in ministry…or much of anything else for that matter. Honestly, he was lazy, uncaring, and unmotivated. He wasn't a bad guy. He was just stuck.

What do you do when you feel like God isn't calling you to do anything? You take responsibility. He is ALWAYS calling. You are just not hearing him. Make it a priority. Get started now!

Ask him. Try to figure it out according to your passions and your burdens. But don't wait to begin serving even though you don't have a clear understanding of it yet. By beginning to serve, you'll find out what your passions are. Don't consider yourself too good to serve in simple ways. Serving and seeking will give you a great foundation for discovering your personal calling. Even doing those "simple things" for a lifetime could give you an opportunity to lead people to Christ in amazing ways!

THINK ABOUT IT!

*Are you volunteering or just sitting around
waiting for something to happen?*

DAY 136

*The difference between something good and
something great is attention to detail.*
CHUCK SWINDOLL

*Work willingly at whatever you do, as though you were
working for the Lord rather than for people.*
COLOSSIANS 3:23

Have you ever looked in the "self-help" section of a bookstore? You'd be amazed to see all the books that attempt to help you organize your life. Aristotle said: "We are what we repeatedly do. Excellence, then, is not an act, but a habit." Many people have a system that works well for them, but may not be just right for you. But there is one thing that they all have in common: attention to detail. It's your attention to the details—the little things in life—that pay off big time.

Our identity is not defined by our actions. Aristotle, though, makes a good point: doing something for a long time will become part of our character. The self-help books will all tell you that if you can repeat something long enough and it becomes a habit, you stand a good chance of becoming a success. The Bible, then, takes it one step further in Colossians. When you take the advice from Chuck Swindoll and Aristotle, and combine it with this great principle from the Bible, you have a winning combo! Be diligent, pay attention to detail, and when combined with the leading of the Holy Spirit, you have success!

THINK ABOUT IT!

How much effort do you put into the details of your life?

DAY 137

Is it easier to say "Your sins are forgiven," or "Stand up and walk?"
MATTHEW 9:5

When Jesus forgave sins, it raised anger among the Jewish leaders. By doing this he showed he was equal with God, because only God had the authority to forgive sins. Jesus proved he was God by healing the paralyzed and the sick. He thereby proves that he has the authority to forgive sins. He has the authority to forgive your sins as well.

When we look back at our lives, we see an enormous amount of sin that Jesus has forgiven. There are so many things we could feel guilty about. Sometimes, our conscience feels like a black hole. But God doesn't see our sin. He has forgotten about them. Jesus has paid the price, and we're set free from a guilty conscience.

We need to remember that Christ's sacrifice was perfect. Whatever you may have done, he has taken your punishment. There's nothing you could have done that would be too big for him to forgive. Just learn from your mistakes, praise Jesus for salvation, and move on.

THINK ABOUT IT!

Have you let go of your guilt?

DAY 138

Personality is only ripe when a man has made the truth his own.

SØREN KIERKEGAARD

Let the wise listen to these Proverbs and become even wiser. Let those with understanding receive guidance.

PROVERBS 1:5

We are all critics at heart. Some more than others. When listening to a sermon or reading a book, it's easy to look for flaws. It's good to be a critical thinker, but when it becomes our main focus, then something is wrong. Instead of focusing on finding flaws, we need to be better at looking inside and finding the flaws in ourselves. If focusing on the flaws in others stops us from growing spiritually ourselves, then we've certainly lost our focus.

When you hear someone preaching the Word, your main focus should be on your own life. Look for something that speaks to you—both encouraging and critically. And, should the teacher say something that you don't agree with, put it in perspective. You will automatically notice it if you have been reading the Word of God for yourself. It's important to find someone you can trust theologically, but don't let a few mistakes from the speaker distract you from the many mistakes in your life. It'll harden your heart and stop you from maturing in your relationship with the Lord. The Bible says: "So don't bother correcting mockers; they will only hate you. But correct the wise, and they will love you" (Proverbs 9:8). Which of these two are you? If you're spiritually mature, you'll find something good to positively impact your life even in a mediocre sermon.

THINK ABOUT IT!

Are you looking for flaws in the preacher or yourself?

DAY 139

I have told you all this so that you may have peace in me.
Here on earth you will have many trials and sorrows. But
take heart, because I have overcome the world.

JOHN 16:33

L ooking at political systems around the world, we can end up feeling very small against such a giant machine! In the history of planet earth, we have had many who have risen through their political agenda only to kill, steal, and destroy. And these days it's difficult to see many world leaders who don't have power and greed as a motivation. It can all seem overwhelming, unless we remember these words from Jesus: "I have overcome the world." In other words, the most important things— sin and death—have been defeated. The Bible tells us that we will always have wars and rumors of wars. There will always be people who will try to take advantage of you and whatever finances you have. There will be times when evil tyrants rise to power, murdering and pillaging from the very people they are supposed to serve. That's why Jesus says we will have many trials and sorrows. But that isn't the end of the story. Death is dead. Your sin has been erased. There is no longer any barrier between you and God. No matter what is going on around us, we can say, "We have overcome this world!"

THINK ABOUT IT!

Have you taken your position as an overcomer?

DAY 140

Love never gives up, never loses faith, is always
hopeful, and endures through every circumstance.

1 CORINTHIANS 13:7

Do you feel beat down by life today? After a long period of struggle and pain our outlook on life changes. We almost feel "stuck" in gloom. In the Bible, Job described his experience by saying "Depression haunts my days" (Job 30:16). During difficult times, thoughts of depression and suicide can take over. We begin to believe there is no hope of things ever getting better. You are close to giving up on yourself, and perhaps God is giving up on you as well?

NO! Absolutely not! We might feel so miserable that it seems even God is considering giving up on us. But that is never the case. The Bible is not silent about these feelings. The Book of Psalms gives us the key: "Come quickly, Lord, and answer me, for my depression deepens. Let me hear of your unfailing love each morning" (Psalm 143:7-8). God doesn't ignore the ugly parts of life. The Bible is filled with stories of depression, suicide, anger, pain, and frustration—and He's present in all of these situations.

God's love never quits. He will never give up on you, even when you give up on yourself. He will stay by your side through your difficult times. The proof of this is in Jesus Christ. He came to earth and endured a pain that we could never even imagine. He carried the sins of the world to the cross.

THINK ABOUT IT!

You may feel like giving up on yourself when times
are tough, but God will never give up on you!

DAY 141

…I am on the path of victory right now
PETE SANDOVAL (MORBID ANGEL)

*But thank God! He gives us victory over sin and
death through our Lord Jesus Christ.*
1 CORINTHIANS 15:57

We have victory in the end! But how do I make it through today? Sometimes we feel as if we are making every mistake possible! We know better, but it seems our flesh is stronger then our desire to succeed! You feel like a big loser! However, your identity is in something else. In the end, you win, since Jesus already won this battle.

You will experience success in life many times before you leave this earth. And, unfortunately, you will also experience loss. No matter if we are encouraging to those around us, or we get rejected because of our beliefs, we know that we WIN in the end. That is a guarantee. We might lose many small battles throughout life, but that doesn't change the fact that the big battle has already been won. Although the losses will be temporary, the victory will last forever!

THINK ABOUT IT!

*Do you feel like a winner today? You should! The Lord
has made you a part of his winning team. So today you
can walk with your head held high as a conquerer!*

DAY 142

Underneath the anger and hate, it's hurt. A lot of times those that have the deepest hurt are the most vocal about their hatred for God.
TED KIRKPATRICK (TOURNIQUET)

I have told you all this so that you may have peace in me. Here on earth you will have many trials and sorrows. But take heart, because I have overcome the world.
JOHN 16:33

Instead, you must worship Christ as Lord of your life. And if someone asks about your hope as a believer, always be ready to explain it.
1 PETER 3:15

I met him for coffee. We sat in the back corner of the coffee shop so no one would recognize him. His fame and fortune as one of America's most popular singers had only lead to more misery. "I want to have a relationship with Jesus, but I don't trust him. I know he is supposed to be loving, but I have also experienced his cruelness." He grew up in a very legalistic Christian home, where he always felt like God was mad at him. His father whipped him a lot, and always explained that he was doing this so he would be a better Christian. "How can I trust a God like that" he asked?

So many in the world are hurting. Many of them have had such bad experiences with Christians that they no longer trust God as a result. You can't simply tell someone that Jesus loves them. They need to experience his love through YOU! As this verse says, when you live a life of hope and love, people who need God's love will ask you about it!

THINK ABOUT IT!
Do people see God's HOPE in you?

DAY 143

*Okay, I'm going to pray for some of these things
that I'm a slave to. It went in steps.*
REGINALD "FIELDY" ARVIZU (KORN)

*No one can serve two masters. For you will hate one and
love the other; you will be devoted to one and despise
the other. You cannot serve both God and money.*
MATTHEW 6:24

When we try to improve ourselves, we realize that it doesn't necessarily work on a deeper level. We're only capable of scratching the surface, while our inner thoughts and feelings stay the same. We simply cannot discipline ourselves to be holy. I know that sounds depressing...but I do have some exciting news: The Holy Spirit lives permanently in you! When Jesus died on the cross, the curtain into the holy of holies in the temple was torn in half, from the top to the bottom. The New Testament calls us the new temple. Our body is now the temple of the Holy Spirit who works from our innermost being. He dwells in us deeper than our feelings and thoughts—deeper than anything. He works from the inside out.

This truly is a game changer! Whatever is going on inside of us, the Holy Spirit is deeper. While we might be able to "make ourselves better" on the surface, he makes us better on the inside. John 7:38 says: "Rivers of living water (the Holy Spirit) will flow from his heart." By allowing the Holy Spirit to work in us, we actually can be changed for the better. In time, we become a slave to less and experience more freedom. So how do we allow him to work in us? The best way is to surrender to God. When we let go of our own agenda, we allow him to work in us.

THINK ABOUT IT!

*Have you surrendered to God today? Have you learned
to recognize the Holy Spirit working inside of you
in those areas of your life that you can't fix?*

DAY 144

The Christian faith is about the inside, not the outside.
SIMON "PILGRIM" ROSÉN (CRIMSON MOONLIGHT)

*But the Lord said to Samuel, 'Don't judge by his appearance
or height, for I have rejected him. The Lord doesn't see
things the way you see them. People judge by outward
appearance, but the Lord looks at the heart.'*
1 SAMUEL 16:7

If you're a metalhead, chances are that someone has told you that you don't "look like a Christian." Long hair, tattoos, piercings, black clothing all of this doesn't fit with what is normally thought of as Christian appearance. Honestly, that's the part I've always enjoyed. I've had long hair for almost 50 years now. My hair has been every style and color you can imagine. The tunnels in my ears continue to expand, and the stories I love to tell are illustrated through the tattoos on my arms. They tell the INSIDE story of what Jesus has done in my life.

I get excited when people ask what my tattoos mean. Little do they know they're in for an illustrated testimony! It's one of those things I use to take what is obvious in my outward appearance and bring it inside to my heart and experiences. Even better than being able to be different and still have a life-changing testimony is the fact that God only cares about the inside of me. My heart is the hub of our spiritual communication center!

THINK ABOUT IT!

*If your heart is the "hub" of your communication center
with God, are you keeping it open to his transmission?*

DAY 145

All the current and past members of BTA are born-again Christians who are not ashamed of the gospel of Jesus Christ.
SETH HECOX (BECOMING THE ARCHETYPE)

For I am not ashamed of this Good News about Christ. It is the power of God at work, saving everyone who believes
ROMANS 1:16

You're lookin' good!" Those are words we all want to hear! We want to look good in front of others. But it isn't just about the clothes on your back, or the way you comb your hair. "The message of the cross is foolish to those who are headed for destruction!" (1 Corinthians 1:18). Shouldn't Christianity look attractive to people so they will actually want to hear about it? While the music needs to be good for people to actually listen (practicing is important!), some will write you off when they hear the lyrical content.

This also applies to the Christian faith. 2 Timothy 2:15 says, "Work hard so you can present yourself to God and receive his approval. Be a good worker, one who does not need to be ashamed and who correctly explains the word of truth." It's going to take a bit of work to get to know the Bible enough to share its truths with people. We need to be prepared for people's questions!

Your friends may think you're a religious nutcase! They may think you have gone off the deep end! But even if your friends think your beliefs are silly, you should not be ashamed of them. Christ was not ashamed of us. And he actually had some very good reasons to be! The message of the Gospel is the very power of God. Don't be ashamed of the One who took your guilt and shame. It is this power that actually gives us eternal life!

THINK ABOUT IT!

When people around you think you're foolish for following Christ, how do you handle it?

DAY 146

I see saints in the cellblocks. I see revival in chains

LYRICS FROM "FINISHED PEOPLE"

BY SLEEPING GIANT [FINISHED PEOPLE]

*In this new life, it doesn't matter if you are a Jew or a Gentile,
circumcised or uncircumcised, barbaric, uncivilized, slave, or
free. Christ is all that matters, and he lives in all of us.*

COLLOSSIANS 3:11

One of the beautiful things about the early church was that people of all social classes began to believe in Jesus. Christians considered each other as equals. There's even an example of a slave becoming a bishop. Today, unfortunately, many look down on people who have been raised in the poor side of town, or have lived less than perfect lives. People in prison are considered lesser than others. They are the outcasts of our society.

Every time we look down on someone and consider them lower than ourselves, we are guilty of sin. We have a distorted and perverted view of God's creation. Even though they are paying for their past failures, there are people in prison who have an amazing faith, who are sharing the Gospel right where they are. They're reaching people who you and I could never reach.

Don't consider yourself better than others. "Pride goes before destruction, and haughtiness before a fall" (Proverbs 16:18). The Lord has already given you great value. There's no reason to compare yourself to others to feel better. Just listen to what God says about you and use that confidence to build up others.

THINK ABOUT IT!

*Do you sometimes look down on people because they have
different values, or sin differently than you do? If you know
someone in prison, please write an encouraging letter to him!*

DAY 147

It's so funny how we see things so clearly
when we have no time left to live
LYRICS FROM "A MOMENT SUSPENDED IN TIME"
BY UNDERØATH [DEFINE THE GREAT LINE]

For all of God's promises have been fulfilled in Christ
with a resounding "Yes!" And through Christ, our "Amen"
(which means "Yes") ascends to God for his glory.
2 CORINTHIANS 1:20

There is nothing like a near-death experience to put your life into perspective! We quickly realize what's important and what isn't. For some, you feel an overwhelming surge of thanksgiving for your life and friends. But for others, this becomes a brutal realization. They may regret spending too much time at the office, or not enough time with friends and family. Those are simply not the important things in life!

The more we understand God's heart, the better perspective we have on life in general. Money and security seem less important. Instead of a selfish desire to bless ourselves, we have a new desire to bless others. We begin to care more about relationships, because we know they'll last forever. We develop an honest burden to bring healing to this world. While insignificant things become less important, we take greater joy in the smaller things in life. We begin to appreciate things that seem like minor details compared to the bigger picture.

Having a larger perspective on life doesn't mean we want to escape it. Rather, it means getting involved helping to change things for the better. Since your eternity has been secured giving your time and money away become easier.

THINK ABOUT IT!

Are you involved in the world around you? Have you
learned to get involved in making this world a better
place and sharing the Good News of Jesus Christ?

DAY 148

"My scars are telling the story I am human"
LYRICS FROM "CANVAS" BY SACRIFICIUM [ESCAPING THE STUPOR]

Those who...honor the faithful followers of the Lord, and keep their
promises even when it hurts...Such people will stand firm forever.
PSALM 15:4-5

L ove hurts! It just does. We all experience it. If we love others as God
tells us to, we'll end up feeling hurt many times. It's a simple fact.
People hurt each other. We never know when we'll end up at odds
with someone who is close to our heart. We'll feel wounded. But what
story will our wounds tell? Some view their wounds as defeat. They
adopt a victim mentality which make them slaves to their past. This
mentality will keep you from loving as much as you can since the fear of
being hurt again will control you.

Other people go through rough times but end up at peace with the
outcome. Their wounds tell a story of having the courage to love even
when it hurts badly. They will always have reminders of the pain that
relationships can bring. They don't regret getting involved but learn from
whatever happened and move on in a healthy way.

THINK ABOUT IT!

Don't get trapped into the mindset of being a victim. Let
your wounds tell your story of love and healing.

DAY 149

Flaws found in all thought to be pure
LYRICS FROM "FOREVER IN FLAMES"
BY BROKEN FLESH [BROKEN FLESH]

As the scriptures say, "No one is righteous — not even one. No one is truly wise; no one is seeking God. All have turned away; all have become useless. No one does good, not a single one."
ROMANS 3:10-12

We usually have an unrealistic picture of the people we admire. We view our idols as being almost superhuman. We tend to see them as bigger-than-life. "If I could just be more like that guy, I would be a lot happier and more successful!" Not necessarily. Even those people you idolize have their problems no matter what you may think about them—or what they believe about themselves. Even pastors sometimes begin to believe their own "hype" and judge themselves by a different standard, justifying their sin and still calling themselves "a good man." The truth is, there is no one who is "good." And none of us are good enough on our own before God.

No one throughout history was found to be good. No man was without sin. No man was ever able to live up to God's standards. We can't even live up to our own standards! We need righteousness to stand before God—HIS righteousness!

Jesus came to earth because there were no righteous people here. He alone lived a life of perfect righteousness, even though he was tempted in all the ways we are. He is completely good. Not just by human standards, but by heavenly standards. We cannot stand before God, if we aren't covered in his righteousness. He alone is our righteousness!

THINK ABOUT IT!

Do you have a realistic view of your idols? Do you understand that none of us are good enough, and we need His righteousness?

DAY 150

"Empowered, prepared—on a mission. We are the ministry"
LYRICS FROM "MINISTERS" BY EXTOL [EXTOL]

As a result of your ministry, they will give glory to God.
For your generosity to them and to all believers will prove
that you are obedient to the Good News of Christ.
2 CORINTHIANS 9:13

S till looking for something meaningful to do with your life? As Christians, we're already given this! No matter what situation you find yourself in, there are meaningful elements to everything you do. Whenever there are people around you, you're on a mission. You need to be both empowered and prepared.

The Holy Spirit empowers us. He changes us on the inside, and helps us develop the necessary character to do God's work. He also guides us toward people. Get ready for it! Preparing for a concert takes many hours of practice. Preparing to speak with people may take some preparation as well. Reflect on your own Christian experience so that you may be ready to give an honest answer when you have the opportunity.

"We are the ministry." This is very exciting and a little frightening at the same time. Be prepared. Allow the Holy Spirit to guide you. He already knows your weaknesses and your strong points. How exciting that we are called to his mission. And the greatest thing is seeing people giving thanks to the Lord as a result of him living through us! That's the greatest joy of life!

THINK ABOUT IT!

Are you prepared, empowered, and on a mission?

DAY 151

Wrapped so tight, in the cold embrace of pride
LYRICS FROM "EN HAKKORE" BY THE BURIAL [IN THE TAKING OF FLESH]

For the world offers only a craving for physical pleasure, a craving for everything we see, and pride in our achievements and possessions. These are not from the Father, but are from this world.
1 JOHN 2:16

Pride sucks. And yet, most of us are hypocrites when it comes to pride. We despise it in others, and tolerate it in ourselves! Man's pride leads to destruction. Wars have been started. People have died. CS Lewis calls it "the great sin" and "spiritual cancer." Pride is always thirsty. It only enjoys having more and more. Its desire is to outdo those around him. Having a nice car doesn't matter. Having a *better* car than his neighbors is what's really important

Pride is horrible on a personal level. The proud are always looking down on others. When we are blinded by pride, we cannot see God. It hinders our intimacy with God as well as our love for others. Pride is a root cause of many sins. Because it always needs to stroke the ego, it can't afford to accept God as the higher power.

We need humility. As always, this isn't something we can do ourselves. It's a fruit of the Holy Spirit. He is the only one who can save us from ourselves. Have pride in your relationship with God. 1 Corinthians 15:31 says, "For I swear, dear brothers and sisters, that I face death daily. This is as certain as my pride in what Christ Jesus our Lord has done in you."

THINK ABOUT IT!

Is Pride ruining parts of you relationship with God and others?

DAY 152

"Cheap grace is the deadly enemy of our church. Cheap grace means grace sold on the market like cheapjack's wares."
DIETRICH BONHOEFFER

You do not belong to yourself, for God bought you with a high price. So you must honor God with your body.
1 CORINTHIANS 6:19-20

This blows our minds! It is difficult for us to understand how the God of this universe would become human and sacrifice himself for us. Actually, this was one of the things that brought C.S. Lewis to Christianity. He believed no one would be able to come up with such a crazy plot like this. We used to be slaves of sin. But God bought us with the most expensive price to set us free.

The fact that we were bought with a price has major implications for our lives. Legally we belong to God, not ourselves. Grace, in a way, is tremendously expensive for us. We're selling ourselves to God, and no longer have the right to just do as we please. God is our Father, but he's also our Master. When we disobey him, we take control ourselves and steal what belongs to him. When we try to be our own master, we become slaves to sin ones again.

Be completely obedient to the one who will give you freedom. No matter what you do in life, you're serving something or someone. By serving yourself you'll become a slave to sin. What seems like pleasure in the beginning will quickly turn into disappointment. In the end, it becomes death. Serve the One who will satisfy your ultimate needs.

THINK ABOUT IT!

Do you realize you don't belong to yourself?

DAY 153

"The same sun which melts wax hardens clay. And the same Gospel which melts some persons to repentance hardens others in their sins."
CHARLES H. SPURGEON

Today when you hear his voice, don't harden your hearts as Israel did when they rebelled, when they tested me in the wilderness. There your ancestors tested and tried my patience, even though they saw my miracles for forty years.
HEBREWS 3:7-9

There is no middle ground! When facing the cross, you'll either surrender to its message or be offended by it. The only thing you cannot do is be neutral. It's either the truth or the biggest lie in history.

Many people don't consider Christianity because of a lack of understanding. They need to know that there can be no neutral response. Many people claim to have intellectual problems with Christianity. It usually comes down to either a lack of personal investigation, or wanting to be the master of their own lives. It's a hardened heart towards a worldview which has an amazing explanatory power in morality, history, psychology, art, the beginning of the universe, even the laws of nature.

The biggest reason for rejecting Christianity is that people want to be the master of their own life. When you admit God's existence, you also admit to not being the center of the universe. By choosing yourself above God, you begin to harden your heart. Guard your heart for the things that harden you. Pray for a soft heart that melts you!

THINK ABOUT IT!

Does your heart gets softer as you mature?

DAY 154

But you're probably like a lot of us who what you hate and what you despise is man's corruption of the word, man's religious creation. Religion is of man, not of God. There's a huge difference between religion and true faith and discipleship in Jesus Christ as the Messiah.
ERIC CLAYTON (SAVIOR MACHINE)

They will act religious, but they will reject the power that could make them godly.
2 TIMOTHY 3:5

Are you religious?" The woman caught me off guard. I was shopping in a grocery warehouse for our homeless ministry. I was so intent on what I was doing that I hardly noticed this store employee standing beside me—until now. "No, actually I'm not. But I am a Christian though!" She looked confused. I quickly explained that I was a follower of Jesus Christ and had a personal relationship with him, instead of simply being a follower of some belief system. A smile came across her face, and she replied, "Great! You are just the one I am looking for then."

She explained to me that her brother was in the hospital dying, and she felt helpless to do anything. "I was just thinking that I could pray for him, but I don't know how. I've seen you in the store before and you look like a nice man, so I thought I would take a chance and ask you to help me." As we prayed together right there in the middle of the warehouse, she didn't seem bothered. And she was very excited to learn that she could invite Jesus into her life and pray to him on her own. Every time I go into the store, she loves to tell me how she is still praying and getting to know Jesus Christ. As Eric Clayton says above, "There's a huge difference between religion and true faith and discipleship in Jesus Christ as the Messiah." And let's not forget there are many people around us who also need to understand the difference!

THINK ABOUT IT!

Are you aware of those around you who may need to know the difference between religion and a relationship with Jesus?

DAY 155

Be not angry that you cannot make others as you wish them
to be, since you cannot make yourself as you wish to be.

THOMAS A KEMPIS

Don't grumble about each other, brothers and sisters, or you
will be judged. For look—the Judge is standing at the door!

JAMES 5:9

"Get your act together!" The sins of others can be really frustrating to us. They need to just pull themselves together, right? Well, not exactly. The world is actually tired of being judged by Christians instead of being helped. And the world is right to feel this way! When we judge others, we become vulnerable to judgement ourselves.

We need to be more involved in people's lives instead of simply telling people what they are doing wrong. We have to earn the right to give advice. If we truly engage in somebody's life, the whole dynamic changes. If we've shown them love and helped them out first, then when we speak into their lives they will truly listen. People receive advice from others when they feel loved and trusted. As Christians we should understand we don't personally have what it takes to be righteous. We needed Christ's righteousness. We need the Spirit to work inside us. We understand that we are unable to make ourselves good so how can we expect others to be? Instead, we need to encourage others! Don't simply judge. Engage in others' lives and earn the right to help them out.

THINK ABOUT IT!

Have you given up the right to judge in order to engage?

DAY 156

*To all the non-Christians, I really encourage you to read
for yourself who Jesus is...find out for yourself.*
LUKE RENNO (CRIMSON THORN)

*And this is the way to have eternal life—to know you, the only
true God, and Jesus Christ, the one you sent to earth.*
JOHN 17:3

Just Google it!" That's our advice for finding almost any piece of information you can imagine! But it can be extremely confusing as well. When you Google "God," "Christianity," or "Jesus Christ" you find a real variety of comments and opinions. Who is correct? When I ask people why they have decided to reject the claims of Christianity, their arguments and opinions have usually been shaped by someone's agenda. Luke Renno's advice to "read for yourself" is a very compelling one.

Your eternity and the true meaning of life hang in the balance. It isn't enough to simply have someone else's opinion. You need to hear from an authority. The Bible is a good place to start. If you approach it as a skeptic, you'll always find something wrong. Your search will be full of misunderstandings! But if you allow the Holy Spirit to "guide you into all truth" (John 16:13), it'll amaze you how the windows to understanding will open up!

THINK ABOUT IT!

*Are you simply allowing people around you to dictate
your belief system, or are you asking God to personally
reveal himself to you through the Holy Spirit?*

DAY 157

These people told me about Jesus, but I never understood who
he was. What I remember is that I wanted what this family had.
BRIAN "HEAD" WELCH (KORN)

...if someone asks about your hope as a
believer, always be ready to explain it.
1 PETER 3:15

Hope. It's what we all want but don't know how to obtain it. We hope for our future. We hope for our present circumstances. From the time we wake up in the morning we hope it's going to be a trouble-free day. But that doesn't always happen. At best, our hope is unsure. When we hope in our own security and the world around us, we can easily be left feeling hopeless.

One of the wonderful gifts God has given us as believers is HOPE. His Hope. Philippians 1:6 says, "...I am certain that God, who began the good work within you, will continue his work until it is finally finished on the day when Christ Jesus returns." That's where my hope begins! I have his assurance that he will continue what he started in me. I am becoming that new creation that he promised I would become. I am learning to love with his unconditional love. And all of this doesn't go unnoticed! Just as Brian "Head" Welch saw a family that followed Jesus and wanted what they had, people will ask you the same question when they see Jesus in you!

THINK ABOUT IT!

Is your relationship with Jesus at the point where people
are asking about the hope they see within you?

DAY 158

Life is not a problem to be solved, but a reality to be experienced.
SØREN KIERKEGAARD

*Knowing this, I am convinced that I will remain alive so I can continue
to help all of you grow and experience the joy of your faith.*
PHILIPPIANS 1:25

Are you dead or alive? That may sound like a strange question, but there are so many today who are barely existing. Are you so focused on all the problems of your daily life that you forget to really live? With a busy lifestyle, it's easy to feel wiped out. Focusing too much on the future can have the same effect. But, there are many ways to solve this. The answers for you personally may be unique, since we all have our own set of circumstances.

Dare to follow your passions. That is a great place to begin! Chose a path you find exciting, meaningful, and practical. Work hard, but play hard as well! Have some fun once in a while. It'll help you relax which will make you more focused in your work and make you more pleasant to be around. Be emotionally involved in the people around you. Take an adventurous vacation. Volunteer somewhere. There are many worthwhile causes where your help is really needed. Learn thankfulness towards the things you take for granted. Have small, reflective pauses throughout the day.

Most importantly, allow the Holy Spirit to produce his fruit in your life! He really is an emotional game-changer who will do awesome stuff in a seemingly boring day. Life is short. Make sure you feel alive while you actually live. Be people-oriented and enjoy life instead of being focused on your problems. You can have a profound effect on the world around you, so be creative!

THINK ABOUT IT!
Are you focused on the exciting things in life or the problems?

DAY 159

*If you have two shirts in your closet, one belongs to
you and the other to the man with no shirt.*

AMBROSE

*When you are harvesting your crops and forget to bring
in a bundle of grain from your field, don't go back to get
it. Leave it for the foreigners, orphans, and widows.*

DEUTERONOMY 24:19

When I began working with the homeless, I had a huge closet filled with clothes. As I began to encounter people in need, I started sharing my wardrobe. I was left with three shirts and three pairs of pants. Now, 10 years later, that's what I still have. It's an awesome opportunity that God has given us to share what we have. After sharing in the Lord's Supper, the early Christians would take the rest of the food and distribute it to the poor. It was the obvious thing to do after being reminded what God had done for them.

When we start viewing our role as givers instead of hoarders, it completely changes our perspective. Even the things we've worked hard for aren't necessarily meant for us to keep to ourselves. Pass it forward. God has given us so much, we cannot even begin to pay him back.

Reevaluate your life in this aspect. Money is the obvious thing to consider, but what about your lifestyle? Are there clothes in your closet you don't use? Are there things in your house you don't need? Not only can you pass it along, but it may be the answer to someone's prayer! "...the godly are generous givers" (Psalm 37:21). Don't let guilt motivate you; rather, be motivated by thankfulness. As you let the things on God's heart be on yours as well, you'll find plenty of motivation to be generous.

THINK ABOUT IT!

*What do you possess that someone
else might need more than you do?*

DAY 160

Concepts create idols; only wonder comprehends anything. People kill one another over idols. Wonder makes us fall to our knees.

GREGORY OF NYSSA

Trust in the Lord with all your heart; do not depend on your own understanding. Seek his will in all you do, and he will show you which path to take.

PROVERBS 3:5-6

How does the Bible speak to you? People read the Bible under different circumstances, depending on their culture, the period in history, and according to their own baggage and emotions. It helps to see how others have read and understood the Bible in other cultures and throughout history.

Many have tried to be very structured in their reading in order to write dogmatically about life. In doing so, they may actually miss the whole point! As we experience more depth in our understanding of life and scripture, we grow more in our relationship with God, and not just in our dogma of the Bible. There will always be questions that life doesn't really answer. The Bible fits so well with life. It speaks to us in all circumstances.

Life will continue to be filled with things that seem illogical. Worldly logic is always changing, but the Bible and its truths are never-changing. The Bible speaks clearly on the most foundational parts of life. While we may be unable to solve the difficult theological questions as quickly as we would like to, we can be thankful that scripture speaks to our hearts. While we grow in wonder and amazement of God, he continues to guide us into all truth.

THINK ABOUT IT!

Have you allowed God to guide you into all truth—even when you have difficulty understanding the Word?

DAY 161

The fruits of the earth are not brought to perfection immediately, but by time, rain and care; similarly, the fruits of men ripen through ascetic practice, study, time, perseverance, self-control and patience.

ANTHONY THE GREAT

Gray hair is a crown of glory; it is gained by living a godly life. Better to be patient than powerful; better to have self-control than to conquer a city.

PROVERBS 16:31-33

This verse makes me feel a lot better about my long gray hair! There are many quotes about getting older. "Age is just a state of mind." "You're only as old as you feel." "You're not getting older, you're just getting better." Or my favorite from Mae West, "If I had known I was going to live this long, I would have taken better care of myself." If you're one of the gray haired ones, someone could really use you as a mentor. If you are a younger person, don't be so quick to dismiss the benefit of the older folks in your life and glean their wisdom!

Maturing in holy living takes time. When we look at ourselves daily, it doesn't seem like much has happened. But when you consider your life even a year ago, hopefully it becomes evident how much you have grown. Anthony thought the right thing to do was to wander out into the desert so he could live away from all temptations, and thereby live the holy life. Though he became an inspiration, we're called to be where people are. Live a holy life. Even though the Bible says you are now a citizen of Heaven, living among people here and now might get a little dirty. Be mentored, mentor others, grow patiently in holiness, and be a light in a darkened world.

THINK ABOUT IT!

Who helps you in spiritual growth, and who are you helping?

DAY 162

Patience is necessary, and one cannot reap
immediately where one has sown.
SØREN KIERKEGAARD

And the seeds that fell on the good soil represent
honest, good-hearted people who hear God's word, cling
to it, and patiently produce a huge harvest.
LUKE 8:15

Slow down, you move too fast. You got to make the morning last. Just kicking down the cobblestones. Looking for fun and feelin' Groovy!" Lyrics from an old song called The 59th Street Bridge Song by Simon and Garfunkel. It was very popular when I was in high school in the 1960's. Of course, not very metal! I remember thinking a lot about the lyrics. "Slow down, you move too fast." We get so busy with life that we forget to actually stop and reflect upon it. The greatest things in life take time, and we need to slow down to experience them. Nature. Playing with children. Friends. Sexuality. Peaceful moments. If we adopt a consumer-mentality where everything has to become more efficient, we'll lose out on the greatest pleasures of all.

This applies to the Christian life and ministry as well. Efficiency is good when dealing with practical assignments. But when it comes to people, we must lose that mindset. Here the Holy Spirit's patience is needed. "Patience can persuade a prince, and soft speech can break bones" (Proverbs 25:15). In most cases, changing one's whole worldview takes a lot of time. Most adopt this "get-saved-quick" mentality. But, mentoring someone into spiritual growth also takes time. Sometimes years! Expect "wasted" time. People need to move and process at their own pace. That time isn't really wasted. It's all part of walking through life with someone. And, at the same time, it will help you develop the necessary relationship that gives you the right and trust to actually speak into someones life!

THINK ABOUT IT!

Are you always patient when it comes to people?

DAY 163

*There seems to be a force, to some degree anyway, to
drive Christianity out of our schools, off television,
out of our movies, and on and on and on.*
MICHAEL SWEET (STRYPER)

*If the world hates you, remember that it hated me first. The
world would love you as one of its own if you belonged
to it, but you are no longer part of the world.*
JOHN 15:18-19

I have always been the target of gossip and slander. I have been single
my whole life. People assume that I am either gay or I have women
on the side. Neither are true. But the truth doesn't stop people from
talking—and writing! More than once I have been crucified in the press.
It has also been a wake-up call. I don't believe anything that I read. I am
the biggest "news skeptic" around. I could have coined the phrase "fake
news" if I had just thought of the term first!

I realize the world hates me. As do many Christians. Because I have
done something wrong? Not necessarily. Simply because they don't agree
with me and don't condone my viewpoints and philosophies. But that
doesn't stop us from being change-agents in the world around us. I am
not here to force my opinions and beliefs down people's throats. I am
here to demonstrate unconditional love to a world that gossips, hates,
slanders, and misunderstands me. It isn't personal. If they understood
Jesus, they would understand his followers a bit better also.

THINK ABOUT IT!

How do you react when the world hates you?

DAY 164

*"Sometimes we don't need another chance to express how
we feel or to ask someone to understand our situation."*
DIETRICH BONHOEFFER

*So encourage each other and build each other
up, just as you are already doing.*
1 THESSALONIANS 5:11

I t's important for all of us to express how we feel. We shouldn't bury our emotions. It always makes you feel a bit vulnerable when you share the deeper things in your heart. But don't let that vulnerability stop you! Don't walk around with concerns for days when you can express them to a friend today. Don't be slow to say what's on your mind. Don't wait until tomorrow to ask for prayer or advice.

This also applies to encouraging the people around you. Small things can make a big difference in someone's life. Simple comments can make a big difference. It can help other people believe in themselves, and may give them the confidence to follow what God has put on their hearts.

In the face of death, many people regret not telling others how much they loved them. This is a difficult thing to deal with. We never know when it's going to happen. That gives us even more reason to say it today! Tell those you love how much you care about them. Get into the habit of paying someone a compliment every day. Encouragement has the power to help somebody move forward and take the first steps towards great things.

THINK ABOUT IT!

Who have you complimented today?

DAY 165

For God has said, "I will never fail you. I will never abandon you."
HEBREWS 13:5

It is popular within the American church for people to "re-dedicate" their lives to Jesus Christ. It is an interesting concept since we are not even capable of dedicating our lives to Jesus in the first place. We ALWAYS fall short. This concept of "re-dedication" would need to be done multiple times a day! It was for this reason that Christ died on the cross for us. He knew it was impossible to have that kind of dedication so he took the burden of it away from us. No matter what you do, he promised to never fail or abandon you!

You can't earn his love or his forgiveness. He gives you both as a gift. This is the foundation you have as you live the Christian life. You are never disqualified. You were never qualified in the first place. Romans 5:8 says, "But God showed his great love for us by sending Christ to die for us while we were still sinners." We all get off-track from time to time. When you do, simply remember that God is still there. All he asks you to do is connect with him, and get on track again.

THINK ABOUT IT!

*Do you sometimes feel guilty when you get
off-track? What can you do about that?*

DAY 166

For Christ himself has brought peace to us.
...he broke down the wall of hostility that separated us.
GALATIANS 2:14

Sometimes life just sucks. It may suck for a long period of time. For example, when you end a relationship, you feel rejected, hurt, and maybe even betrayed. It is so tempting during a tough time like this to harden your heart and bury your emotions. When life hurts, it doesn't feel like it's worth feeling at all.

It may take a long period of time to get to the point where life is worth "feeling" once more. You may have to learn to trust again. It may seem like you're taking a big risk to begin loving again. And, honestly, you are! When we choose to love another person, we become very vulnerable. The other person has an opportunity to do some serious damage to us emotionally! We realize how little we're actually able to control. But one of the biggest joys of life is actually having something to lose. If we protect ourselves to the point of holding our feelings back, then our life doesn't have much meaning.

Do you have those feelings of being "stuck" because someone has hurt you? It's difficult to get through! God calls all of us to love people so we need to deal with the wounds that keep us from doing that. It's true that loving others will make us vulnerable and will open us up to the possibility of getting hurt again. Nonetheless, we have to do it! Don't build a wall around your heart. Loving relationships are also the very best part of life!

THINK ABOUT IT!

Are there hurts in your life that keep you from daring to love?

DAY 167

So I say, let the Holy Spirit guide your lives. Then you won't be doing what your sinful nature craves.
GALATIANS 5:16

Your word is a lamp to guide my feet and a light for my path.
PSALM 119:105

Every day brings a new set of challenges and an opportunity for you to make wise choices. How you act and react will largely depend on how closely you allow the Holy Spirit to work through you. For many years, I have started the day with a time of peaceful contemplation. Sometimes I read the Bible. Sometimes I pray. Sometimes I simply read a book. Sometimes I just sit still and dream. It's important time for me.

I can honestly say it sets the mood for how the rest of my day will turn out. Perhaps you will make a habit of reading your Bible or this devotional every morning when you wake up as preparation for the day. It will give you something to think about as you work, and many times will give insight into the very things you will encounter throughout the day. Hopefully with time, then, it'll turn into action—into wisdom.

THINK ABOUT IT!

Have you established a morning quiet time?

DAY 168

We give thanks to you, Lord God, the Almighty, the one who is and who always was, for now you have assumed your great power and have begun to reign.

REVELATION 11:17

A friend once told me that the only thing we can know for sure is that "God is real and I'm not him." This is a good place to start! We often feel tempted to be the "god" of our own lives. We want to create the illusion that we have control over the things around us. We don't want to admit that our lives are extremely fragile. We are not promised a tomorrow. We don't know when our lives will end. And God would still be God if humans ceased to exist.

There's something liberating in accepting your own humanity. We are set free from the pressure of needing to accomplish what only the Lord can do. Instead of trying to become something "more," our focus is on becoming who we are in Christ. He wants us to become the person he intended for us to be. Being the "god" of your own life is a heavy burden. When a relationship ends or you lose your job, it can feel like your life is falling apart. That's an overwhelming burden that only God is strong enough to carry. If you let God be God, he will always keep his promises. God is almighty, and wants the best for you. He will never break under pressure. Even in death, this foundation will last!

THINK ABOUT IT!

What do you cling to in painful, difficult situations?

DAY 169

We represent eternal life and we defy your suicide
LYRICS FROM "OVERTHROW"
BY SLEEPING GIANT [FINISHED PEOPLE]

*But the Holy Spirit produces this kind of fruit in our
lives: love, joy, peace, patience, kindness, goodness,
faithfulness, gentleness, and self-control.*
GALATIANS 5:22-23

Most people experience times when there's something "dead" in them. For many, this can turn into suicidal thoughts. These feelings don't come from out of nowhere. They have a message for us: something in our lives needs to die! And that's the thing that needs to be killed—never yourself!! The struggles, the pain can become so overwhelming that it feels like there's no way out of it. No light at the end of the tunnel. No hope…

What makes you feel like dying? A relationship? Something from your past? Those are the things that need to be dealt with. If you're in an overwhelming situation, remember that you're not alone. The Holy Spirit works in you. And he's able to give you peace so that you'll have something to hold on to in the middle of the storm. Ask for his peace! This may be a long process to get back to a state where life's worth living, but don't quit! I have seen the Holy Spirit bring people out of suicidal thoughts.

Sometimes we experience a friend's suicide as a total surprise. But most people send out signals and cries for help before doing so. Be aware of others who are desperate for help and reach out to them. Suicide is never the answer. And if you feel this way yourself consider what needs to die in you. Let the Holy Spirit work in you. He can change your situation. He'll never leave you alone!

THINK ABOUT IT!
What needs to die in your life?

DAY 170

*For myself, I find I become less cynical rather than more--remembering
my own sins and follies; and realize that men's hearts are not often
as bad as their acts, and very seldom as bad as their words.*

J.R.R. TOLKIEN

*People can tame all kinds of animals, birds, reptiles, and fish,
but no one can tame the tongue. It is restless and evil, full of
deadly poison. Sometimes it praises our Lord and Father, and
sometimes it curses those who have been made in the image
of God. And so blessing and cursing come pouring out of the
same mouth. Surely, my brothers and sisters, this is not right!*

JAMES 3:7-10

*Yes, I am the vine; you are the branches. Those
who remain in me, and I in them, will produce much
fruit. For apart from me you can do nothing.*

JOHN 15:5

Some of the most severe emotional pain I have endured in my life
has been through the power of someone's words aimed at me. As a
public figure, so many feel like it is fair game to take pot shots at me,
whether the information is true or not. I have been accused of everything.

My father gave me some great advice at the beginning of my ministry. He said, "Don't let them stop you, or even slow you down. In the end,
your testimony and God's good work through you will speak for itself." 1
Peter 3:16 says, "Keep your conscience clear. Then if people speak against
you, they will be ashamed when they see what a good life you live because
you belong to Christ." Watch your mouth! Be careful what comes out of
it. Make sure the Holy Spirit is tempering what you have to say!

THINK ABOUT IT!

What would others have to say about the power of your words?

DAY 171

Wake up and step outside your box. Wake up
LYRICS FROM "IN REGARDS TO MYSELF"
BY UNDEROATH [DEFINE THE GREAT LINE]

This is my command—be strong and courageous! Do not be afraid
or discouraged. For the Lord your God is with you wherever you go.
JOSHUA 1:9

Stepping out of your comfort zone is very uncomfortable. It involves giving up those feelings we love: control and safety. We need to be sure we are able to "make" it. We want to make sure we are secure. But, it isn't about you! It is important that you begin to have a broader perspective. It creates confidence when you take risks.

It's actually a delusion when we believe we can control things around us. This is extremely difficult to accept, but no less true. Life is fragile. We don't know if tomorrow will come. One of the key aspects of faith is trust. If we really trust the Lord, we must have faith to step out of our comfort zone when he calls us to do so. In life and in death, we're in his hands. However frightening it may seem, to truly experience that he is faithful we have to step out into unknown territory when he asks.

Are you letting fear or insecurity keep you from being where God wants you to be? It's time to step out of your comfort zone despite your fear of failure. It may feel like going from the shallow end of the pool to the deep end. But in the deep end, there's so much more of life to experience. Trust the Lord!

THINK ABOUT IT!

Dare to dive into the deep end, and he will show you
that he's faithful. Have you taken the leap?

DAY 172

Prayer does not change God, but it changes him who prays.
SØREN KIERKEGAARD

*Search me, O God, and know my heart; test
me and know my anxious thoughts.*
PSALM 139:23

*Yes, I am the vine; you are the branches. Those
who remain in me, and I in them, will produce much
fruit. For apart from me you can do nothing.*
JOHN 15:5

"CHANGE ME LORD!" I think those are the three words that
God loves to hear the most! It certainly should be our heart's
desire in prayer. I used to rattle off the things that I wanted God
to give me when I was a younger Christian. I envisioned him as a "Santa
Claus" figure, or a magical genie ready to grant my wishes, if I simply
rubbed him the right way.

As a more mature Christian, I realize that my understanding of
prayer was immature at best. The purpose of prayer is to connect my
heart to God's heart. He is wiser and more intelligent than I'll ever be. To
tell him what I need, and expect him to gift it to me is ridiculous. That
is why the psalmist says, "Search me and know my thoughts." And why
Jesus later said, "...apart from me you can do nothing." It's all about the
change that God is performing in my heart. It's about praying, "Change
me Lord!" Allow God to complete his work in your heart, and make you
into the new creation that he wants you to be!

THINK ABOUT IT!
Have you prayed, "Change Me Lord?"

DAY 173

We are here to serve and worship our creator.
TED KIRKPATRICK (TOURNIQUET)

*But you are not like that, for you are a chosen people. You are
royal priests, a holy nation, God's very own possession. As
a result, you can show others the goodness of God, for he
called you out of the darkness into his wonderful light.*

1 PETER 2:9

I live on a lake. My home is 300 square feet. Even though my home
is small, the great outdoors with a breathtaking view of the lake is
right outside the windows that line the front of the house. Every
day I have ducks and geese in my yard. I am their food supply! In the
mornings, deer walk through the yard. And today as I write this, there
are 50 turtles sitting on the boat dock. It is a little piece of paradise. I am
thankful every day for this wonderful place to live. Why this narrative
to connect the above scripture? Because thanksgiving has to come from
somewhere. I have to first FEEL the thankfulness in my heart before I
am able to express it.

The same is true with our worship to God. I haven't always had a
heart for worship. It has grown inside of me as a result of my relationship with my creator. It isn't a chore to serve and worship God. It is the
very thing that my thankful heart desires to do. If you are not at that
place yet in your own heart, give it some time. Thanksgiving and worship come from a heart that is being transformed by God. Simply allow
him to fill it!

THINK ABOUT IT!

Are you growing in your desire to worship God?

DAY 174

I've waved that flag high for thirty some odd years and I will continue to do so. I'm proud to be a Christian.
MICHAEL SWEET (STRYPER)

I am a special messenger from Christ Jesus to you Gentiles. I bring you the Good News so that I might present you as an acceptable offering to God, made holy by the Holy Spirit. So I have reason to be enthusiastic about all Christ Jesus has done through me in my service to God.
ROMANS 15:16-17

What would make a Christian band continue in ministry for many decades? Money? Fame? A love for hotel rooms and airplanes? I think not. It has been exciting to watch Stryper all of these years serving God, and continuing to proclaim the Gospel of Jesus Christ. When Michael Sweet says that he is proud to be a Christian, it doesn't stop there. His desire to reach people with the Good News of Jesus Christ is the whole reason for the ministry. Stryper has taken more than a few beatings. They've been knocked them down a few times. But each time, they got up again and realized there was a greater purpose than simply just playing music.

Paul says here in Romans 15 that "I bring you the Good News so that I might present you as an acceptable offering to God, made holy by the Holy Spirit." I can't count how many people have been affected by the ministry of Stryper and other Christian metal bands throughout the years. And we are not finished yet. Our burden is for the metal culture to know Christ, and begin a relationship with the God who made them!

THINK ABOUT IT!

Do you consider yourself a "special messenger?"

DAY 175

*In one moment God totally changed me. I had true
joy that didn't end at the end of a concert.*
SCOTT WATERS (ULTIMATUM)

*I have told you these things so that you will be filled
with my joy. Yes, your joy will overflow!*
JOHN 15:11

There's a huge difference between "happiness" and "joy." I always say that happiness is that feeling you have in-between catastrophes! Happiness usually depends on outward circumstances and not on your actual state of being. Joy, on the other hand, is not dependent on circumstances. It's a state of being that can only come from God.

When the Bible lists the attributes of the Holy Spirit (his fruit), it lists joy second, right after love. Can you manufacture joy? Do you have the ability to produce it? No! This scripture tells us that once he has filled us with *his* joy, our joy overflows. We depend on him. We allow him to make his changes in us to improve and change our lives. It's an amazing opportunity that we have to demonstrate his fruit in our lives. People around you will see the difference. Nothing speaks more loudly about God's ability to transform us than personally demonstrating it to those around us. Letting the Holy Spirit produce his fruit is easy. You simply ask. Then, as a result, he'll show you the the areas of your life you need to let go of. When you surrender these areas to him, he begins to produce even more fruit!

THINK ABOUT IT!

*Have you experienced the difference between
happiness and joy in your life?*

DAY 176

*I really just want people who hear our music to
know they have a purpose. To know that Jesus
loves them, more than they love themselves.*
BROOK REEVES (IMPENDING DOOM)

*And we know that God causes everything to work
together for the good of those who love God and
are called according to his purpose for them.*
ROMANS 8:28

Did you know that God has a purpose for you? Besides forgiving you and setting you free, he has a specific purpose for your life. I know so many believers who are feeling hopeless with a lack of purpose. That isn't God's fault, nor is it his promise to you. YOU have a purpose—a God-given purpose in life—that will give you the energy to get up in the morning. His purpose will spark your creativity, and give you hope.

How do you find your purpose? Great question! What are your interests? What occupies your free time? That would be a good place to begin looking. Once you have an idea what your purpose might be, ask God to open the doors to show you how to live in your purpose. It's been said that when you find your true purpose in life, you will never have to "work" another day in your life.

THINK ABOUT IT!
Have you discovered your purpose in life?

DAY 177

With whatever big problem that seems insurmountable that someone walks up with, we don't necessarily give them the answer to the problem, but we point them to the One that does have the answers.

KEVIN YOUNG (DISCIPLE)

God sent a man, John the Baptist, to tell about the light so that everyone might believe because of his testimony. John himself was not the light; he was simply a witness to tell about the light.

JOHN 1:6-8

If we saw John the Baptist today, he would certainly make an impression. The description in Matthew 3 describes him dressed in a camel's hair garment, secured by a leather belt, and his diet consisted of locusts and wild honey. His clothes were the same as a Bedouin Shepherd at that time, and the diet was very nutritious. John's coming was a fulfillment of prophecy from the Old Testament. Even though he carried God's message, and was actually a blood-cousin to Jesus Christ, he knew his own shortcomings. When people asked him about his own importance, he told them he was not worthy to "tie his [Christ's] shoelaces."

John was a voice in the wilderness heralding the coming messiah. And, as the scripture records, he had the awesome opportunity to actually baptize Jesus. John the Baptist is our example of what a real witness is all about. We're not personally the "light"—although some misguided Pastors and Evangelists would like to think they are! We are simply a witness to tell about the light. As John the Baptist who went before us, we follow this great tradition. We have the same wonderful opportunity to herald the second coming of Jesus Christ. We are his witnesses, pointing to his death, resurrection, and announcing his coming return!

THINK ABOUT IT!

Are you tempted to have people look at you, or do you point to Christ with your life?

DAY 178

With knowledge unsearchable, You bestow Your thoughts on man. If only in fragment, I wish I understood Your ways.
LYRICS FROM "LIGHTS" BY THE BURIAL [LIGHTS AND PERFECTIONS]

That is what the scriptures mean when they say, "No eye has seen, no ear has heard, and no mind has imagined what God has prepared for those who love him." But it was to us that God revealed these things by his Spirit. For his Spirit searches out everything and shows us God's deep secrets. No one can know a person's thoughts except that person's own spirit, and no one can know God's thoughts except God's own Spirit. And we have received God's Spirit (not the world's spirit), so we can know the wonderful things God has freely given us. When we tell you these things, we do not use words that come from human wisdom. Instead, we speak words given to us by the Spirit, using the Spirit's words to explain spiritual truths. But people who aren't spiritual can't receive these truths from God's Spirit. It all sounds foolish to them and they can't understand it, for only those who are spiritual can understand what the Spirit means. Those who are spiritual can evaluate all things, but they themselves cannot be evaluated by others. For "Who can know the Lord's thoughts? Who knows enough to teach him?" But we understand these things, for we have the mind of Christ.

1 CORINTHIANS 2:9-12

The Christian life is full of mysteries and miracles. The works of the Holy Spirit inside of us certainly fall in these categories. I am amazed at the insight and guidance God has given me throughout the years. Because the Holy Spirit inside of me searches the deep things of God, I begin to understand them and be guided by them. So many times people without the Spirit have questioned my rationale. At those times my only comment is, "I just feel God is leading me in this direction." With his Spirit leading, it's a very exciting adventure!

THINK ABOUT IT!

Are you allowing the Holy Spirit to guide your life?

DAY 179

*This means that anyone who belongs to Christ has become
a new person. The old life is gone; a new life has begun!*

2 CORINTHIANS 5:17

I can't believe I did that!" It's difficult remembering mistakes we have made in the past. We get that sick feeling in our stomachs when we recall how foolish we were! We feel like those mistakes still define who we are. But honestly, they shouldn't! When Christ died on the cross, he took our guilt as well. He gave us a clear conscience. This is extremely difficult to understand. "How can I have a clear conscience when I was so horrible?!"

It's hard for us to comprehend the magnitude of the message of the cross. Jesus didn't take away our sin without also dealing with our guilt. He died for our guilt, too! In fact, guilt can often be a form of self-righteousness—a way of feeling like we deserve forgiveness since we feel very badly about what we did.

Because of Jesus' death on the cross, you have a new beginning. You are a new person. The old life is gone. In the new life your sins are forgiven and your guilt has been taken away. Today you can live with a clear conscience.

THINK ABOUT IT!

Do you use feelings of guilt as a form of self-righteousness?

DAY 180

*But my sin was this, that I looked for pleasure, beauty, and
truth not in Him but in myself and His other creatures, and
the search led me instead to pain, confusion, and error.*
SAINT AUGUSTINE

*We do this by keeping our eyes on Jesus, the champion who
initiates and perfects our faith. Because of the joy awaiting
him, he endured the cross, disregarding its shame. Now he
is seated in the place of honor beside God's throne.*
HEBREWS 12:2

Man has been guilty of worshiping the creation instead of the creator for centuries. When we try to find truth in anything else, we fail miserably. One of the biggest mistakes many new believers make is following people instead of God. You may have a favorite pastor or speaker. Or maybe you have a favorite band, and you're able to quote their lyrics. All of that is great, but it's not following God.

The Apostle Paul said, "Follow me as I follow God." In other words, realize that I am trying to follow him just like you are. I can't count how many times I have been disappointed by Christian leaders around me. So many have had their sins exposed in public. Others have been guilty of getting involved in false doctrine. Several of these situations have caused me to rethink my own faith, and have honestly shaken my determination to follow Christ. For this reason, I love this quote from Saith Augustine. The only place you will find absolute truth is in Jesus. And don't forget: we are all on this road together!

THINK ABOUT IT!
Is your focus on God or on people?

DAY 181

The Bible talks a lot about prayer. Yet, it remains one of the most misunderstood practices in our walk with the Lord. I have listened to a lot of sermons and opinions on the subject which has only served to confuse people even more. If there was one word that sums up what prayer is all about, it would be "communication."

Communication is the foundation of any relationship. That's why prayer is so important for us. To develop an intimate relationship with God we need to communicate. What does that look like in practical terms? I really don't have a very good answer for you. It's always different for me. There are times when my prayer is one word: "HELP!" There are other times when I am quiet and listen to God as he speaks to my heart. And other times when I need to get some things off of my chest I simply talk with God about them. If your foundation for prayer is "communication" with God, then you cannot go wrong.

THINK ABOUT IT!

*Have you discovered a way of communication or
communicating with God that works for you?*

DAY 182

Hated may I be. But love shall then abound.
LYRICS FROM "DARKNESS THAT CAN BE FELT"
BY A HILL TO DIE UPON [OMENS]

If the world hates you, remember that it hated me first. The world would love you as one of its own if you belonged to it, but you are no longer part of the world. I chose you to come out of the world, so it hates you.
JOHN 15:18-19

We struggle most of our lives to "fit in." School. Church. Our Job. With our friends. We want to be loved, recognized, and appreciated. Why do we care so much? Because our connection with other people is important. God didn't create us to be alone. When our connections are positive, it is a wonderful feeling. But when they fail, it can leave us depressed and lonely. I have learned to value the friends and family that I have, but that hasn't always been true. There have been periods in my life where I didn't honor these connections and did little to nurture them. I have hurt people by not responding to them when they needed me. And there have been times when I have seen people as a means to accomplishing goals.

I have learned a lot about friendship. I have learned the importance of people around me who believe in me, and I have the opportunity to believe in them as well. They are the ones who stand with me when the world decides to hate me. They have my back when I come under attack. And they love me through my mistakes and shortcomings. The value of God's people in your life is huge. When you come under attack (and you will!), then you have a safety net.

THINK ABOUT IT!

Have you surrounded yourself with friends and family whom you love—that will encourage you and protect you from the world's hatred?

DAY 183

*Let us go right into the presence of God with sincere
hearts fully trusting him. For our guilty consciences have
been sprinkled with Christ's blood to make us clean, and
our bodies have been washed with pure water.*
HEBREWS 10:22

I AM FORGIVEN! Wow! How exciting to be able to say that! Think about that for a moment. Jesus died on the cross for your sins. And you are forgiven. Completely. Forever. It is finished! The Bible tells us that your sin is now separated from you as far as "the east is from the west." It is no longer there! When we come to God, he accepts us as if we had never sinned. Christ's blood has made us clean. When you say, "God, remember all of those horrible things I did in my past?" He replies, "No, I don't." He has forgiven you. He has forgotten your sins. He has actually forgotten that he has forgotten. There is no record anywhere of them!

In essence, Christ's death on the cross was for your sin AND for your guilt. God doesn't want you to carry either any longer. You are a new creation. The old life is GONE! How exciting that he has given you a new beginning. You have a brand new start in life! Like Nicko, we can celebrate this good news—and live accordingly. Now we are free to pursue holiness and righteousness, where we were not able to before. As a result, we can have a deeper relationship with God!

THINK ABOUT IT!

*Have you been holding on to the guilt of your
past? What would happen if you let it go?*

DAY 184

I look back on a time in my own life that in Biblical terms probably could be called "the valley of the shadow of death." It was a time when I faced the deepest sorrow and despair a man could ever feel. In the situation I was in I saw two possibilities: either to throw myself down a steep cliff, away from everything, or throw myself into God's arms and care. God was there at the edge of the cliff even before I went there. His arm reaches farther than the deepest deep.

SIMON "PILGRIM" ROSÉN (CRIMSON MOONLIGHT)

And God will raise us from the dead by his power, just as he raised our Lord from the dead.

1 CORINTHIANS 6:14

Have you ever been on the edge of this cliff that Pilgrim is talking about? Most of us have! There are times in our lives when our faith is stretched to the limit. We feel hurt, forgotten, confused, and alone. These are defining times. It's easy to follow the Lord when everything is easy and hassle free. But what do you do when you go through "the valley of the shadow of death" as Pilgrim puts it?

Our spiritual lives are largely shaped by what we do and where we turn during the trials of life. Now, don't get me wrong. I hate them as much as you do. And as I write this, I am secretly praying that my worst trials are behind me. Whew! But I do understand that the reason I have an intimate relationship with God is largely due to the trials in my life that have both corrected my path and have taught me to trust him!

THINK ABOUT IT!

How have the trials of your life defined you?

DAY 185

*On the last day, the climax of the festival, Jesus stood and shouted
to the crowds, 'Anyone who is thirsty may come to me! Anyone
who believes in me may come and drink! For the scriptures
declare, Rivers of living water will flow from his heart.' (When
he said "living water," he was speaking of the Spirit, who would
be given to everyone believing in him. But the Spirit had not yet
been given, because Jesus had not yet entered into his glory.)*
JOHN 7:37-39

This is one of the most powerful verses in the Bible. It defines your relationship with God. Since Jesus has now been glorified, we have now received the Holy Spirit. "Rivers of living water will flow from his heart." The word 'heart' here actually means "innermost being." Many times we look for the Holy Spirit outside of ourselves. We ask for signs and wonders. We want to see him with our eyes. But his desire is to be closer than a simple vision. He has decided to live in the depths of your being. Deeper than your emotions, thoughts, passions—deeper than anything you feel or experience, is the Holy Spirit.

He desires to work from the inside out. He isn't there for your enjoyment only, but also to transform you into a new creation. How do you recognize him? Galatians 5:22-23 gives us a list: "But the Holy Spirit produces this kind of fruit in our lives: love, joy, peace, patience, kindness, goodness, faithfulness, gentleness, and self-control." These are qualities you cannot produce. When you begin to see his fruit at work in your life, you will know that God's Spirit is a work in your heart—working from the inside out!

THINK ABOUT IT!

Have you recognized the Holy Spirit working in your life?

DAY 186

*God will enlighten you and inspire you. He will show you
what you need to know, maybe not everything you want
to know, but everything that you need to know.*
ERIC CLAYTON (SAVIOR MACHINE)

*And the Holy Spirit helps us in our weakness. For example, we
don't know what God wants us to pray for. But the Holy Spirit prays
for us with groanings that cannot be expressed in words. And the
Father who knows all hearts knows what the Spirit is saying, for
the Spirit pleads for us believers in harmony with God's own will.*
ROMANS 8:26-27

I have been frustrated with God many times in the past. I couldn't understand why he didn't answer my simple prayer for understanding in a situation, or why he hadn't changed the outcome of it as I had asked him to do. Age has its benefits. One of them is the ability to look back over your life, and be thankful that God didn't answer specific prayers and demands you made. I have never been able to see the whole picture. I still can't. It used to bother me. I wanted a lot more control, as I was still learning to trust God in my life. Now, it is easier. I have enough life-experience that I have learned to trust him. He has proven himself to be trust-worthy!

When I don't understand what is going on, I no longer demand that he solve the situation according to my short-sided understanding. Instead, my prayer has become more about trusting him to do the right thing, and showing me his plan and perspective. We would all be in great trouble if God answered all of the ridiculous prayers that we offer in times of trouble and confusion. "Not my will, but your will be done" is a better prayer. That's the reason God gave us his Holy Spirit. When he is able to inspire our prayers, we begin to have his understanding.

THINK ABOUT IT!

Have you begun to allow the Holy Spirit to guide your prayers?

DAY 187

Dear brothers and sisters, I want you to understand that the gospel message I preach is not based on mere human reasoning.

GALATIANS 1:11

When Jesus enters your life, you begin to feel things more deeply. Maybe your heart is broken for friends and family that you love deeply. This is a difficult thing to live with. We have a strong desire for those we love to know Jesus. But taking full responsibility for their salvation is too heavy for you to bear. That belongs to God.

Work as hard as possible on the things he calls us to do. Allow his word to affect your life so you can communicate it correctly. Remain faithful to him and to the things he teaches you. That's your responsibility. But whether or not our friends receive it or not, that is God's responsibility.

We must be emotionally involved with our friends. That means getting our hearts broken from time to time because they may not receive our message. But we're not strong enough to carry the weight of their rejection. Only God has the strength to do so. We must simply be tools for the Holy Spirit to speak through us and remain true to that message.

THINK ABOUT IT!

Are you trying to be strong enough to carry other people's eternal destiny on your shoulders?

DAY 188

Brace yourself for what will come next.
LYRICS FROM "ENDSEEKERS"
BY OH, SLEEPER [CHILDREN OF FIRE]

The thief's purpose is to steal and kill and destroy.
My purpose is to give them a rich and satisfying life.
JOHN 10:10

In 1979, Folk/Rock singer songwriter Bob Dylan released this song called "Gotta Serve Somebody." Here is a sampling of the lyrics:

> You may be a preacher with your spiritual pride
> You may be a city councilman taking bribes on the side
> You may be workin' in a barbershop,
>   you may know how to cut hair
> You may be somebody's mistress,
>   may be somebody's heir
> But you're gonna have to serve somebody
> Well, it may be the devil or it may be the Lord,
>   but you're gonna have to serve somebody

Satan's ultimate purpose is to destroy you. Period. His continued lies and manipulation take its toll on this world every day. Many claim not to be "religious" or to have any kind of belief system. But, as Bob Dylan puts it, "You're gonna have to serve somebody." If you don't belong to Jesus, then you are serving the desires of Satan. Pretty harsh statement? Especially when all of us know some really "good" people who are not Christians. One pastor friend of mine made the statement that many times non-Christians act more Christian than Christians! What about those people? Goodness doesn't get us to Heaven. If it could, Jesus wouldn't have died on the cross. Besides, the Bible says that no one is good—no one! Good people are not going to Heaven. "Saved" people are going to Heaven!

THINK ABOUT IT!

Who are you serving?

DAY 189

"Unless he obeys, a man cannot believe."
DIETRICH BONHOEFFER

*Jesus replied, "My mother and my brothers are all
those who hear God's word and obey it."*
LUKE 8:21

God is our Father, friend, and comforter. He cares deeply for each one of us. But he's also our Master and King. We must not lose sight of those aspects of God as well. When life becomes difficult, sometimes we try to create a God that will fit into our situation. We don't want him to be judgmental or demanding. Instead, we feel more comfortable with him if he just does what we ask, fits into our emotional state. You wouldn't like a god like that!

Jesus didn't die on the cross to simply make you feel better. He died to give you new life, and eternity at the end of it. He came to bring your life a foundation. And, like any good brother, sometimes he needs to tell us things we would rather not hear. That's because he is God. He sees a bigger picture, and knows where we are headed.

There will be many times in your Christian life when you don't feel that God is being fair with you. There will be times when you interpret his correction as silence. And, there will be times when his answers to your desperate questions are not what you want to hear. Like any father who loves his child, he is willing to take whatever negative feelings you might have temporarily to achieve the best outcome for your life. He knows what he is doing!

THINK ABOUT IT!

Do your emotions dictate your view of God in some areas?

DAY 190

I hated Christians and all they stood for—
or at least what I thought they stood for.
MICHAEL HERO (SONS OF THUNDER)

"Well then, if you teach others, why don't you teach yourself?
You tell others not to steal, but do you steal? You say it is
wrong to commit adultery, but do you commit adultery? You
condemn idolatry, but do you use items stolen from pagan
temples? You are so proud of knowing the law, but you
dishonor God by breaking it. No wonder the scriptures say, "The
Gentiles blaspheme the name of God because of you."
ROMANS 2:21-24

Many times, the only thing standing in someone's way of becoming a Christian is… well… other Christians! When we present ourselves as judge and jury to the world, we are guilty of being hypocrites! The biggest problem we have with the sin around us is that they are sinning differently than we do! Romans 3:23 says, "For everyone has sinned; we all fall short of God's glorious standard."

The Apostle Paul, who wrote much of the New Testament, said that he was the "chief" of sinners. His strategy was "follow me as I follow Christ." We should adopt the same strategy! The fruit of the Spirit (the characteristics given to us by the Holy Spirit listed in Galatians 5) is "Love, joy, peace, patience, kindness, goodness, faithfulness, gentleness, and self-control." Judgment, condemnation, and hatred are not part of his fruit. And, in my opinion, they shouldn't be part of ours either!

THINK ABOUT IT!

Are you a help or a hindrance in someone finding Christ?

DAY 191

We're nothing but hollow vessels in search of what makes us alive
LYRICS FROM "THERE COULD BE NOTHING AFTER THIS"
BY UNDERØATH [DEFINE THE GREAT LINE]

Elijah replied, "I have zealously served the Lord God Almighty."
1 KINGS 19:10

What are you passionate about? What makes you feel alive? Too many people are stuck in a job they hate. The pay and security may be good, but to continue to do something you dislike will eventually takes it toll on you. We need to involve ourselves in things that make us feel alive. We need passion! In work, family, or spare time. Not all of us get to play music for a living. But it can still be a hobby even though you might not play a lot of shows.

Very few people are radicals throughout their lives. But Christians can be! Our faith is filled with passion by its very nature. Get in tune with the Holy Spirit. Let him guide you in your everyday life. Even if you have a job that you're not excited about, God can use you there in ways you cannot anticipate! When he produces his fruit within your life, things start to get exciting. Some people work at a job they find less than exciting, but they still love it since it gives them the opportunity to meet people and share their life with them.

Find passion! Find something you enjoy doing. Even during those times in your life when you are not enjoying your labor, find opportunities to shine! Allow the Holy Spirit to make you his ambassador no matter what your situation may be.

THINK ABOUT IT!

Are you on a mission from God?

DAY 192

He was taking care of me even when
my back was turned to Him.
TOMMY ALDRIDGE (WHITESNAKE)

If we are unfaithful, he remains faithful,
for he cannot deny who he is.
2 TIMOTHY 2:13

So you're not perfect. Welcome to the human race! How many times do we walk away from God and imagine that he is walking away from us as well? No matter what, he remains faithful, even when we're not! Isaiah 49:16 says, "I have written your name on the palms of my hands." The longer you live the Christian life, the more you will realize that it is an impossible life. You know it. I know it. God knows it, too! That's the reason he sent Jesus to die on the cross for us. Jesus paid the price to make what was once impossible, possible! Because of Jesus' sacrifice, God always has your back.

When Tommy Aldridge came back to the Lord, he realized that God was taking care of him even through those times when his back was turned and he was going a different direction. This is great news! It means that no matter where you are at and what you are doing, you can always turn to God in your time of need and he will hear you. He won't give you a lecture about how long it has been since you talked. Rather, he will guide you from the position you are currently in. This is the miracle of his grace!

THINK ABOUT IT!

Do you sometimes hesitate to come to God because
you imagine he has walked away from you?

DAY 193

In a strange way I was longing for a more meaningful
life, but at the same time, I was afraid to take a step.
ULF CHRISTIANSSON (JERUSALEM)

But when you ask him, be sure that your faith is in God alone.
Do not waver, for a person with divided loyalty is as unsettled
as a wave of the sea that is blown and tossed by the wind.
JAMES 1:6

Ulf is like so many of us who are afraid to take a step of faith! We want a relationship with God, but we also want what the world has to offer. Many begin to play a game called "Build-A-God!" We formulate all of the attributes that we would like God to have, and then we begin to place our faith in our own ideas. We make statements like, "I believe in a God that" or " I don't believe God would truly object to" Build-A-God.

Faith is an interesting concept. So many, who are playing this game, have placed their faith in their own misconceptions of God. Their personal faith is in their misguided faith! But that is where true Christianity is different. God has given us an "object" of our faith: Jesus Christ! Jesus actually told us that "if you have seen me, you have seen the Father." (John 14:9). So to play an accurate Build-A-God game, we would need to use Jesus as our guide. That is the step of faith Ulf is talking about. It is a step where we can honestly say, "I am willing to see the real attributes of God, and get to know him for who he really is!

THINK ABOUT IT!

Are you playing "Build-A-God?" How much of your
personal faith is misguided instead of in Jesus Christ?

DAY 194

Crushing the legalist agenda, defying the hypocrites mentality
LYRICS FROM "OVERTHROW"
BY SLEEPING GIANT [FINISHED PEOPLE]

T hen Jesus went over to their synagogue, where he noticed a man with a deformed hand. The Pharisees asked Jesus, 'Does the law permit a person to work by healing on the Sabbath?' (They were hoping he would say yes, so they could bring charges against him.)' " Matthew 12:9-10

Some preachers are very legalistic. They spend their energy condemning everyone and telling people what they cannot do. They care more about people behaving properly than about their relationship with the Lord. This can be really confusing since this speaks to the core of your identity. Instead of hearing everything you are doing wrong, wouldn't it also be a great idea to tell you about your opportunities as a dearly loved child of God?

Jesus actually spoke harshly against this kind of thinking. During Christ's life the Pharisees didn't understand the real heart of Jesus' teaching. They constantly tried to catch Jesus doing something wrong instead of listening to His message of love and freedom. When Christian leaders take on the role of moral police, it creates confusion for all of us. It creates a sin-based mindset as the foundation for our spiritual lives. Instead of pursuing holiness, we try to get as close to the world as possible without falling in.

Our focus should be on Jesus Christ. The Bible tells us to seek him with all of our heart. When this happens, we begin to seek him in freedom. We understand what Romans 13:10 means when it says, "love fulfills the requirements of God's law." When this happens, our focus changes. We simply don't have a desire to do the things that make us a slave to the world.

THINK ABOUT IT!

Are you focusing more on all the things you cannot do than on him?

DAY 195

Are your mental and spiritual lives connected? Some people try to separate the two. But to live a full and complete life, that is not the way to process. Body and spirit affect each other. Your spiritual life affects you mentally, emotionally, sexually, socially, and physically.

In a period of doubt about God's existence, the worst thing you can do is to ignore the questions. Doubt needs to be taken seriously, without letting it take over your whole life. If you ignore it, it'll grow bigger. If you let doubt control you, you'll stop praying and seeking the Lord. When doubt knocks on your door, welcome it inside. Engage in rational discussions with it and fight back. There are many extremely talented Christian thinkers who can help you find good answers to your questions. The Christian worldview is by far the most intellectual. It just takes some work and reading to find the solid answers.

You're called to love God with your entire mind. Therefore, you cannot separate your intellectual and spiritual lives. The two affect each other. By finding answers to some of your questions your trust in the Lord will grow, and you will be more complete in your surrender to him, which will deepen your spiritual life.

THINK ABOUT IT!

*Have you considered how your mind and
spirituality affect each other?*

DAY 196

I think comfort can often be a killer.
RYAN CLARK (DEMON HUNTER)

A lazy person is as bad as someone who destroys things.
PROVERBS 18:9

We are creatures of comfort. We love to make our surroundings as comfortable as we possibly can. But, can too much comfort be a problem? Yes! It can make us greedy and lazy. But even worse, we forget to depend on God in our daily lives. It's difficult to understand that he's all we need until he's all we've got. Many people find they don't learn these lessons until they have lost everything. I hear this lesson from our homeless friends all the time!

Many times, God calls us to a more humble lifestyle. We may not have the newest car or the largest home on the block, but the house is easier to manage, and the car provides the means to get from point A to point B. While financial security isn't a bad thing, it's a blessing to be dependent on the Lord and experience his care for you.

Be thankful for the comfort you have. It's not a bad thing in and of itself. But be careful it doesn't consume your time and focus. Make important decisions about finances and unnecessary comfort. Learn to give to those in need. God's plan for you may very well include leaving your comfort zone and trusting him for everything. He's all you need.

THINK ABOUT IT!

*Does your current comfort zone make you lazy? Are
you trusting the Lord to provide for you?*

DAY 197

As no darkness can be seen by anyone surrounded
by light, so no trivialities can capture the attention
of anyone who has his eyes on Christ.
GREGORY OF NYSSA

But Martha was distracted by the big dinner she was preparing....
But the Lord said to her, "My dear Martha, you are worried and upset
over all these details! There is only one thing worth being concerned
about. Mary has discovered it, and it will not be taken away from her."
LUKE 10:40-42

"Squirrel!" Some days it doesn't take much to become distracted! Usually, those distractions take our focus away from what's important. There are many things that capture our attention in life. Our lives have become very fast-paced. It's easy to feel very busy, even when our time could be better spent. It's always a good idea to reconsider your priorities. Time moves by so quickly. A day. A week. A month. A year. It seems difficult to find time every day to sit with Jesus. There's so much to do!

Mary is a great example for us. She understands her duties but she doesn't let her business get in the way of spending time with Jesus. She sits down and listens to him. She understands what's most important. She doesn't try to stuff her time with Christ into a few spare moments, but realizes there are more important things with eternal values at stake. Is Christ really the center of your life? Do you make time for him? Do the cares and concerns of a busy schedule crowd him out of your day? We need to learn from Mary: "All who heard the shepherds' story were astonished but Mary kept all these things in her heart and thought about them often" (Luke 2:18-19).

THINK ABOUT IT!

How do you prioritize sitting at the feet of Christ?

DAY 198

*Why do we keep what holds us? Why do I keep what holds me
down? Lose the weight of defeat. It's time to stand your ground!*

LYRICS FROM "VICES LIKE VIPERS"
BY OH, SLEEPER [WHEN I AM GOD]

*Sin is no longer your master, for you no longer live
under the requirements of the law. Instead, you
live under the freedom of God's grace.*

ROMANS 6:14

I am a Christian now. Why do I continue to sin?" Even after becoming a Christian, we all continue to have sins that are very difficult to get rid of. Some things even make us addicts and control parts of our lives. Pornography is an obvious example here. It appears to be a pleasing addition to our sexuality, but in the end, we become slaves to it. Christ paid for your freedom with his blood on the cross. Now, for the first time, you have an opportunity to be free!

You serve whatever controls you. 2 Peter 2:19 says, "They promise freedom, but they themselves are slaves of sin and corruption. For you are a slave to whatever controls you." Give sin a finger, and it'll take your whole hand! Sin may be fun and satisfying for a short time, but it will take control over your emotions and thinking. Sin is designed to produce addiction.

As Christians, we find ourselves in sin from time to time. It happens. But continual sin is something we need to take very seriously. Continued, addiction-driven sin will try to steer you away from God. It is a lifelong struggle to get rid of the sin you're addicted to. He is there to help! It's time to stand your ground!

THINK ABOUT IT!

*Do you have continual sin in your life? Don't allow sin
to control your life. Be prepared for the things you know
will tempt you. Be strong. Surrender these difficult areas
of your life to God. Let the Holy Spirit change you.*

DAY 199

I have always felt that heavy metal was the ultimate music and the ultimate form of expression, with Christianity being the ultimate message. The message and the music fit together perfectly, in my opinion.

SCOTT WATERS (ULTIMATUM)

Praise him with a blast of the ram's horn; praise him with the lyre and harp! Praise him with the tambourine and dancing; praise him with strings and flutes! Praise him with a clash of cymbals; praise him with loud clanging cymbals. Let everything that breathes sing praises to the Lord!

PSALM 150:3-6

"He who sings prays twice." What a great quote attributed to Saint Augustine. Powerful things happen inside our hearts when we put our thoughts and prayers to music. I really love Scott Waters' quote here. Metal is the ultimate expression for a powerful message! I've been on the cutting edge of Christian Rock and Metal for 50 years. I've heard all of the arguments against it, to, from, "It's the same drum beat that is used to conjure up demons in Africa" to "It isn't soothing to the soul, so it cannot be from God." But what I really hear is, "It isn't my taste in music, so it cannot be holy."

David's use of music is a great study in the Bible. He talks about soothing music, the kind he used for King Saul: "And whenever the tormenting spirit from God troubled Saul, David would play the harp. Then Saul would feel better, and the tormenting spirit would go away" (1 Samuel 16:33). But then, in Psalm 150, he is definitely not creating soothing music! He gives us the example of two types of music, in my opinion. Worship (in 1 Samuel) and Celebration (in Psalm 150). Both have their place in our expression to God. Heavy Metal would fall in the second category, and for many, the first category as well!

THINK ABOUT IT!

How much of a role does music play in your life?

DAY 200

In 1996 I was diagnosed with leukemia and twice was given just two hours to live....The Bible has given me the words to fight and beat cancer and the devil. I live on to share my hope in Christ with others through the music and concerts of Mortification.

STEVE ROWE (MORTIFICATION)

He personally carried our sins in his body on the cross so that we can be dead to sin and live for what is right. By his wounds you are healed.

1 PETER 2:24

I have known Steve Rowe for many years. Once while staying at my home in Nashville many years ago, I remember he could barely walk. He struggled with almost every bodily function. Yet, he kept going. I've worked with Steve many times since then. He's an amazing man. A true testimony to the healing power of God.

Would his physical healing be the most important work of God in his life? I am sure Steve would tell you "No!" Healing from our old life and becoming a new creation in Jesus Christ is always the ultimate healing. How wonderful to be able to claim God's power for physical healing. I have that same testimony, but it isn't what keeps me going. My daily praise to God is for what he continues to do on the INSIDE of me. His death on the cross so that I could be inwardly transformed will always be the biggest miracle in my life!

THINK ABOUT IT!

Are you still looking for outward signs of God working in your life, or have you begun to experience his divine transformation from within?

DAY 201

To be honest, when I was younger, I think I was writing in a large way—out of insecurity. I felt like I had to prove myself to everybody. LOOK HOW CHRISTIAN I AM! I was writing all these lyrics to prove to everybody that I believed what I said I believed in. In secret, I felt like such a hypocrite.
MATTIE MONTGOMERY (FOR TODAY)

His words are as smooth as butter, but in his heart is war. His words are as soothing as lotion, but underneath are daggers!
PSALM 55:21

H e's not the person I thought he was. He has been a huge disappointment." Her pastor, whom she idolized, had just been caught in an affair. The whole church was devastated. "How could he have done such a thing. He even preached against looking at other women. We just assumed he was following his own advice!" All of us have been disappointed by people in whom we have invested some trust. While it is true that leaders should understand that they're being looked up to and behave as such, we are continually surprised that people sometimes are hypocritical and fall into sin. Again, that is the reason Jesus died on the cross. ALL of us are hypocrites. "For everyone has sinned, we all fall short of God's glorious standard" (Romans 3:23). Paul said, "And you should imitate me, just as I imitate Christ" (1 Corinthians 11:1). Paul knew that his personal example would not be enough. He knew he wasn't perfect. It is important that we lead by our lives, and not by our dogma. I have sinned in front of people many times. My prayer is always that they know my heart, and they know that my Lord is patient and loving—and picks me up every time!

THINK ABOUT IT!

Don't be afraid to make mistakes in front of others. Allow them to experience God's grace in your life as well!

DAY 202

Far better for a man that he had never been born than that he should degrade a pulpit into a show box to exhibit himself in.

CHARLES H. SPURGEON

Watch out! Don't do your good deeds publicly, to be admired by others, for you will lose the reward from your Father in heaven.

MATTHEW 6:1

Everyone wants to be a rock star! From the time you pick up that first guitar, receive your first pair of drumsticks, or scream into a microphone for the first time, you dream about that day that others will see and appreciate your talent! Playing a concert where a large crowd goes wild is a lot of fun. It's awesome playing metal, sharing testimonies from the stage, and seeing the crowd hang on your every word. But the true test is when the crowd is small. Do you then play with the same intensity? Do you share your testimony with the same fire in your eyes?

The danger for many bands is pride and arrogance. Many start out with good intentions, but slowly end up serving themselves. The real test isn't what they can do in front of 5,000 people, but rather what they can do when only 5 people show up for a concert. We need to see each person individually and realize that everyone matters. Jesus didn't consider himself too important to reach out to seemingly unimportant or "too sinful" individuals. He extended his heart with the same care and unconditional love to everyone. No matter whether he taught the masses or just one person, he pointed them to God.

THINK ABOUT IT!

Are you more focused on yourself, or on the people you meet every day?

DAY 203

*He who loves with purity considers not the gift
of the lover, but the love of the giver.*

THOMAS A KEMPIS

*When it was time for the harvest, Cain presented some of
his crops as a gift to the Lord. Abel also brought a gift—the
best portions of the firstborn lambs from his flock. The Lord
accepted Abel and his gift, but he did not accept Cain and his
gift. This made Cain very angry, and he looked dejected.*

GENESIS 4:3-5

Dear God: If you love me, could you give me stuff? I have been good, and I deserve it." We sometimes get Santa Claus and God confused! Have you considered your attitude towards God on this subject? Do you merely become happy because of the gifts he gives you, or do you focus on the amazing love that's behind it? We may ask God for a lot of things, but honestly, there are gifts all around us that we should be thankful for. As we become more mature in our relationship with the Lord, we don't just focus on all the awesome things that await us in Heaven. They are worth being thankful for, and there's nothing wrong with looking forward to them. But our focus becomes the giver, God. And living in perfect union with the Lord.

God looks at us in that way. His main focus isn't having you do a bunch of stuff for him. He doesn't start out by wanting your actions, money, time, etc…he wants you! He wants to be in a relationship with you! Giving gifts to others can be a great way to show them love, especially by not doing it on the obvious occasions like Christmas and birthdays. Hopefully, they'll get to see the love of the giver as well.

THINK ABOUT IT!

*Are you more interested in the stuff God can
give you, or do you just want him?*

DAY 204

Hate is a consuming thing. It's the second most powerful emotion in the world, the first being love. It can confuse you if you don't let it go.
ERIC CLAYTON (SAVIOR MACHINE)

All who fear the Lord will hate evil.
PROVERBS 8:13

For this is how God loved the world: He gave his one and only Son, so that everyone who believes in him will not perish but have eternal life.
JOHN 3:16

"H ater's gonna hate!" It's a term we use a lot for internet stalkers and bullies. You know the type. And many times, Christians are the worst. It almost seems like they're looking for an excuse to dislike people and get upset at things that are going on around them. We have gotten very good at judging the world and people around us. But we fail miserably when it comes to loving each other unconditionally.

Every day I get hate mail from well meaning Christians who want to set me straight about doctrine and appearance. It's interesting since I am doctrinally conservative. Of course, my appearance has always bothered many "conservative" Christians. I'm sure that if I wore a robe and looked more like the Jews at the time of Jesus, they would have an even bigger problem. When we decide to hate and condemn, we travel a slippery slope. That's the reason Jesus asks us to love unconditionally. When I'm able to see others through his eyes, I'm able to love them without seeing their shortcomings or mine!

THINK ABOUT IT!

Is it easier for you to judge, or to love unconditionally?

DAY 205

*We are not very financially rich. We live like royalty,
however, compared to the real poor of this world.*

STEVE ROWE (MORTIFICATION)

*While Jesus was in the Temple, he watched the rich people
dropping their gifts in the collection box. Then a poor widow
came by and dropped in two small coins. 'I tell you the truth,'
Jesus said, 'this poor widow has given more than all the rest
of them. For they have given a tiny part of their surplus, but
she, poor as she is, has given everything she has.'*

LUKE 21:1-4

There's a big difference between giving out of our surplus and giving out of our need. Honestly, this verse isn't about money. It's about our hearts. As I write this I have been involved in feeding the homeless for 12 years. We are currently serving about 8,000 meals per month. Why? Because I feel some kind of pressure from God to do it? No! It has been a real joy to get to know those in need, and be able to respond in a simple way with food. But for me, it hasn't been about obedience to this principle as much as it has been a passion from my heart.

I love it when God loves through me! I love to feel his unconditional love for the man who reeks of alcohol as I hug him. For the woman who will go out that night an sell her body to make ends meet. For the young kids who are suddenly too old for the foster care program, and are now on the streets without family. And that is just Nashville. Our homeless friends have it so much better than the people Steve Rowe is talking about in the rest of the world. When your heart gets involved, and God's Holy Spirit begins to give you his unconditional love, you can't help but get involved!

THINK ABOUT IT!

*Have you allowed God to open up your heart to those
in need close to you and around the world?*

DAY 206

To say that God turns away from the sinful is like
saying that the sun hides from the blind.
ANTHONY THE GREAT

I have called you back from the ends of the earth, saying, "You
are my servant." For I have chosen you and will not throw
you away. Don't be afraid, for I am with you. Don't be
discouraged, for I am your God. I will strengthen you and
help you. I will hold you up with my victorious right hand.
ISAIAH 41:9-10

Do you ever feel like giving up on yourself, believing it's too late for you to make this life-thing work? Welcome to the club. I am the president! Sometimes life beats us down, and it becomes very difficult for us to imagine things ever working out. We feel depression, anxiety, and brokenness. How could anyone become victorious against these odds? Do you realize that God will never give up on you? He loves you and believes in you. He will never let you go.

Maybe you have friends who feel this way. It's very important for them to know that you will never give up on them, either. We all need to be reminded of others' love for us. That is part of the give-and-take that defines friendship! You understand that God would never give up on them so you must do the same.

THINK ABOUT IT!
Do you understand and reflect God's endurance?

DAY 207

*Try to keep your soul always in peace and quiet, always ready
for whatever our Lord may wish to work in you. It is certainly a
higher virtue of the soul, and a greater grace, to be able to enjoy
the Lord in different times and different places than in only one.*

SAINT IGNATIUS

*Now may the God of peace make you holy in every
way, and may your whole spirit and soul and body be kept
blameless until our Lord Jesus Christ comes again.*

1 THESSALONIANS 5:23

Be still, and know that I am God!" (Psalm 46:10). I would have said, "Shut up and listen!" Be quiet. Be ready all throughout the day. Listen for the Lord's calling. Being ready for his guidance is one of the most awesome things in our walk with the Lord. This can turn an ordinary day into an important mission. Turn your thoughts into prayers. In doing so, you're listening to God during your day. When you are sensitive to the Spirit, he will show you people who need your help. The daily routine at your job becomes an opportunity to share your heart with co-workers. Your eyes will begin to focus on those who are hurt. You see, daily devotions like this one shouldn't just be the time we seek the Lord and learn something about him. It should also set the tone for seeking the Lord throughout the entire day. Today, reflect on what you've learned, turning it into wisdom. Be sure to be sensitive to him in every situation throughout the day.

THINK ABOUT IT!

Have you learned to "shut up and listen?"

DAY 208

We used to hate and destroy one another and refused to associate
with people of another race or country. Now, because of Christ,
we live together with such people and pray for our enemies.

JUSTIN MARTYR

When people's lives please the Lord, even
their enemies are at peace with them.

PROVERBS 16:7

I am leaving you with a gift—peace of mind and heart. And the peace
I give is a gift the world cannot give. So don't be troubled or afraid.

JOHN 14:27

It seems everyone has a political opinion these days. And, with their opinions, each has a different political model they believe can bring peace to the world. Many believe they can exchange their worldview for a sense of democracy. These diplomatic solutions only show they don't understand the real problem: People!

A political ideology simply doesn't go deep enough. We need something stronger than our emotions, frustration, anger, and even our sin. We need Christ! Only through Christ can we bring divine peace to a hurting and dying world. Jesus has the power to change the hearts of humans. We can't fix ourselves. We've certainly tried! Only God can change us. It's absolutely amazing how he's able to change us into something better. "I have told you all this so that you may have peace in me. Here on earth you will have many trials and sorrows. But take heart, because I have overcome the world" (John 16:33).

THINK ABOUT IT!

With this in mind, how would you seek to bring peace to the world?

DAY 209

Let all that I am wait quietly before God, for my hope is in him. He alone is my rock and my salvation, my fortress where I will not be shaken. My victory and honor come from God alone. He is my refuge, a rock where no enemy can reach me. O my people, trust in him at all times. Pour out your heart to him, for God is our refuge.
PSALMS 62:5-8

I am totally stressed out!" Sound familiar. I use that phrase more than I should. This can also effect us spiritually. Stress makes it difficult to spend quality time with the Lord. Prayer becomes another thing on the list that needs to be done throughout the day. It becomes extremely difficult to listen to the Lord. Joblessness can create the same challenges for different reasons. When every form of structure gets removed from the week, then our good habits go out the window as well. It's easy to become lazy or even forget to spend time with the Lord. And, during times of extreme difficulty, life may seem to lose its purpose.

It's good to be aware of this. When life is stressful, you need to make sure it doesn't continue to be that way. Otherwise it will sooner or later lead to sickness, and the body can be affected even many years afterwards. Here, simple spiritual habits can come in handy. The same goes for a period of joblessness. Habits can create structure throughout the week that will help you move forward in life until you get a job. Those habits will help bring you through a rough time and help you in deepening your relationship with God, even when everything else is crazy.

THINK ABOUT IT!

How do structural changes in your life affect your spiritual life?

DAY 210

We make music that we think people will enjoy, but over all, we make music to carry the message where it hasn't gone before.
TED KIRKPATRICK (TOURNIQUET)

I waited patiently for the Lord to help me, and he turned to me and heard my cry. He lifted me out of the pit of despair, out of the mud and the mire. He set my feet on solid ground and steadied me as I walked along. He has given me a new song to sing, a hymn of praise to our God. Many will see what he has done and be amazed. They will put their trust in the Lord.
PSALM 40:1-3

I love music! I learned to dance before I could talk. Singing came naturally. I sang a duet in church with my mom when I was just 2 years old. I started playing the piano for Sunday School at 12, and then started playing the piano for church when I was 15. My mom played the organ. I developed a deep love for the hymns during this time, which has served as the foundation for my love of all music.

It has taught me how important music is as a form of communication. I experienced that communication at 2 years of age. Since that time, I have watched thousands of people respond to music with a Gospel message. As David says here in this psalm, as a result of his experience, "many will see what he has done and be amazed. They will put their trust in the Lord." The power of music to carry a message is amazing! If you are a music lover, you already understand the power of music with a message!

THINK ABOUT IT!
How had God used music in your life?

DAY 211

I've seen heroin addicts drop their habit and many anti-Christ type of people make a 180 degree turn for God.
ROBERT SWEET (STRYPER)

For I can do everything through Christ, who gives me strength.
PHILIPPIANS 4:13

This means that anyone who belongs to Christ has become a new person. The old life is gone; a new life has begun!
2 CORINTHIANS 5:17

We have been experiencing revival in the metal community. As you can see from so many personal quotes and song lyrics here in this book, many have come to know the saving power of God through his Son, Jesus Christ. Most are former drug addicts, atheists, alcoholics, and sex addicts. Many struggled with thoughts of suicide and depression even while enjoying success in the music world.

Mark 8:36 asks, "And what do you benefit if you gain the whole world but lose your own soul?" We all have a desire to be happy. We choose those things that give us temporary happiness, and strive for the things we think will bring us inner happiness. But when all of that fails, and we are on the top of our game, we are left with despair. It's as if we live with a God-shaped void that only Jesus can fill. God promises his PEACE. Happiness is fleeting. But peace is totally different. The Bible says we can have God's peace "even in the middle of a storm." In fact, it even tells us that it can't be understood by human wisdom. We don't even know what we are looking for! Thank God that he is still changing people and setting them free!

THINK ABOUT IT!
How has Jesus changed your life?

DAY 212

For God says, "At just the right time, I heard you.
On the day of salvation, I helped you." Indeed,
the "right time" is now. Today is the day of salvation.

2 CORINTHIANS 6:2

I t's too late. I have sinned too much. I have gone too far. I'm sure God hates me by now!" Really? Who says so? According to God, ALL have fallen short of the glory of God. You. Me. Everyone! Because he holds the keys to unconditional forgiveness and eternal life, it all comes down to God's compassion. Through Christ's death on the cross, God made a way for our salvation. But that is where you and I have a decision to make. It is a one-time decision.

Will you accept Jesus as your Lord and Savior, or will you reject him? That is the most important decision you will ever make! It is important that you understand that "right now" is the time for it! TODAY can be your day of salvation if you have never asked Jesus into your life before. And if you have, you can rejoice with Nicko that you are saved, and confirm your desire to see others in Heaven with you as well! NOW IS THE TIME OF SALVATION!

THINK ABOUT IT!

Have you ever had a time when you invited Jesus into your heart?

DAY 213

He knew the pain because He felt it. He knew the rejection
because He knows it firsthand. He knew the loneliness
because He has lived it. He knew all about what I was going
through, and He extended His helping hand to me.
TOMMY ALDRIDGE (WHITESNAKE)

This High Priest of ours understands our weaknesses, for he
faced all of the same testings we do, yet he did not sin.
HEBREWS 4:15

In the middle of an emotional difficulty we usually feel like we're the only ones going through it! We love to remind people that they simply don't understand. "Until you have walked in my shoes, you can't understand the pain and despair I am in!" It's true that I will never know the pain of losing a child, or the difficulty of fighting a drug or alcohol addiction. But that doesn't mean that we aren't tempted in the same ways.

Jesus understands our weakness. He became human so that he could fully understand and have the highest compassion for our difficulties. His compassion is complete. He shares with our emotions, and guides us to a place of healing. It's because of his unique understanding that you can trust him with whatever you are going through. He understands you. He loves you. He believes in you!

THINK ABOUT IT!

Do you sometimes wait until you fail to manage
your trials before you come to God with them?

DAY 214

Sound doctrine does not enter into a hard and disobedient heart.
JUSTIN MARTYR

My child, pay attention to what I say. Listen carefully to my words.
Don't lose sight of them. Let them penetrate deep into your heart, for
they bring life to those who find them, and healing to their whole body.
Guard your heart above all else for it determines the course of your life.
PROVERBS 4:20-23

Sound Doctrine." I know many people who have studied the Bible all of their lives, and yet I wouldn't say their doctrine is "sound." They may be able to quote the original Greek and Hebrew, and give you the context for its meaning, but they miss the whole purpose of its content. What makes doctrine sound? When we understand God's unconditional love toward us, and realize what Christ's death on the cross actually accomplished in our hearts. It isn't about doctrine. It is about relationship and transformation.

The world has its share of hard-hearted pastors. They preach terror and guilt into the hearts of people. Even though they may have an understanding of basic doctrine, they have missed the whole purpose of its foundation. As it tells us here in Proverbs, when God's Word penetrates out hearts it will "bring life to those who find them, and healing to their whole body." And, in the end, it "determines the course of your life!"

THINK ABOUT IT!

Is your heart ready for sound doctrine?

DAY 215

*You alone Shake the core of my being, regenerate that child's
heart Transform my mind to understand, the gravity of your plan.*

LYRICS FROM "APATHY AND PETITION"
BY THE BURIAL [LIGHTS AND PERFECTIONS]

*Don't copy the behavior and customs of this world, but
let God transform you into a new person by changing
the way you think. Then you will learn to know God's will
for you, which is good and pleasing and perfect.*

ROMANS 12:2

The Bible talks about 2 "patterns." The pattern of this world, and the pattern guided by the Holy Spirit. You will follow one or the other. Actually, by not following one, you automatically follow the other. Just because you have become a Christian doesn't mean that you will always automatically follow God's "pattern." You have to decide to do so. Romans says "LET God transform you" Choose to surrender to the Holy Spirit's guidance within you, instead of copying the behavior and customs of this world.

The difference between the two is paramount! When you follow this world, you will always have an inner sense that you are not in control. You will continue to be a product of your circumstances. You will feel defeat and confusion. When you allow the "patterns" of the Holy Spirit inside of you to guide you, a sense of security, wisdom, and peace will accompany your life. Don't forget that this is a daily choice. God is always waiting and willing to guide your life. He just needs you to be willing as well!

THINK ABOUT IT!

*Are you allowing the Holy Spirit to guide your life,
or are you following the pattern of this world?*

DAY 216

A Bible that's falling apart usually belongs to someone who isn't.
CHARLES SPURGEON

*All scripture is inspired by God and is useful to teach us what is
true and to make us realize what is wrong in our lives. It corrects
us when we are wrong and teaches us to do what is right. God
uses it to prepare and equip his people to do every good work.*
2 TIMOTHY 3:16-17

I have worn out several Bibles. They are literally falling apart, and are not really usable any longer. When I pick one of them up and look through it, I am flooded with emotion. I have an old Bible that is actually covered in snake skin. Old Sanctuary followers will remember it. I carried it everywhere. There isn't a page in the whole Bible that isn't underlined and notes written in the margins. It represents some of my sweetest times with the Lord.

These days, I use electronic media. My Bible is in an app. When I write something in it, the app instantly puts that message on all my devices (MacBook, iPad, and iPhone). Technology changes, but the Word of God never does. Whatever way you use the Bible, whether hardcopy or electronic media, make sure you wear it out. Use it. Become familiar with it. Take notes. Fall in love with it!

THINK ABOUT IT!

Are you wearing your Bible out?

DAY 217

I have talked to some big stars about this, some really horrific characters and you'd be surprised. The ones that you would think are the furthest gone are the ones that are more apt to listen.

ALICE COOPER

This is good and pleases God our Savior, who wants everyone to be saved and to understand the truth.

1 TIMOTHY 2:4

Sometimes we get tempted to give up on certain friends. We think, "That person is too far gone." "He never shows any interest in my faith." But when you listen to people tell the stories of their conversion, many of them say they never wanted anything to do with Christianity! They were absolutely positive that they would never convert. You know, God never told us to judge someone's spiritual abilities. That's not our job. What we know is that God wants everybody to repent and come to him. And some of the people who have turned to Christ in the metal scene are honestly some of those you wouldn't have expected!

We need to be sensitive to the Holy Spirit inside of us. He will lead us to the people we are supposed to share our faith with. Other than that, just live your life in front of people: friends, family, people at your job. Let your lifestyle be your testimony. You never know who will be next to ask you about the hope that you have in Christ.

THINK ABOUT IT!

Be open to everyone around you today. Be ready to give an answer to anyone who may ask you about the hope you have in Jesus.

DAY 218

*I did this so you would trust not in human
wisdom but in the power of God.*
1 CORINTHIANS 2:5

When we look at our faith, it's easy to become disappointed. The longer we look, the smaller and weaker it seems. Unfortunately, there are many preachers who teach a "faith-in-your-faith" mentality. "You will be healed if you believe without doubt." "God will make you rich if you truly believe." This isn't the way things work. This isn't the biblical description of faith!

We don't have faith in our faith—we have faith in the object of our faith, Jesus Christ! We are not told to focus on our ability to produce faith. Instead, we need to look at HIM. Jesus was the only one who had a perfect faith. His trust in God never wavered. He held on to God in all areas of his life. Today your faith may seem small and insecure. You may be battling with doubt. Honestly, it ultimately doesn't matter! If you fall over a cliff and grab a branch, you may be in doubt on whether or not the branch will break. But ultimately, it doesn't matter how much faith you have in the branch. What matters is that you grab it. Jesus is the perfect branch that will never break. Don't look at your faith. Look at him!

THINK ABOUT IT!

*Do you spend more energy looking at your
faith than you do looking at Jesus?*

DAY 219

*"For I know the plans I have for you," says the Lord. "They are plans
for good and not for disaster, to give you a future and a hope."*

JEREMIAH 29:11

Every man gotta right to decide his own destiny." That is a quote
from Bob Marley. And, in essence, he is correct. We have a right
to choose our destiny. It's the most important choice you will ever
make. You need to get it right. Your eternity hangs in the balance! "But,"
as Oh, Sleeper says, "What if we're wrong? What if our peace can never
be found on our own?" God doesn't force his way on you. He continues to knock at your heart's door, but he doesn't break the door down.
When we answer and let him into our lives, he comes with a plan! "For
I [already] know the plans I have for you." He doesn't leave you clueless.
He gives you a destiny. And he defines your destiny "They are plans for
good and not for disaster, to give you a future and a hope."

Yes, you have a right to choose your own destiny. Joshua 24:15 says,
"But if you refuse to serve the Lord, then choose today whom you will
serve. Would you prefer the gods your ancestors served beyond the
Euphrates? Or will it be the gods of the Amorites in whose land you
now live? But as for me and my family, we will serve the Lord."

THINK ABOUT IT!

Have you made a decision about your destiny?

DAY 220

In my own weakness, the power of God is my strength.
SIMON "PILGRIM" ROSÉN (CRIMSON MOONLIGHT)

*That's why I take pleasure in my weaknesses, and in the
insults, hardships, persecutions, and troubles that I suffer
for Christ. For when I am weak, then I am strong.*
2 CORINTHIANS 12:10

That guy is a really good Christian!" How many times have you heard someone described like that? Actually, that guy doesn't exist! There is no such thing as a "good Christian." Romans 3:12 says, "No one does good, not a single one." We will always be weak, and in need of God's strength.

When people accuse me of using my relationship with Christ as a crutch, I correct them and explain that he is more like a stretcher! He carries me most of the time. I have come to realize that it's not a sign of weakness. It is the beginning of new strength. But God doesn't stop there. He combines it with wisdom. Not only does God renew my strength day by day, but he gives me his wisdom as a guide to use it.

THINK ABOUT IT!

*Still trying to be a "good Christian?" Give it up.
You can't do it. But then, who would want to? God's
power in your life is a much better option!*

DAY 221

*Bred in gluttony to believe our social standing
is more important than our soul.*
LYRICS FROM "BLOOD HARVEST"
BY BROKEN FLESH [BROKEN FLESH]

*After that the end will come, when he will turn the Kingdom over to
God the Father, having destroyed every ruler and authority and power.*
1 CORINTHIANS 15:24

What does your Christian faith look like to those who are watching you? God calls each of us differently. Some stand behind a pulpit sharing the Gospel. Others perform on a big stage producing epic music. In both cases, there are many who you are not even aware of. What about the guy who get's to the church early every Sunday morning to turn on the lights and make the building ready? What about the guy who sets up the stage and mixes the sound for the concert? And what about the guy who cleans everything up after each event? Do you know who they are? No! They are the ones who go unnoticed.

We face this question: Would you do what God has called you to do us even if no one noticed you doing it? We all need encouragement from the people around us, but do we care more about getting credit from humans than we do following God's purpose for our lives? When we're being honest with ourselves, the answer may not be as simple as we would hope.

Right now there are older retired people praying for us. They are true prayer-warriors. As a result of walking with Jesus through a life-time, they've developed this character and relationship with God, even though we may not even notice it.

THINK ABOUT IT!

*Does your lifestyle reflect that you care more about
your soul and others than social standing?*

DAY 222

*Christians, instead of arming themselves with
swords, extend their hands in prayer.*

ATHANASIUS

*Be strong in the Lord and in his mighty power. Put on all of God's
armor so that you will be able to stand firm against all strategies
of the devil. For we are not fighting against flesh-and-blood
enemies, but against evil rulers and authorities of the unseen
world, against mighty powers in this dark world, and against evil
spirits in the heavenly places. Therefore, put on every piece of
God's armor so you will be able to resist the enemy in the time
of evil. Then after the battle you will still be standing firm.*

GALATIANS 6:10-13

L ife is a gift, I accept it. Life is an adventure, I dare it. Life is a mystery,
I'm unfolding it. Life is a puzzle, I'm solving it. Life is a game, I play
it. Life can be a struggle, I'm Facing it. Life is an opportunity, I
took it. Life is my mission, I'm fulfilling it!" (unknown author). Life can
be difficult at best. It seems that every day is filled with its own challenges,
some more difficult than others. When Athanasius tells us to "extend our
hands in prayer," he isn't telling us that we are not in battle. He is instead
explaining to us the best way to arm ourselves.

It's not with "physical" swords, but with "spiritual" ones. Galatians
6 goes on to say, "and take the sword of the Spirit, which is the word of
God" (verse 17). We need to remember that our battles are fought spiritually more than physically. Peace of mind doesn't come from punching
someone out and taking revenge. It only comes when you have learned
to love your enemies—a product of the Word in prayer.

THINK ABOUT IT!

Have you learned to fight your battles in prayer?

DAY 223

Even Gentiles, who do not have God's written law, show
that they know his law when they instinctively obey it, even
without having heard it. They demonstrate that God's law is
written in their hearts, for their own conscience and thoughts
either accuse them or tell them they are doing right.
ROMANS 2:14-15

Can we know with certainty if something is right or wrong? Is it an individual decision, or is there an impartial standard? Everyone has an opinion. Some would argue that each of us have our own truth that changes from individual to individual. We would all agree that there are no situations where rape or ethnic cleansing is okay. And yet, thousands followed Hitler. Why?

Philosophy attempted to explain this, but falls short. Only Christianity holds an honest answer. Morality must reflect God's nature. He has written his law on our hearts. Of course, that doesn't mean we have a perfect understanding of it. But it does mean that we can know right from wrong. Morality isn't simply left to the individual. That's how Hitlers are made!

It's a breath of fresh air to know there are moral absolutes. We all need a pattern to live by. It is one of the main reasons people consider the Christian faith. As we personally live by his standards, we demonstrate that we live by an ethical code that reflects the heart of our Creator.

THINK ABOUT IT!

Have you considered the moral absolutes of Christianity?

DAY 224

*I was in my room, preparing a drug dose, when I just stopped,
looked straight up and said, "Jesus, if you are real, set me free
from my drug addiction" What happened was something that no
therapy, and not even love for my daughter, could accomplish. Within
a week's time, I was completely free from my drug addiction.*
BRIAN "HEAD" WELCH (KORN)

*Keep on asking, and you will receive what you ask for. Keep on
seeking, and you will find. Keep on knocking, and the door will be
opened to you. For everyone who asks, receives. Everyone who
seeks, finds. And to everyone who knocks, the door will be opened.*
MATTHEW 7:7-8

God is faithful. I can't count how many times I have called out to him in my time of need and he has rescued me! You and I may not have had a critical drug addiction like Brian "Head" Welch, but we have all had those things in our lives that are larger than we are! We feel powerless. We feel defeated. But God knows all of that.

This is the amazing part of his love. He is faithful to deliver us from our struggles. There have been times in my life when I asked for his help, and the answer came instantaneously. But there have been other times when I had things to learn about the situation I found myself in, and his greatest concern was teaching me the lessons within the crisis. Those lessons have, for the most part, kept me from returning to my sin. Ask. Seek. Knock. He is still answering the door!

THINK ABOUT IT!

*Don't be afraid to call out to the Lord at
any time. He is ready to respond!*

DAY 225

Spoke matter into substance, outside of time and space
LYRICS FROM "IN THE TAKING OF FLESH: THEANTHROPOS"
BY THE BURIAL [IN THE TAKING OF FLESH]

In the beginning God created the heavens and the earth.
GENESIS 1:1

Bang!? From philosophy and modern physics, we learn that the universe came in to existence. This sounds obvious to us, but until 1965 physicists actually didn't believe this. Have you ever thought about how this happened? There must be some sort of cause. Atheists don't have a cause for this. For them, it simply "just happened." But that doesn't make much sense. Something just doesn't pop into existence out of nothing.

Sometimes people ask "Who created God?" Only created things need a cause. God is eternal, and not created. We need an explanation for the beginning of the universe. Whatever or "whoever" created the universe would need to be immaterial and outside of space and time. You can't help thinking about the God of the Bible. This is exactly how he is described.

The Almighty God, who made the universe and everything in it, made you as well. You are the main focus of his attention. This is really humbling when you put it all in perspective. Looking up at the stars so far away, we realize we're just a small speck in the whole universe. Christians have always said what physicists discovered not long ago. The Bible was right! God, the mighty power who created a vastly complex universe, made you, too! He didn't make a mistake. He had *you* in mind!

THINK ABOUT IT!

Are you aware of Gods awesome power?

DAY 226

For in him we live and move and exist. As some of your own poets have said, 'We are his offspring'" (Acts 17:28).

Some Christians get stuck at the foot of the cross. They simply see themselves sitting there day by day, reflecting on what Christ did there, and on his wonderful gift of eternal life. Although that is a wonderful perspective, it isn't the end of our experience. Rather, it is the beginning; the foundation for our very existence and daily life. It dictates how we love others, how we work our jobs, and how we live above the circumstances each day brings to us. "In him we live and move and exist."

In fact, we're told to observe communion as a memorial service. Why? We can be so busy living our Christian lives that we need to be reminded of how we obtained that foundation in the first place. There are two ways your love for God will continue to grow. First, by allowing the Holy Spirit to continue to give you his unconditional "agapé" love. And second, to get moving. Live your life on the solid foundation that God has given you, and stand firm on his promises to you. It's the greatest thing after many years to look back and say: "I know and love God better than I ever have!"

THINK ABOUT IT!

Are you stuck, or are you moving forward?

DAY 227

My comfort is my vice, and greed I have misplaced as virtue.
Wisdom is of no worth if it has only my own interest in mind.
LYRICS FROM "APATHY AND PETITION"
BY THE BURIAL [LIGHTS AND PERFECTIONS]

For wherever there is jealousy and selfish ambition, there you will find
disorder and evil of every kind. But the wisdom from above is first of
all pure. It is also peace loving, gentle at all times, and willing to yield
to others. It is full of mercy and the fruit of good deeds. It shows no
favoritism and is always sincere. And those who are peacemakers
will plant seeds of peace and reap a harvest of righteousness.

JAMES 3:16-18

We're a society of self-seekers. "I just need to spend some 'me' time." "I need to take care of myself before I can take care of someone else." "I need to go away and 'find' myself." Really? Wherever you go, there you are! We're so preoccupied with ourselves, we fail to see the needs in others. While it is true that introverts need alone time, the mentality that says we have to "take care of ourselves first" before we can help someone else is ludicrous.

Nothing will help your own stability and give you insight into your own situation more than serving other people. It has been said, "Go and live among the poor, and they will heal you." I have experienced this in my own life after working with the homeless for many years. I began to serve them thinking I would change them. I was confident in my ability to motivate and to encourage. And even though I have used those gifts, it hasn't been the core of the ministry. They've changed me. I believe God has this in mind when he asks us to get involved with people in need. It isn't just for their benefit; it is also for yours!

THINK ABOUT IT!

Have you made the transition from being self-centered to being motivated to serve others?

DAY 228

*"Nobody ever outgrows scripture; the book
widens and deepens with our years."*
CHARLES H. SPURGEON

*And may you have the power to understand, as all God's people should,
how wide, how long, how high, and how deep his love is. May you
experience the love of Christ, though it is too great to understand fully.*
GALATIANS 3:18-19

he Bible is just too difficult to understand. I will let the profession-
als handle it!" The Bible may seem difficult. It takes a little time to
understand its principles and purpose. And it seems overwhelming
at first! The pages are many and the letters are small. But once you get
started, it isn't as difficult as you think! That's the amazing thing about
the Bible: the Gospels are simple enough for a child to understand them,
but so deep that even the wisest scholars are never really finished studying them.

Everyone is different. Some like to reading a few chapters every third
day. Others enjoy reading just one verse a day, but then really think about
it. Whatever you enjoy—go for it! But don't be discouraged by not being
able to understand how it all ties together. Just take one step at a time.
The overview will come at some point. The more you read and get to
know the Bible, the better it gets! No other book has such an amazing
depth that you can spend a lifetime on it.

THINK ABOUT IT!

*Have you found an enjoyable reading method that
helps you dig into the deep layers of the Word?*

DAY 229

Jesus became what we are that he might make us what he is.
ATHANASIUS

*This High Priest of ours [Jesus] understands our weaknesses, for
he faced all of the same testings we do, yet he did not sin. So let us
come boldly to the throne of our gracious God. There we will receive
his mercy, and we will find grace to help us when we need it most.*
HEBREWS 4:15-16

I have never tried drugs before. Nor do I drink alcohol. And, I am still
a virgin. I am excited that God has given me his grace to live above
those things. But that doesn't mean that I am not tempted just like
everyone else. Many people tell me that I can't be a very good counselor
since I have never actually been addicted to those things. But I do understand the temptation. I have the same pop-up ads on my computer with
barely dressed or even naked women. It is a temptation every time to
look at them, and to follow the links!

Does even Jesus understand that temptation? Sure he does "…for
he faced all the same testings we do." He truly understands our weaknesses. That is why this scripture in Hebrews is so powerful. "So let us
come boldly to the throne of our gracious God." Boldly because he has
the answers. Boldly because he has gone through exactly the same temptations and understands. Boldly because he promised to deliver you!

THINK ABOUT IT!

Have you learned to come to God with your temptations?

DAY 230

*Being a Christian is something you just progress in. You
learn. You go to your Bible studies. You pray.*
ALICE COOPER

*Like newborn babies, you must crave pure spiritual milk so that
you will grow into a full experience of salvation. Cry out for this
nourishment, now that you have had a taste of the Lord's kindness.*
1 PETER 2:2-3

Picture this: You bring a newborn baby home from the hospital. You want to make him feel welcome so you say, "Please make yourself at home. The bathroom is down the hall to the left, and the refrigerator is well stocked with all your favorite foods." Silly, isn't it? Of course that baby is going to need a lot more personal care than that. You will need to feed the baby, and change his diapers. But what if, when he turns 20 years old, he's still counting on you to feed him and change his diapers?

I wonder if God feels that way about us sometimes. How many times are we still acting like babies in the faith, instead of growing into maturity? Like Alice Cooper says, faith is something you need to progress in. Learn. Study. Pray. Good advice!

THINK ABOUT IT!

Are you growing in your spiritual walk with the Lord?

DAY 231

*Patience is necessary, and one cannot reap
immediately where one has sown.*
SØREN KIERKEGAARD

*We can rejoice, too, when we run into problems and trials, for we know
that they help us develop endurance. And endurance develops strength
of character, and character strengthens our confident hope of salvation.*
ROMANS 5:3-4

*You, too, must be patient. Take courage,
for the coming of the Lord is near.*
JAMES 5:8

Learning how to type came easy to me. I am a piano player so I aced the class. We had manual typewriters with blank keys so you were forced not to look at your hands when you type. I remember when in my senior year in high school the typing class got an electric typewriter. We thought it was amazing! In 1982 I purchased my first Apple computer. Again, it was a game changer. And then, in the mid 90's, the internet was made available. We started with dial-up. It took a few minutes to download a page, but it was still fantastic! We didn't know any better. Then when higher speed internet was born, I no longer had the patience for dial-up. Now my download speed is 300 Mbps, and my upload speed is 150 Mbps. That's lightning fast compared to dial-up. And the whole system is amazing compared to the original manual typewriter that I used at the beginning.

But my patience has changed, too. I used to have patience for the typewriter and even for dial-up. Today, as I travel, I usually check the hotel's internet speed before booking a room! We live fast and furious. And I know that it carries over into our spiritual lives as well. Rest in the Lord. Be patient in listening to his voice and to living your life in his divine plan. There are times when God feels like "high speed internet fast," and other times when he feels like "dial-up slow and sure." Be ready for either!

THINK ABOUT IT!
How would you rate your patience in following God?

DAY 232

Jesus is the reason I still breathe.
DAN SPITZ (ANTHRAX)

*For in him we live and move and exist. As some of your
own poets have said, "We are his offspring."*
ACTS 17:28

I love how the Bible reflects the arts and culture of the time. The Apostle Paul was probably exposed to Greek literature when he studied with Gamaliel. Here he is quoting a line from one of their poets, showing that he also had an interest in poetry. I am sure this surprised and kept the attention of the audience. Much the same as poetry and music do today!

When an artist stands on stage and sings (or growls) his lyrics, he communicates in a very special way. I really love this quote by Dan Spitz. He understands his shortcomings. Even though he is able to stand on stage and perform to thousands of people, he realizes his very breath is grounded in the Lord. How exciting to communicate to people through the arts. We just have to remember where our talent comes from in the first place!

THINK ABOUT IT!

How often do you realize your complete dependence on God?

DAY 233

I was supposed to die overnight. So, I've come very close to death....I just think that God hasn't finished with me yet...The doctors say it's a miracle and they're not Christians.

STEVE ROWE (MORTIFICATION)

The Lord is my shepherd; I have all that I need. He lets me rest in green meadows; he leads me beside peaceful streams. He renews my strength. He guides me along right paths, bringing honor to his name. Even when I walk through the darkest valley, I will not be afraid, for you are close beside me. Your rod and your staff protect and comfort me. You prepare a feast for me in the presence of my enemies. You honor me by anointing my head with oil. My cup overflows with blessings. Surely your goodness and unfailing love will pursue me all the days of my life, and I will live in the house of the Lord forever.

PSALM 23

Life is short, especially when you compare it to eternity to come. We always view our life on earth as the center of our existence, but it is anything but that! It is brief, fragile, and temporary. And in the course of this momentary existence, God has a definite plan for us. Not even a life-threatening illness can interfere with his plan.

Steve Rowe came to visit me 15 years ago in the USA. At that time he was very ill. The Doctors had advised him not to travel, as they were still a bit perplexed as to why he was still alive! But here he was—not only traveling, but doing shows! I remember his band-mates helping him to climb the steps, as his brain was not able to connect with his feet at the time. But he continued. Why? He didn't believe God was finished with him yet, no matter what everyone else advised. And now as I write this 15 years later, he is still alive and involved in ministry. No matter what life may throw at you, God is still large and in charge!

THINK ABOUT IT!

Have you learned to trust God for your existence here on earth?

DAY 234

*When you read God's Word, you must constantly be
saying to yourself, "It is talking to me, and about me."*
SØREN KIERKEGAARD

*And I am certain that God, who began the good
work within you, will continue his work until it is finally
finished on the day when Christ Jesus returns.*
PHILIPPIANS 1:6

Have you ever had a friend correct your behavior, and then tell you, "Please don't take it personally." Really? It's difficult not to take correction personally. That's the point that our Danish friend Kierkegaard is making. Reading the Bible isn't simply about collecting thoughts and principles. It's about being transformed by those thoughts and principles.

Very many times while reading the Bible I run across a scripture that I think would be good for a friend who might benefit from its principles. Less often, I find those that are correcting me! Keeping in mind that the Bible is God's personal love letter to you will transform your life. It will give you clarity on your path and focus on your destination. So please, take it personally!

THINK ABOUT IT!

Are you taking the Bible personally?

DAY 235

*There's just so much power of being used in Korn. I can
reach so many people and know what I'm about, not what
Korn's about. I want to try to follow the Bible the best I
can, because I know it's going to give me the best life.*

REGINALD QUINCY "FIELDY" ARVIZU" (KORN)

*And you yourself must be an example to them by doing
good works of every kind. Let everything you do reflect
the integrity and seriousness of your teaching.*

TITUS 2:7

If you are reading this, you probably play music. Maybe you are in
a band. Your dream for the band is to be popular and sell a lot of
albums. To have a song hit number one on the music charts. You
envision standing in front of thousands of screaming fans that chant
your name, and ask for your autograph after the concert. Just imagine!
Okay back to reality.

All of us have been given some kind of responsibility for our walk
with the Lord. It isn't just a personal thing. Nothing really is. Every minute you are around people you are living your life in front of them. What
they see and hear from you will not only shape their opinion of you, but
also of the God you follow! Following the Bible will not only give you
the best life possible, as Reginald Quincy "Fieldy" Arvizu says, but it will
also be a witness to those around you!

THINK ABOUT IT!

*Would your spiritual life change if you became a rock star?
What would people see if they were following you?*

DAY 236

Work willingly at whatever you do, as though you were working for the Lord rather than for people. Remember that the Lord will give you an inheritance as your reward, and that the Master you are serving is Christ.
COLOSSIANS 3:23-24

Metalhead. Goth. Punk. Hipster. We use a lot of labels these days. And for most of us, when we fit into a label, most of our lives revolve around it. I fall in the "metalhead" category mostly. You know black clothes, long hair, tattoos, piercings, etc. When people ask me what kind of music I like, they are usually surprised by my answers. I grew up in the 1950's, so Elvis was the most extreme then. And I loved Elvis. I still do! I was a Sam and Dave fan. A Beatles Fan. A Rolling Stones fan. A Queen fan. You get the idea. And today, I listen to a lot of Metal. So when someone asks me about my musical tastes, I usually tell them that I like "good" music. Music done well. Music that speaks to me. And especially music that reflects my lifestyle. That is why 80% of the music I listen to is Christian based. It is what I believe in, and what my heart naturally desires to sing (growl) along with!

THINK ABOUT IT!

Does your music match your lifestyle?

DAY 237

*Unwanted by man, this world hates me now, I
no longer choose to run from my fate*
LYRICS FROM "UNWORTHY" BY BROKEN FLESH

And all nations will hate you because you are my followers.
MATTHEW 10:22

We sometimes use this verse as an excuse for the reason people don't like us. In my experience, the majority of the time people haven't liked me is because I was being stupid! When Christians continue to hate certain groups of people, and pass judgment on everyone they meet, they give the world a good reason not to like them.

But, this is not what this verse is talking about. When someone feels conflict between their lifestyle and yours, the conflict is really about who they will decide to serve. The Bible says you can't serve two masters. You will hate one and love the other, or love one and hate the other. It is this conflict that sometimes separates Christians from the rest of the world, but it is also this conflict that brings people to Jesus Christ! Make him your master above everything else. Even your belief-system. Focus on loving your brothers and sisters in Christ, instead of the things you disagree upon.

THINK ABOUT IT!

Do the people around you describe you by your love?

DAY 238

The Bible is alive, it speaks to me; it has feet, it runs after me; it has hands, it lays hold of me.

MARTIN LUTHER

For the word of God is alive and powerful. It is sharper than the sharpest two-edged sword, cutting between soul and spirit, between joint and marrow. It exposes our innermost thoughts and desires. Nothing in all creation is hidden from God. Everything is naked and exposed before his eyes, and he is the one to whom we are accountable.

HEBREWS 4:12-13

An amazing, supernatural thing happens when you begin reading the Bible. With the Holy Spirit as your guide, you actually begin to understand the deeper things of God. Not only that, but you begin to adopt them. Its principles and life-giving guidelines become part of your very being. It comes alive. That is what Luther is talking about here. He has developed a relationship with God through his Word. The Bible has come alive, with a voice, feet, legs and hands. It wraps its arms around us, and ushers in new life and breath.

THINK ABOUT IT!

Has the Bible truly "come alive" to you?

DAY 239

*And I believe that while I was trying to understand some
of the scriptures, the Word of God, I believe that God
came into my heart and he opened my eyes.*
PETE SANDOVAL (MORBID ANGEL)

*But you have received the Holy Spirit, and he lives within you, so you
don't need anyone to teach you what is true. For the Spirit teaches
you everything you need to know, and what he teaches is true—it is
not a lie. So just as he has taught you, remain in fellowship with Christ.*
1 JOHN 2:27

I have read the Bible many times. I've used it for enjoyment, for study, for teaching, and for advice. There have been so many times when the words seem to jump off the page and into my heart. It feels supernatural because it is! There is a deeper connection for me than simply reading words on a page. It is life-transforming.

My love affair with the Bible didn't kick into gear until a few years after I had become a Christian. I had never really thought about allowing the Holy Spirit to teach me. Like Pete Sandoval says, it happens when you open up to the Holy Spirit. When you open your heart, he opens your eyes!

THINK ABOUT IT!

*Have you allowed the Holy Spirit to open
up the Word of God to you?*

DAY 240

Christ was the impetus and driving force for us to do this from the beginning. We still feel that way today and hope that what we do is inspiring spiritually.
BRUCE FITZHUGH (LIVING SACRIFICE)

Then I observed that the basic motive for success is the driving force of envy and jealousy! But this, too, is foolishness, chasing the wind.
ECCLESIASTES 4:4

What is your driving force? Money? Success? Job? Fame? Family? Ministry? What consumes you and drives you? This is an important question to answer from time to time. It is so easy to get caught up in the cares of this world that we lose track of the things that are important! Many people around us are driven by "envy and jealousy" which this verse in Ecclesiastes calls "foolishness, chasing the wind."

Bruce Fitzhugh tells us that Christ was the "impetus" for the ministry of the band. He is the force that sets the band's ministry in motion. That's a great reminder for us every day of our lives. Beginning each day saying, "What is my impetus? How can I best let Christ be my driving force today?" So many of life's little detours can be avoided when we simply have perspective. Know where you are going, and who is getting you there! Bruce goes on to say that he wants to "inspire spiritually." Not simply inspire. It isn't about the band or the music. It is about the message. That is a great life lesson!

THINK ABOUT IT!

What is your driving force today?

DAY 241

Only truth will satisfy, and only You are true. Grant me strength to live
in You, in spirit and in the truth. The Father hears a heart uninterrupted.
LYRICS FROM "PEARLS, THE FRAILTY OF MATTER"
BY THE BURIAL [LIGHTS AND PERFECTIONS]

For God is Spirit, so those who worship him
must worship in spirit and in truth.
JOHN 4:24

As I write this, I am sitting at a table with a guy from Denmark, and a guy from Portugal. They are both speaking English with me. If each of them were to speak in their native languages, we wouldn't understand each other. English is the common language that we share. Communication with God is a little different. He understands everything you say, no matter what or how you communicate. But when he communicates back with you, his language is always the same: "Truth." That's why we miss what he is saying so many times. We are waiting for him to tell us what we want to hear. But for him to do that, he would have to violate his own nature!

Successful communication involves giving and receiving. When you speak to God, he speaks back. Your prayers are not falling on deaf ears. And when you are communicating in his language of spirit and truth, you will hear his reply. So many view their Christian life as simply talking to God, but never expecting him to talk back. We recite prayers. We sing songs. We preach and talk about him. But to actually communicate with him, you need to remember that "truth" will always be your common language!

THINK ABOUT IT!

Are you communicating with God in Spirit and in Truth?

DAY 242

Everyone wants to be a rock star now. Everybody wants the million-dollar check. They want to do whatever they can to make it to that point when they make money, they become completely different people, even with Christians greed is such a powerful thing.
BROOK REEVES (IMPENDING DOOM)

Then he said, "Beware! Guard against every kind of greed. Life is not measured by how much you own."
LUKE 12:15

I have a confession to make. I am an addict. No, it's not about sex, alcohol, or drugs. It's about sports cars. Seriously. In my lifetime, I have been very frugal in almost every area of my life except for this one! I'm ashamed to say that I have spent tens of thousands of dollars during my lifetime on expensive sports cars.

I can imagine myself standing up at a local AA meeting (AUTOholics Anonymous) and saying, "Hello. I'm Pastor Bob. And I am a Autoholic!" I am better now. I haven't owned a sports car for 20 years. But the desire is still there—especially when I see something I like on the streets. Greed is like that. It never goes away. We all have those areas in our lives. What we do with these desires determines who and what we will serve. Remember, life is about what is on the inside, not about the "stuff" you own!

THINK ABOUT IT!

In what areas of your life are you tempted by greed?

DAY 243

It makes me sick that it's hard to distinguish an honest leader who preaches a cause that's not made and not based on the profit they'll receive from telling the world

LYRICS FROM "IN THE WAKE OF PIGS"
BY OH, SLEEPER [CHILDREN OF FIRE]

Those false teachers are so eager to win your favor, but their intentions are not good. They are trying to shut you off from me so that you will pay attention only to them.

GALATIANS 4:17

You've seen them on TV. You hear them on the radio. Their books overpower the "religious" section of the bookstore. These "Super-Pastors" have become quite wealthy sharing their brand of Christianity to the masses. Some honestly have a real heart for God—while others enjoy being famous and getting the attention. In a time when we almost don't know who to trust, how do we find honest teachers? John 16:13 says, "When the Spirit of truth comes, he will guide you into all truth." You don't necessarily have to be a scholar of theology to have a heart for sharing God's truth. When we find those who display their deep love for God, we can better trust their teaching. That doesn't mean they're right about everything, but when they're wrong they're willing to be corrected.

We all need teachers who can answer our questions. Look for people who have had an intimate relationship with the Lord through many years. And if you're a teacher yourself, test yourself on the things you're teaching. Every time you speak take a good look inside yourself to see if your own life reflects what you're saying. Be honest about the difficulties of life instead of sugarcoating them. People look for something real. Be real!

THINK ABOUT IT!

Do you have the courage to both practice what you preach and preach what you practice?

DAY 244

In other words, people know what the truth is. What I see is
people in the search of the truth. They're all on a journey, the
people that are attracted to this genre are people who are
really a lot more in tune with it than they think they are.
BLACKIE LAWLESS (W.A.S.P.)

They demonstrate that God's law is written in their
hearts, for their own conscience and thoughts either
accuse them or tell them they are doing right.
ROMANS 2:15

There are many people in the metal-crowd who are searching for something real. Metal tends to be one of the most honest genres in music since it reflects every aspect of life; the good, the bad, and the ugly. This is one of the things that draws people to Heavy Metal. How many other styles of music have lyrics that reflect both pain and joy, suffering and happiness? We need to keep this in mind when we meet people at the shows. They don't, and shouldn't, want a simple answer to life's complex questions. They want to see a real person living a real life with struggles and difficulties.

Remember that we are all on a journey through life! We all search for truth and happiness. This applies to Christians, the religious, and to atheists. It isn't a matter of us vs. them. It is a matter of taking someone along with you on your journey and finding answers together. And even though we know that Jesus answers us at the foot of the cross, we need to be vulnerable enough to people of different world views to let them see our whole life and not just the pretty parts. The metal crowd is a great place for such a journey!

THINK ABOUT IT!

When asked about your faith are you answering
honestly, or as you'd like things to be?

DAY 245

*The more completely we focus our attention on our Creator and
Lord, the less chance there is of our being distracted by creatures.*
SAINT IGNATIUS

*They traded the truth about God for a lie. So they worshiped
and served the things God created instead of the Creator
himself, who is worthy of eternal praise! Amen.*
ROMANS 1:25

*We do this by keeping our eyes on Jesus, the champion who
initiates and perfects our faith. Because of the joy awaiting
him, he endured the cross, disregarding its shame. Now he
is seated in the place of honor beside God's throne.*
HEBREWS 12:2

As I write this, the ducks and geese in my yard are walking down my driveway. It is a most endearing sight to see. Although I have lived here for a number of years, it never gets old. But it does distract me from whatever I am doing every time! If you're like me, you get distracted easily, too. Most people do. And yet, the world offers us so many distractions.

Many of these distractions lead us away from God's plan for our lives. 1 Corinthians 7:35 says, "I am saying this for your benefit, not to place restrictions on you. I want you to do whatever will help you serve the Lord best, with as few distractions as possible." After all these decades following Jesus, I have learned the benefit of keeping my eyes on Jesus. My distractions only put me at a disadvantage. The more I trust him and keep him in focus, the more clearly I can see his path in front of me!

THINK ABOUT IT!

Are you learning to keep your focus on Jesus throughout the day?

DAY 246

*Success puts you in a different point in life and
there's new things that you have to deal with.*
ROBERT SWEET (STRYPER)

*Don't be afraid, for I am with you. Don't be discouraged,
for I am your God. I will strengthen you and help you. I
will hold you up with my victorious right hand.*
ISAIAH 41:10

Where God guides, he provides." I heard that reminder from my parents many times while growing up. It is one of those little slogans that has meant a lot to me. There have been many times when I've stepped out in faith, not knowing how to accomplish what God was asking me to do. It is easier not to go down that path. I suppose being a couch potato has its attractions at times. But the adventure of following the Lord and accomplishing the impossible has always been a "drug of choice" for me.

After these 50 years in ministry, I have watched God open impossible doors and break through impossible situations. The most difficult one? ME! I have watched him change me from the inside out. Oh, I am not finished yet. I still have a long way to go. But I am not what I used to be, and I am not what I am going to be, either. Why? Because he is beside me, walking with me every step of the way. I have learned to recognize his partnership, and count on his wisdom and guidance. And after all these years, I wouldn't change a thing!

THINK ABOUT IT!
How is God guiding you?

DAY 247

Therefore, we never stop thanking God that when you received his message from us, you didn't think of our words as mere human ideas. You accepted what we said as the very word of God—which, of course, it is. And this word continues to work in you who believe.

1 THESSALONIANS 2:13

Social media is full of Bible-thumpers. You know the ones. They seem to find something wrong with everything you post, and then use scripture (usually out of context) to back it up. They spew hatred for certain groups of people who simply sin differently then they do. And, in essence, they have missed the whole point of Jesus' death on the cross—God's unconditional love toward us!

There's a difference between a belief system and a relationship. I believe that my car will take me to the grocery store. But unless I get into the car and begin to drive, it is only a belief. The same is really true when it comes to the Bible. I can read it to increase my knowledge, which isn't a bad thing. But it won't take you anywhere until you actually develop a relationship with Jesus. THEN your life is changed by it. You not only have an owners manual that instructs you how to live, but you have an in-depth guide telling you why you live! God's desire isn't that you simply increase your knowledge, but that you are also transformed!

THINK ABOUT IT!

Have you allowed the power of the Word of God
through his Holy Spirit to transform you?

DAY 248

Commit everything you do to the Lord.
Trust him, and he will help you.
PSALM 37:5

For I can do everything through Christ,
who gives me strength.
PHILIPPIANS 4:13

My father always told me not to be afraid to dream big. He reminded me often, "God is always dreaming bigger than you are!" Good advice from one of the wisest men I have ever met. When I look at any success that I have had in my life, there are two factors that stand out. First, I have always had this feeling of divine intervention and wisdom. And second, I have never surrounded myself with people who tell me I can't do it!

Many times I attribute my personal success to simply not knowing any better! God said it. I believe it. Let's do it! The above verse gives us the key to success: "I can do everything through Christ who gives me strength." Did you catch that? "Through Christ!" Where God guides, he provides. I realize after all these years that the most difficult part isn't the journey, but rather, it is deciding which road to take. Once you are on the path that God has laid in front of you, he will complete it!

THINK ABOUT IT!

Have you allowed yourself to dream big?

DAY 249

The Lord is close to the brokenhearted; he rescues those whose spirits are crushed. The righteous person faces many troubles, but the Lord comes to the rescue each time.
PSALM 34:18-19

Sometimes life sucks. It just does. There is nothing you can do about that. How you handle things when life throws you a curve will determine how you navigate through the difficult times. Many people feel suicidal during these times. They want an escape. They feel dead. That feeling is to be expected, actually. When life sucks, something does need to die. Just not you!

The biggest challenge you will have when you go through these dark times is identifying what needs to die. It may be a relationship that needs to come to an end. It may be letting go of the past. It may even be a job or vocation that is no longer tolerable. LET IT DIE. But don't kill yourself. That feeling of "death" that you have is for a reason. It will help you to identify and feel the problem. And then you will be able to begin the process of change—allowing the difficulty to die, and going another direction with your life. Psalm 30:5 says, "…but joy comes with the morning." The sun will come up tomorrow—each day things will get a little easier, and you will get through the rough patch.

THINK ABOUT IT!

Have you considered taking your own life in the past?

DAY 250

Smack your own pride. Treat it with disgust when looking in the eyes of our borrowed time. Strip down to the basics of your own soul and think.

LYRICS FROM "THE KAKISTOCRACY CATACOMBS"
BY DROTTNAR [WELTERWERK]

Yet you do not know what your life will be like tomorrow. You are just a vapor that appears for a little while and then vanishes away.

JAMES 4:14

We struggle with temporary thinking. When we are having a good day, we feel like every day from now on will be great! And when we have a bad day, we imagine that our life is simply full of bad days and it isn't going to get any better. We are truly short-sighted. It's hard to imagine what the future might hold. Now put that in terms of eternity, and we get totally freaked out! When you consider eternity, our lives are "just a vapor." Very small and insignificant.

Isn't it strange that we put all of our effort into this split second of eternity, instead of looking at what's ahead? This great song by Drottnar tells us to "strip down to the basics of your own soul and think." Get honest with yourself. Make sure the things that occupy your mind are eternal in nature. If you are living your whole life for the temporary things of this life, then you have missed the whole point!

THINK ABOUT IT!

Are you eternally minded?

DAY 251

The veil was torn, the temple destroyed
LYRICS FROM "IN THE TAKING OF FLESH: DIAKONOS"
BY THE BURIAL [IN THE TAKING OF FLESH]

*By his death, Jesus opened a new and life-giving way
through the curtain into the Most Holy Place.*
HEBREWS 10:20

A quick study in Old Testament 101: The Tabernacle was a transportable temple from the time of Moses. Inside of it was the Ark of the Covenant. It was a way for the Holy God to be near his sinful people. In 2 Samuel 6 the Ark of the Covenant is taken to Jerusalem. In 1 Kings 5-8 we read about the Temple of Solomon. This is the most important event since Exodus. The temple had two important parts: The holy place and the holy of holies. The temple was destroyed and rebuilt before Jesus time.

When Jesus died, the curtain into the holy of holies was ripped apart from top to bottom. The "closeness" of God is now no longer in a temple built of stone and gold. In the New Testament the people are called the Temple of God. He now lives in us. Jesus says: "Rivers of living water will flow from his heart" (John 7:38), and this he said about the Spirit (John 7:39). We are the temple from the Holy Spirit! This is a major game changer!

He lives deep inside of us and works from the inside out. His purpose is to guide us into all truth and wisdom. His personality can help us with ours. His fruit is love, joy, peace, patience, kindness, goodness, faithfulness, gentleness, and self-control (Gal 5:22-23). He will do all the work; we just need to surrender! His power and unconditional love flow through us. We're the temple, and he'll never leave us for a second.

THINK ABOUT IT!

Are you letting him fix the difficult inner parts of your life?

DAY 252

He is the same though another to me
LYRICS FROM "THE ALTERATION"
BY ASCENDANT [THE ALTERATION]

I am the Lord, and I do not change.
MALACHI 3:6

S ince Adam sinned in the Garden of Eden, we've been affected by this fall physically, emotionally, mentally, and spiritually. Our theology will always be affected by our thoughts and emotions. It's difficult for us to separate God's truths from our emotional state. In periods like this, we need to hold on to the things that are true: God's goodness. God's love. Jesus death for our sins. The Holy Spirit's presence in our lives. We may not be stable enough to feel them, but we need to hold on to them, and these foundations of our faith will help us.

We will also have a different view of the Lord. We may complain to him, and give him a list of everything we feel he is doing wrong. But in reality, he hasn't changed. He is still perfect. He still has a plan for us, though through the eyes of our emotions, it is difficult to understand this at the time.

When we come through our difficulties (and we always do!), we'll realize that we were wrong. What we accused God of in a time of anger and frustration wasn't fair, nor was it correct. We move to a clearer picture of him once again. Are you angry at God today? Go ahead and tell him! Are you getting past a period of confusion? Thank him that he stuck by you.

THINK ABOUT IT!

Are you moving towards a healthier understanding of God as you go through different periods of emotions?

DAY 253

*The hairsplitting difference between formed and unformed
makes no difference to us. Whoever deliberately commits
abortion is subject to the penalty for homicide.*

SAINT BASIL

*You made all the delicate, inner parts of my body and knit me
together in my mother's womb. Thank you for making me so
wonderfully complex! Your workmanship is marvelous—how well I
know it. You watched me as I was being formed in utter seclusion,
as I was woven together in the dark of the womb. You saw me
before I was born. Every day of my life was recorded in your book.
Every moment was laid out before a single day had passed.*

PSALM 139:13-16

Saint Basil called abortion "homicide." You might think this is a recent quote since abortion wasn't legalized until 1973. But actually, this quote is over 1,600 years old! And abortioon was practiced a long time before then. Man has always had a desire to hide and dispose of what he considers "his mistakes." Although sex is a gift from God for a married couple, it does come with consequences. They are happy consequences if you are married, but those consequences may be unwelcome if you are not.

Jesus made it very clear what our attitude should be about children. "Anyone who welcomes a little child like this on my behalf welcomes me, and anyone who welcomes me welcomes not only me but also my Father who sent me" (Mark 9:37). A child is always a blessing. Even though the situation may be difficult for the parents, the miracle of birth is always a cause for celebration. To eliminate a life because it makes life more "difficult" for a parent, is the highest form of selfishness and pride. And, in the end it robs you of the blessing that children always bring!

THINK ABOUT IT!

Have you considered how sacred life really is?

DAY 254

*The void in my heart and the emptiness has been filled—filled
with the most amazing feeling one can ever experience!*
PETER BALTES (ACCEPT)

*Jesus replied, "I am the bread of life. Whoever comes to me will never
be hungry again. Whoever believes in me will never be thirsty."*
JOHN 6:35

Human beings need to connect. Mothers and Fathers connect with their children. Men and women can feel lonely until they find their "soulmate" and marry. Many of us have friendships that we have nurtured for many years that have also become very important to us. But there is another void that is even stronger. It has been said that all of us walk around with a God-shaped void in our hearts. Until we connect with our Creator, we feel the emptiness of that void.

My sister was adopted when she was just 9 months old. What a joy it was to welcome her into our family! That was 50 years ago. I always forget that she was actually adopted since she is a wonderful part of the family. Even though I have always loved her as my sister, she had always felt like something was missing. She had a strong desire to meet her birth mother. A few years ago, through a series of miracles, she was able to reconnect with her birth mom for the first time since the day she was born. It was a wonderful meeting for both of them. They connected immediately. Even though she regards our mom as her "MOM," it has filled a void that she had in knowing who her birth mom was. When we connect with God, we find out who we are. Our lives make a lot more sense when we actually have a relationship with our Creator!

THINK ABOUT IT!

Have you filled that God-shaped void in your heart?

DAY 255

*Jesus, heal me of this cancer, but Your will be done, I would like to
live on and keep doing things for You and bless other people.*
STEVE ROWE (MORTIFICATION)

*But he was pierced for our rebellion, crushed for our sins. He was
beaten so we could be whole. He was whipped so we could be healed.*
ISAIAH 53:5

God knows your heart. We get that. But sometimes, that is not
the question. Rather, do you know God's heart? Are you aware
of what God has in store for you, and what his plans are for your
future? The more I get to know God, the more I can see glimpses of what
he has planned for me.

I have never, in my 60+ years of being a Christian, been able to see
the whole picture. That's why Steve Rowe prayed, "…but Your will be
done." He didn't know God's whole plan for him. He only knew what
his desire was. When we pray demanding that God do according to our
desires, we forget that we don't see the whole picture. We actually try to
play God, and assume we know best. A better prayer would be modeled
after Steve's, "Lord show me your will. I know what my desires are, but
I don't see the whole picture. Please show me your perfect will, and help
me get my own will out of the way!"

THINK ABOUT IT!
Are you guilty of trying to tell God what to do?

DAY 256

Since we live by the Spirit, let us keep in step with the Spirit
LYRICS FROM "AGAINST SUCH THINGS THERE IS NO LAW"
BY BARRICADES [BLOOD COMBINES]

For God called you to do good, even if it means suffering, just as Christ suffered for you. He is your example, and you must follow in his steps.
1 PETER 2:21

I remember as a young child trying to keep in step with my mom. I remember grabbing ahold of her dress (they were longer then!) and holding on tight. As I write this, she is 87 years old, and I am still trying to keep up with her.

Christ asks us to "follow in his steps." There are basically two kinds of followers. Some people are very driven. They may try to do more than they can actually handle. In their fast pace, they sometimes forget to be in tune with the Spirit and listen to his guidance. God is never calling any of us to "burn out" for him! On the other hand, most people move too slowly. Many worry about the outcome. They don't want to take risks. They prefer not having to leave their comfort zones. When God calls them, they hesitate and overthink it all. They need to have the courage to get started.

What all of us need is to be in tune with Christ. We need to walk in "yoke" with him. Matthew 11:30 says, "my yoke is easy to bear, and the burden I give you is light." The yoke in this verse refers to a wooden harness that connected two oxen. The best way to train an ox was to have it walk beside an older, more experienced ox. Together the two would drag the plow on the field. The same is true when walking with Jesus. He teaches us while he's the one carrying the heavy load. But we need to walk in the same pace as he is! Don't sit still. Don't run. Make sure that you're always in tune with him, and listen to his plans for you.

THINK ABOUT IT!

Are you walking in the right pace?

DAY 257

God give me the strength I need
LYRICS FROM "PSALMS"
BY WAR OF AGES [RETURN TO LIFE]

"My power works best in weakness." So now I am glad to boast about my weaknesses, so that the power of Christ can work through me For when I am weak, then I am strong.
2 CORINTHIANS 12:9-10

Wait. What? "When I am weak, then I am strong?" That doesn't make much sense, does it? How can a person be strong, when he is weak? In this verse, Paul reveals one of the great truths about the Christian life. It's difficult to understand because it is contrary to what we have been taught. We are told that we need to be better educated and build up our reassume. We're instructed to be stronger and more self-sufficient. So how can we be strong in our weakness?

When we rely on our own strength, we depend on nothing but ourselves. We think we can handle life on our own. But when we're weak, we realize that we need strength from the Lord. When we surrender to him he starts to work through us. Surrendering weakness is so much better than self-sufficient strength. At our best, we are nothing compared to the power of God working through us!

Do you feel weak today? Congratulations! The Lord is ready to use you and do awesome things through you. Rely on his strength. Maybe you are having a good day, and you feel fine on your own. Remember that it never stays that way. No doubt you will encounter times during your day when you will need his strength and his wisdom!

THINK ABOUT IT!

Is God's power working through you?

DAY 258

Now, in retrospect, to think about…I consider myself a pretty strong person, but when that [depression] happened, it just totally rocked my world and I wasn't able to cope with it at first; I really wasn't.
JESSE LEACH (KILLSWITCH ENGAGE)

Our yesterdays present irreparable things to us; it is true that we have lost opportunities which will never return, but God can transform this destructive anxiety into a constructive thoughtfulness for the future. Let the past sleep, but let it sleep on the bosom of Christ. Leave the Irreparable Past in His hands, and step out into the Irresistible Future with Him.
OSWALD CHAMBERS

Give your burdens to the Lord, and he will take care of you. He will not permit the godly to slip and fall.
PSALM 55:22

I have heard it said that that Bible is a crutch, that people use it instead of standing on their own. But I would go one step further. I would call it a stretcher. It isn't something I simply lean on; it actually carries me—especially during times of despair and anxiety. It's not an option, but a necessity during those times.

When the people around Jesus were leaving during difficult times, he turned to his disciples and said, "Are you also going to leave?" Simon Peter replied, "Lord to whom would we go? You have the words that give eternal life" (John 6:67-68). The real test of our faith and our relationship with Jesus isn't what happens during the easy times of life, but rather, how do we handle things when life falls apart? If we have developed a relationship with Jesus, then he becomes the one we run to. His words in the Bible are not only comforting, but transforming.

THINK ABOUT IT!
Have you learned to go to God with your anxiety and despair?

DAY 259

Let me drift within your reach where I'm blameless and pure.
LYRICS FROM "OPEN THE GATES " BY EXTOL

Yet now he has reconciled you to himself through the death of Christ in his physical body. As a result, he has brought you into his own presence, and you are holy and blameless as you stand before him without a single fault.
COLOSSIANS 1:22

How does God see you? That is an important question for you to ponder. Your answer will determine the quality and magnitude of your relationship with him. If you believe God see's you as a horrible person, always messing up, then you will cower and feel guilty when you approach him.

Since Christ's death on the cross, you have been reconciled to him. There's no more reconciling to do. As a result, he has brought you into his presence. How does that affect you? This verse says you are now "holy and blameless as you stand before him without a single fault." Wow! When God sees you, he sees Jesus. His death on the cross was a wonderful gift to you, and the most significant gift you will ever receive!

THINK ABOUT IT!

How does God see you?

DAY 260

*He has changed me from the inside. I'm still Tommy, but
I'm closer to the Tommy He created me to be.*
TOMMY ALDRIDGE (WHITESNAKE)

*"This means that anyone who belongs to Christ has become
a new person. The old life is gone; a new life has begun!"*
2 CORINTHIANS 5:17

I am a senior citizen now. It's very strange to me. I had imagined that when I got to this point in my life that I would mellow out a bit. Maybe I would enjoy chiller music. Maybe I would even cut my hair! Of course, none of that has happened. I have been a Christian for 60 years. I honestly thought I would be further along spiritually than this! I had imagined when I got to be this age, I would be a spiritual giant. That hasn't happened either.

It's sometimes difficult for me to remember that I am a new creation. Especially when I sin the same way as everyone else does. I imagine God in Heaven looking at me and shaking his head, saying, "I thought you would have learned these lessons by now!" Of course, he doesn't. I continue to be imperfect, but I'm getting better. He continues to change me from the inside. I realize my biggest challenge is to put this in perspective. I can either get wiped out when I see how far I still have to go, or I can rejoice that he has brought me this far! And, like Tommy Aldridge says, I am closer to being the Pastor Bob that he created me to be!

THINK ABOUT IT!

*Do you have the right perspective? Are you focused
on the person God is molding you to be?*

DAY 261

Purity of heart is to will one thing.
SØREN KIERKEGAARD

If you need wisdom, ask our generous God, and he will give it to you. He will not rebuke you for asking. But when you ask him, be sure that your faith is in God alone. Do not waver, for a person with divided loyalty is as unsettled as a wave of the sea that is blown and tossed by the wind. Such people should not expect to receive anything from the Lord. Their loyalty is divided between God and the world, and they are unstable in everything they do.
JAMES 1:5-8

No one can serve two masters. For you will hate one and love the other; you will be devoted to one and despise the other.
MATTHEW 6:24

I am constantly reminding myself to "choose one thing and do it well." It has always been tempting for me to want to accomplish more than I'm able to. I've learned over the years that when I take on too much, I end up not doing a very good job of anything. I have learned that with the homeless ministry. People come with many needs. They need housing and clothing. Their immediate need is food. I used to try to supply everything. Tents. Sleeping bags. Sox and underwear, etc. I still try to do what I can in those areas, but I always tell our homeless friends that we will always feed them well. We specialize in food, and as I write this, we're serving 8,000 meals per month to our homeless friends.

It's easy to lose focus if there are too many things occupying our time. You simply can't go in an unlimited number of directions. It is important that you choose one thing—and do it well. Love God, and love him only!

THINK ABOUT IT!

Are your loyalties to God divided?

DAY 262

*Ray was watching a TV movie about Jesus Christ, and when the
movie ended with Jesus hanging on the Cross, Ray in disgust,
said to himself, 'NO! The cross is Barren and Jesus LIVES Today!
[Explaining how they came up with the name for the band]*
STEVE WHITTAKER (BARREN CROSS)

*The message of the cross is foolish to those who
are headed for destruction! But we who are being
saved know it is the very power of God.*
1 CORINTHIANS 1:18

I remember when the musical Jesus Christ Superstar came out. Ian Gillan, who had just become the singer for Deep Purple, sang the part of Jesus Christ. You have no idea how exciting that was for a rock enthusiast like me. Christian rock didn't really exist at the time so this was monumental. I memorized every word of the album. To this day, I can sing with the album and play most of it on the piano. But it always bothered me that they didn't finish the story. Christian critics of the rock opera pointed this out over and over again. And they were right. What good is the story unless you know the ending? If Jesus had stayed in the tomb, we would not be here talking about him today.

According to C.S. Lewis, Jesus is either a liar, a lunatic, or lord! The only thing that makes him Lord is his resurrection. He died for your sins, and then conquered death as well. The fact that the cross is barren proves his Lordship! The end of the story "…is foolish to those who are headed for destruction!" Why? Because they don't understand the relevance of the resurrection. That is a very important part of the whole salvation message. He is risen!

THINK ABOUT IT!

Who do you know that needs to hear the "end of this story?"

DAY 263

*I have seen and met a lot of hypocrites over the years, and I would
rather know someone who is being real with me that does not put on
a front, than someone trying to impress with how much they can talk
about Jesus. I think that the ones who are not sincere are easy to spot.*
BRUCE FITZHUGH (LIVING SACRIFICE)

Preach the gospel at all times; when necessary, use words.
ATTRIBUTED TO ST. FRANCIS OF ASSISI

*You see, we are not like the many hucksters who preach for
personal profit. We preach the word of God with sincerity and
with Christ's authority, knowing that God is watching us.*
2 CORINTHIANS 2:17

Live your life in front of people! That is the greatest ministry a Christian will ever have. There are a lot of hypocrites out there who claim one thing and live another. The world isn't looking for us to be perfect. They do, however, expect us to be honest, and for our lives to be different. When you live your life in front of people, they will begin to see the fruit of the Holy Spirit inside of you "…love, joy, peace, patience, kindness, goodness, faithfulness, gentleness, and self-control." (Galatians 5:22-23).

If they know you at all, they will realize that something is different about you. You are not the same person you used to be. When you live your life in front of people, you are preaching the Gospel. You are demonstrating the Good News of Jesus Christ. Obviously, the Gospel needs some verbal clarification. But it all begins with your example of the Holy Spirit's transformation inside of you! Once people see Christ in you, and begin to ask you questions about it (1 Peter 3:15), then you have an opportunity to share the wonderful news of Christ's sacrifice on the cross for them!

THINK ABOUT IT!

*How do you feel about this phrase:
"Live your life in front of people?"*

DAY 264

I knew now that this faith in Jesus thing wasn't actually what I and so many other people had previously thought is was: a finger in your face, prim and proper religion designed to keep people in line.
BRIAN "HEAD" WELCH (KORN)

Not everyone who calls out to me, 'Lord! Lord!' will enter the Kingdom of Heaven. Only those who actually do the will of my Father in heaven will enter. On judgment day many will say to me, 'Lord! Lord! We prophesied in your name and cast out demons in your name and performed many miracles in your name.' But I will reply, 'I never knew you. Get away from me, you who break God's laws.'
MATTHEW 7:21-23

You need God in your life! Only God can give you true happiness!" I heard these words from a red-faced street preacher as he screamed at people passing by. As I stopped to talk to him, he didn't believe me when I told him I was a Christian. "You have long hair and tattoos. God hates those things!" I asked him if he was happy. He didn't answer me. I knew he was just another so-called Christian who was talking about things he hadn't experienced himself.

Was that judgmental? No. Jesus told us that we would know they are true Christians by the way they LOVE each other. Brian "Head" Welch had only experienced fake Christians. It wasn't until he met someone who actually LIVED what they were talking about that he began to realize his need for God in his life. In these verses from Matthew, Jesus tells them, "I never knew you. Get away from me" It's the name of Jesus that has the power. But there are so many who don't have the relationship!

THINK ABOUT IT!

Being a Christian isn't something you do. It is the result of a transformation inside of you.

DAY 265

A lot of times we've seen the most belligerent people are the first ones who have the deepest needs for God in their lives.
TED KIRKPATRICK (TOURNIQUET)

We are made right with God by placing our faith in Jesus Christ. And this is true for everyone who believes, no matter who we are.
ROMANS 3:22

Who would make the best Christians? It's difficult to predict. There have been people in my life who have totally surprised me! And then there have been those who I thought would make great candidates, who have turned out to be the biggest nay-sayers of the Christians faith. We're simply not able to judge who will receive Christ, and who will not. We have friends that we love dearly, and obviously those are the ones we want to see receive Christ the most. That's completely fine. But we still need to broaden our horizons. God wants everybody to become his children, so we can't view any one as a lost cause.

God uses all of us in different ways. I have friends who used to be drug addicts, sex addicts, alcoholics, and the like. They relate so well to those still struggling with those addictions. I don't have the same experience. I have never struggled in those areas. But all of us are called to patiently share the Gospel with anyone who desires to know. Christ reached people who were extremely hostile to Christianity. The people who hate your faith the most might actually be the most willing to convert. We simply do not know.

Listen intimately to the Holy Spirit. Allow him to lead you to those he chooses. There are no lost causes. Paul was seemingly a completely lost cause, but Christ turned him around and made him the main author of the New Testament.

THINK ABOUT IT!
Who is God leading you to chat with?

DAY 266

The name of the Lord is a strong fortress;
the godly run to him and are safe.
PROVERBS 18:10

Then the name of our Lord Jesus will be honored because of the
way you live, and you will be honored along with him. This is all made
possible because of the grace of our God and Lord, Jesus Christ.
2 THESSALONIANS 1:12

Starting your family is a very exciting event. The addition of children in your life changes you completely! But one of the most difficult tasks at the beginning is coming up with the perfect name for your child. You'll want the name to have meaning. You also want it to define your hopes and aspirations for the child. Many books have been written, listing suggestions and meanings for names. God's "name" is like this. If we were to sum up his attributes, they would be the embodiment of Jesus Christ.

John 3:16 says, "For this is how God loved the world: He gave his one and only Son, so that everyone who believes in him will not perish but have eternal life." LOVE. If we were to sum up the meaning of Jesus' name in one word, it would be "love." 1 John 4:8 tells us, "…for God is love." Agapé. Unconditional love. When you speak his name, you also speak his character. You're reminded that he loves you so much that he died for your sins. You're also reminded that, because of his unconditional love, that nothing can separate you from him. You were bought with a price. It's difficult to truly understand this kind of love since we don't possess it naturally. That is why Gregory of Nyssa says that God's name is not known (easily understood), but only wondered at!

THINK ABOUT IT!

Begin to remind yourself what the name of Jesus
means whenever you speak it. Then you will always
be aware of just how much he loves you!

DAY 267

And I am convinced that nothing can ever separate us from
God's love. Neither death nor life, neither angels nor demons,
neither our fears for today nor our worries about tomorrow—
not even the powers of hell can separate us from God's love.
No power in the sky above or in the earth below—indeed,
nothing in all creation will ever be able to separate us from
the love of God that is revealed in Christ Jesus our Lord.
ROMANS 8:38-39

It's so great to know that God isn't going anywhere. Even when we struggle and walk away, he follows us to get our attention. Why? Like any good father with his child, he dearly loves you and desires a relationship with you. When you say "yes" to him and invite him into your life, he makes a pact with you. He accepts Jesus death on the cross as the payment for your sin and the foundation for your relationship. And now, NOTHING can separate you from his love. Not even you!

There are many times I struggle in my faith. I've told God I no longer desire to follow him. But he keeps pursuing me! He understands what I am going through. He also understands that I say things out of my pain that I don't really mean. After all of these years, he has proven his love for me over and over again. The security that I feel in my relationship with God is the foundation for my life.

THINK ABOUT IT!

Do you feel secure in your relationship with God?

DAY 268

*Let your roots grow down into him, and let your lives be
built on him. Then your faith will grow strong in the truth you
were taught, and you will overflow with thankfulness.*
COLOSSIANS 2:7

What should your attitude be when life sucks? We usually
want to cuss someone out, or blame God for not taking good
enough care of us! You may be surprised to know the Bible
asks you to have an attitude of thankfulness. What? Seriously?! Some
people go through life complaining about everything. It's always somebody else's fault. You know those people. They are not very pleasant to
be around. On the other hand, people who seem to exude thanksgiving
are always a pleasure to be around.

Thankfulness isn't rocket-science! It's easy and simple. It's a matter of
putting things into perspective. God's grace is the only thing keeping us
going. We were given life. We screwed it up. God fixed it. What else can
we do but say, "thanks!"

"Make thankfulness your sacrifice to God" (Ps 50:14). As we reflect on
life, it becomes obvious how many things we take for granted. Water and
air are amazing things! A roof over our heads isn't something everyone
has. But most of all, we understand more deeply how much Christ has
saved us from. Without him we would face an unbearable destiny. We
would be overcome by sin and death. Instead, our destination is glorious, and our face-to-face fellowship with our wonderful Savior is ahead!

THINK ABOUT IT!
Are you steadily growing in thankfulness?

DAY 269

But if you remain in me and my words remain in you, you may ask for anything you want, and it will be granted! When you produce much fruit, you are my true disciples. This brings great glory to my Father.

JOHN 15:7-8

Oh Lord. I know that you love me and that you told me to ask you for anything I want. Have you seen that nice new Shelby Mustang at the car dealership? I want it. And I claim it in 'JESUS' name. Amen." Can I expect God to answer this prayer? Some would say, "Yes! God desires to give you the desires of your heart." I would argue that this request is more lust than true desire. How can you tell the difference? "If you remain in me and my words remain in you" is the foundation.

You see, God places the desires of our (his and mine) heart within me. When I am listening to his Spirit, I am able to respond with his heart. How do I know what to ask? He tells us to ask for anything! But first, make sure you are asking from a heart motivated by God's love, as this will give you insight into what to ask for and desire. The results of those answered prayers? "...you [will] produce much fruit"—the fruit of the Holy Spirit. You see, it's not about claiming that new car in "Jesus name!" It's about asking for those things that "bring great glory to God!"

THINK ABOUT IT!

How would understanding this verse affect your prayers?

DAY 270

The greatest argument against the Bible is an unholy life;
and when a man will give that up, he will convince himself.
CHARLES SPURGEON

Humans can reproduce only human life, but the
Holy Spirit gives birth to spiritual life.
JOHN 3:6

We are all on a journey. We are all searching for truth. Everyone searches differently, depending on their unique circumstances. At the university level many think it's only an intellectual thing. They may try to be all brain and no body, but the truth is, emotions play a role as well. People who have family and ordinary jobs are often more interested in knowing how Christianity will affect their current lives. Most people today care more about how religion can affect their current life, not just the afterlife.

The quest for truth looks differently to different people. Our unique circumstances, interests, and priorities make the search for truth diverse. Everyone is different. Everyone is looking for a different aspect of truth. As a result, you may be able to reach people I can't. As the church, the body of believers, we need people who are both good with their hands and with their minds. But since most people want to know what Jesus can do for them in this life, we all need to demonstrate the difference he makes for each of us. The greatest argument for Christianity is a life changed radically by Jesus. If you reflect peace, patience, and joy during trials, a larger perspective, and unconditional love for the people considered outcasts, then it gets very difficult rejecting your convictions. If it "works," then it's probably truth. People are looking for something that works. And the Holy Spirit most certainly does!

THINK ABOUT IT!

Is your life an argument for Christianity?

DAY 271

There's a huge difference between religion and faith.
BLACKIE LAWLESS (W.A.S.P.)

*This Good News tells us how God makes us right in his sight. This
is accomplished from start to finish by faith. As the scriptures
say, "It is through faith that a righteous person has life."*
ROMANS 1:17

The major thing that distinguishes Christianity from other religions is that it's not performance based. Actually, Christians were called "athiests" in the early church by the Roman Empire. In every other religion you have to work to inherit eternal life. But in Christianity our salvation is based on what Jesus did. He lived a perfect, faultless life. He lived the life that we couldn't. He died for our sins. Through faith, his perfect record becomes our record. His holiness becomes our holiness. And our punishment becomes his punishment. Wow, what a trade!

Here's the good news: Whatever bad things you may have done, his forgiveness is bigger. Whatever evil thoughts you may have had, his death on the cross covers it. There is literally nothing you could have done that isn't dealt with on the cross! Today you have a clean slate. Today you have been set free. From now on, your life is covered by the blood of Christ. So you can live today with a clean conscience knowing that whatever you have done, Jesus' death on the cross has dealt with it.

THINK ABOUT IT!

Do you realize what trading records with Jesus means?

DAY 272

All I know is I walk by faith and not by sight and
take baby steps and drink baby milk.
DAN SPITZ (ANTHRAX)

I had to feed you with milk, not with solid food, because
you weren't ready for anything stronger.
1 CORINTHIANS 3:2

In my book "Seriously!? Letters to myself at 21," I made the observation that I believed I knew everything when I was 21. Now that I am older, I realize there are a lot of things I still don't know. That feeling will continue throughout my lifetime! Socrates said: "I am the wisest man alive, for I know one thing, and that is that I know nothing." This might be an exaggeration, but he makes a good point.

This may seem frustrating in the beginning, but it has become one of the biggest joys of life. It makes me desire to grow deeper in the simple, most important truths of life: Jesus loves me. I have been saved, God is my Father. I'm made in his image. Many of us have heard this from childhood, but when we start growing in wisdom about these things, they give us a foundation to live our whole life by. When we're able to do this, we can then make peace with all the other questions.

As you get caught up in theology and complex questions about life, remember to return to the foot of the cross where you will find all the answers you need to live by.

THINK ABOUT IT!
Have you built a life on simple truths while
still being curious about the complex?

DAY 273

*I didn't understand at the time—however now
I know that you were right beside me.*
LYRICS FROM "WITH HONOR"
BY WAR OF AGES [RETURN TO LIFE]

*I know the LORD is always with me. I will not
be shaken, for he is right beside me.*
PSALM 16:8

*Even when I walk through the darkest valley, I will
not be afraid, for you are close beside me.*
PSALM 23:4

It was a chilly night in the Red Light District in Zurich, Switzerland. Since I have a burden for the streets, I asked a friend to show me around. She had been a prostitute from a young age, and had since found the Lord and left the streets. As we began our tour, we encountered young girls standing in doorways. Many of them were being "used" against their will by men with money and lust to burn. We sat in a pub and watched some of the older prostitutes working the tables. We walked from dark alleys to darker alleys. The whole time the burden in my heart increased for these forgotten souls on the streets.

It wasn't until I told a friend of our adventures a few days later that I realized how dangerous it all was. He said, "Weren't you aware that your life was in danger?" I hadn't been. I just felt moved by the Holy Spirit to learn a little about the streets, and begin to find people willing to reach out. I have really learned to love this verse in Psalm 23 the last few years. As we continue ministry on the streets, it gets a bit dark sometimes. But "even when I walk through the darkest [street], I will not be afraid, for you are close beside me."

THINK ABOUT IT!

How often are you aware of God's presence "close beside you?"

DAY 274

And every knee in heaven...on earth, and below
the earth, shall bow to the name Yeshua
LYRICS FROM "EXALT" BY BROKEN FLESH

Therefore, God elevated him to the place of highest honor
and gave him the name above all other names, that at the
name of Jesus every knee should bow, in heaven and on
earth and under the earth, and every tongue declare that
Jesus Christ is Lord, to the glory of God the Father.
PHILIPPIANS 2:9-11

Why was Jesus elevated? Because of his extreme sacrifice on the cross. Jesus took on the sin of the whole world. Yours. Mine. Jack the Ripper's. Hitler's. Stalin's. Donald Trump's. Mother Teresa's. The fact that Jesus Christ is actually king means everything to us. It's because of his high position that he can reach down to our low position and save us.

Not only that, but the Bible tells us that we have now received his inheritance. With that, he has given us all power and authority in his name. We have a lot to be thankful for. Not only has he given us new life, but he has given us an abundant supernatural life here on earth. If we could just begin to understand a tiny bit of what that means, it would change us completely!

THINK ABOUT IT!

Has God transformed your life here and now?

DAY 275

P ractice what you preach!" It's an old saying we use for people who don't actually live up to what they tell others to do. Sometimes we are aware of the things we ought to do, but we are still struggling with them ourselves! It can become extreme as well. Many times we're like the kids bullying others at school because of their low confidence. So it is with adults having trouble in their relationships. If a spouse is very insecure in themselves, they can become very jealous at the others' success since they crave the attention. If a person doesn't feel valuable, they will try to drag others down to their level to feel better.

People with confidence and self-worth act differently. Those who have found their identity in Christ will always try to lift others up. Why? Because they feel uplifted themselves. If you want revival, you must ask God to set a fire in you first. If you want to bring peace, you'll have to seek your own peace in him. If you want to bring hope and healing to a broken world, you must find your hope in him and let him heal you. We have to realize that we cannot discipline ourselves to be good. There's only one who is good! We even fall short in our own vague ethical standards. Surrender to God, receive Jesus' sacrifice, and let the Holy Spirit work in you to produce his fruit. Then you'll be ready to bring healing, peace, hope, and love into all your relationships.

THINK ABOUT IT!

*Do you ever feel tempted to talk down to
people, instead of building them up?*

DAY 276

My father was a minister…I have been in organized religion my whole life and I see definite contradictions that anger me to the point where (I get grouped in) with people who say stuff like, "God hates fags," and who are pointing the finger at people and judging them—when I firmly believe that we're not supposed to judge, we are supposed to show love.
JESSE LEACH (KILLSWITCH ENGAGE)

Spiritual abuse happens when a leader with spiritual authority uses that authority to coerce, control or exploit a follower, thus causing spiritual wounds.
KEN BLUE (HEALING SPIRITUAL ABUSE)

You are the salt of the earth. But what good is salt if it has lost its flavor? Can you make it salty again? It will be thrown out and trampled underfoot as worthless.
MATTHEW 5:13

Are we "salting" or "assaulting?" I have to be honest. Some days when I peruse my Facebook comments I am ashamed to be called a "Christian." Some of the posts from outspoken Christians are not only embarrassing, but misrepresenting the faith as well! I know that many of these people have been trained by spiritual abusers. The abuse has been passed from one generation to the next. Abused Pastors Abuse.

Jesus warned us not to return to this yoke of bondage, and yet so many churches throughout the world have done just that. What do you do if you find yourself in a condemning, judgmental, and abusive church? RUN! Get out of there. Find a place that is nurturing and encouraging, where the Bible is taught with love and grace. Christ's death on the cross was a game-changer, and brought a very clear message: agapé love. Unconditional love. And when they asked Jesus what the greatest commandment was, he told us to agapé. Love God. Love Your Neighbor. Love Yourself. If you follow this, the greatest commandment, you will find it difficult to abuse others!

THINK ABOUT IT!

Have you learned to love unconditionally?

DAY 277

To live in the faultless law of liberty. My darkness drowned in the depths of the sea enter through the gates of righteousness.
LYRICS FROM "OPEN THE GATES " BY EXTOL

So Christ has truly set us free. Now make sure that you stay free, and don't get tied up again in slavery to the law.
GALATIANS 5:1

F reedom. A very misunderstood word, especially when it has to do with our freedom in Christ! The Apostle Paul was concerned for the Christians there in Galatia, as well as those who would live in future generations. He knew that there would always be those false teachers who would distort the Gospel, and try to lead us into slavery to the law again.

His advice is two-fold. First, he wants us see that we are truly free. Really free. Actually free. We have trouble with that. We usually say we are free, but then add a little bondage to the law with it. That's why Paul gives us more advice. He says, "Make sure you stay free" How do you stay free? By realizing you ARE free in the first place! By not wanting to compromise your freedom for anything that tries to tie you down. As Extol so eloquently states it in "Open The Gates," enter through the gates of righteousness!

THINK ABOUT IT!

How can you stay free and avoid becoming a slave to the law again?

DAY 278

I'll stand for the fires of the victims left to die.
LYRICS FROM "THE MARRIAGE OF STEEL AND SKIN"
BY OH, SLEEPER [CHILDREN OF FIRE]

The Spirit of the Sovereign Lord is upon me, for the Lord has anointed me to bring good news to the poor. He has sent me to comfort the brokenhearted and to proclaim that captives will be released and prisoners will be freed. He has sent me to tell those who mourn that the time of the Lord's favor has come, and with it, the day of God's anger against their enemies. To all who mourn in Israel, he will give a crown of beauty for ashes, a joyous blessing instead of mourning, festive praise instead of despair. In their righteousness, they will be like great oaks that the Lord has planted for his own glory.

ISAIAH 61:1-3

We do this by keeping our eyes on Jesus, the champion who initiates and perfects our faith. Because of the joy awaiting him, he endured the cross, disregarding its shame. Now he is seated in the place of honor beside God's throne.

HEBREWS 12:2

What is your responsibility to those who are lost and dying? To simply attend services in a church building while people are poor, brokenhearted, captive, and held prisoners right outside the walls of your church? Once you are saved, you have no greater purpose on this earth than to minister to people who need you, and to bring as many people to heaven with you as you can!

It amazes me how ineffective the church has become. So many people are hurting and in need of our help. Men, women, and children go to bed every night dealing with their shame and discontent. Because Jesus died on the cross, he put an end to sin and shame. That is an important message that people need to hear. What people? The ones right outside the door of your church. The ones that live just down the street from you. The homeless living on the side of the road that you pass by on the way to work.

THINK ABOUT IT!

Are you waiting for someone else to touch people's lives? What about you?

DAY 279

*Today the darkness begins to grow shorter and the light to lengthen,
as the hours of night become fewer…. Realize that the true light is now
here and, through the rays of the gospel, is illumining the whole earth.*

GREGORY OF NYSSA

Your word is a lamp to guide my feet and a light for my path.

PSALM 119:105

*For you are a chosen people. You are royal priests, a holy nation, God's
very own possession. As a result, you can show others the goodness
of God, for he called you out of the darkness into his wonderful light.*

1 PETER 2:9

*God's light came into the world, but people loved the darkness
more than the light, for their actions were evil. All who do evil hate
the light and refuse to go near it for fear their sins will be exposed.*

JOHN 3:19-20

There is light at the end of the tunnel." Without the Lord, that light can be an oncoming train! But with him, it is the light of God's goodness. It is our nature to try to hide—from others, from God, and from ourselves. We think we are doing just fine until "the light" exposes our darkness. It is at that point that you have a choice to make. Will you continue to live in darkness, and hide in the corners, or will you allow the light to expose the dark parts of your life, and bring healing?

God's invitation to you is "come out of the darkness into the light." Why? That's the beauty of the 1 Peter reference above. "For you are a chosen people. You are royal priests, a holy nation, God's very own possession." That's powerful, and yet it is the truth of where you stand as a result of Christ's death on the cross!

THINK ABOUT IT!

Are you allowing the light to expose your dark corners?

DAY 280

It was a very tough call, it was difficult to make this decision
— in a way the band is part of the family too, after all.
SIMON KOCH (ELUVEITIE)

It was by faith that Abraham obeyed when God called him to
leave home and go to another land that God would give him as
his inheritance. He went without knowing where he was going.
HEBREWS 11:8

I love this story! Can you imagine? Abraham gets on the road and begins to walk. His friends yell, "Hey Abe! Where are you going?" "I have no idea!" he answers. We wake up in the morning and think we know exactly what we're going to do and what we'll encounter for the day. And then one morning we feel change in the air, and we no longer feel at peace with our plans. God is "up to something!"

I was excited to get "Sanctuary: The Rock and Roll Refuge" started in 1985. The first Heavy Metal church. It was a huge surprise when, in 1993, God began to move me. I fought the idea for a year. Looking back, I should have responded right away when God called. That would've saved me a lot of struggles. I moved to Tennessee to begin the international part of the ministry. It was the right move, and has been successful for the most part. But it was the most difficult thing I have ever done.

I remember driving away from California. I had no idea what was ahead. Where would I live? What would the ministry look like? I had more questions than answers. I was on the road driving, "…without knowing where [I] was going." Now, many years later, I realize I could never have orchestrated this! It was a matter of simply trusting God and moving when he told me to!

THINK ABOUT IT!

Have you had a time when God told you to "move,"
even though you didn't know all of the details?

DAY 281

For I can do everything through Christ, who gives me strength.
PHILIPPIANS 4:13

*No, dear brothers and sisters, I have not achieved it, but I focus
on this one thing: Forgetting the past and looking forward to what
lies ahead, I press on to reach the end of the race and receive the
heavenly prize for which God, through Christ Jesus, is calling us.*
PHILIPPIANS 3:13-14

To dare. To take risks. To move in boldness. All of us have a desire to move forward with some sort of security. It is that lack of security that keeps us stuck. "I hate my job, but I am afraid I can't find anything else." "I'm not really in love with my girlfriend, but what if I break up with her and then can't find anyone else?" "What if I follow the passions of my heart and fall on my face?" We would all be lying if we denied having these kinds of thoughts. All of us are paralyzed from time to time from moving forward.

The biggest question we seek to answer in times like this is: "What if I try and then fail?" But honestly, that's not the most important question. In fact, it really isn't even a consideration! The real question is: "What passions has God placed in my heart, and what is he leading me to do?" Where God guides, he provides. He will not leave you stranded. He will provide a way for you if he has truly called you on this path in the first place. Then, as the Apostle Paul says in this verse, "I can do EVERYTHING through Christ, who gives me strength!"

THINK ABOUT IT!

Are you sometimes afraid of moving forward in your life?

DAY 282

It's the same for everything in life. You have to have a vision, you have to have an idea of what you want to do, and then do it.

THOMAS WINKLER (GLORYHAMMER)

For I can do everything through Christ, who gives me strength.

PHILIPPIANS 4:13

My greatest joy in being a Christian these past 60 years has been the adventure of it! Discovering who I am in Christ is only the beginning! It has been a wild and wonderful ride! I could never have planned this life. It has exceeded all of my dreams and expectations. God continues to prove to me that he is always "dreaming bigger" than I am! Once he gives you a vision, NOTHING will stop him from accomplishing it! Well, maybe just one thing. YOU!

There have been many times in my life when I have tried to do things with my own strength and wisdom. Those have been the times when I have failed. The key is doing things "THROUGH" Christ. That is where the strength comes from. How exciting to know that God has a plan for you, and that his plan will succeed no matter what. It is just a matter of keeping my eyes on him, and my mind and heart plugged in to the Holy Spirit through reading the Word and communicating with him.

THINK ABOUT IT!

Is your Christian life an adventure?

DAY 283

*We're not here to preach at people, we're here to
show people that there is something else there.*
TED KIRKPATRICK (TOURNIQUET)

*What good is it, dear brothers and sisters, if you say you have faith but
don't show it by your actions? Can that kind of faith save anyone?*
JAMES 2:14

How do you communicate God's love to others? Do you carry your Bible to school, hoping someone will ask you about it? Do you wear your IMPENDING DOOM T-shirt to work looking for an excuse to share the band with your work-mates? Or are you more bold? Maybe you ask leading questions, or even preach on the street corner. The love of Christ is something to show people, not preach at them. It isn't as much what you say, as how you actually live. Why would your friends believe Jesus can change their lives, if they don't see your life being changed? The love of Christ transforms us. Our lives are changed. That will be our greatest testimony, not our words.

Are you tired of seeing rich preachers speaking without actions? Bring Me The Horizon are critical of Christians. In their song Anti-vist, they sing, "If you really believe in the words that you preach, get off your screens, and onto the streets." And honestly, we need to take their critique seriously! Sadly, this is what a lot of non-Christian people see when they look at Christians. Let Christ shine through you. Start loving each other, and helping people.

A quote that has traditionally been attributed to Francis of Assisi says, "Preach the Gospel, and if necessary, use words." This is awesome! In John 13:35, Jesus says, "Your love for one another will prove to the world that you are my disciples." A Christian shouldn't be all talk. He should be all action accompanied by a few words.

THINK ABOUT IT!

Are your actions speaking louder than your words?

DAY 284

*Some of [our] songs definitely do come from an abusive relationship
that I was in a very long time ago. But I feel very disconnected from
it because it happened a very long time ago. It has been a while
and my life isn't like that anymore…I've disconnected enough from
it to know that I didn't want that section of my life to be a waste.*

CORY BRANDAN (NORMA JEAN)

He heals the brokenhearted and bandages their wounds.

PSALM 147:3

L ove sucks! At least, sometimes it does. There's no greater feeling than
to fall in love with someone. The birds begin to sing, the sun begins
to shine, and all is right with the world… unless they break up
with you! Then the birds stop singing, it begins to storm, and life sucks.
Love is such a strong emotion. It dictates our hearts and our lives. But
when love goes sour, it seems like no one really understands. "You'll find
someone else. There are plenty of 'fish in the sea'" people tell you. "God
will heal your heart. You just need to have faith that he knows what he is
doing." Even though this is true, and they are trying to be understanding, that is about the worst thing you can say to someone who is hurting
from a relationship gone bad. You feel very alone. The one you love is no
longer your sounding board, and it feels like no one truly understands.

You also question God. Why would he allow this to happen to me? It
has been in times like these that this verse in John has meant the most to
me. It is the shortest verse in the Bible, and yet it is so powerful. JESUS
WEPT. Why? Because his heart was broken. He felt the pain of a relationship snuffed out. He cried. Whenever you go through difficulties in
your relationships, you can trust God to help. He understands because
he has walked in your shoes. And while others around you are throwing Bible verses and clichés at you, Jesus says, "I understand. I have been
there. I know what you are feeling. And I will bandage your wounds."

THINK ABOUT IT!

*Have you felt the pain from a relationship
gone wrong? How did you handle it?*

DAY 285

Not in judgement, but discernment I'll follow the true
Shepherd's voice. Lyrics from "sight and sensation"
by THE BURIAL [Lights and Perfections]

My sheep listen to my voice; I know them, and they
follow me. I give them eternal life, and they will never
perish. No one can snatch them away from me.
JOHN 10:27-28

But the Holy Spirit produces this kind of fruit in our
lives: love, joy, peace, patience, kindness, goodness,
faithfulness, gentleness, and self-control.
GALATIANS 5:22-23

There's a derogatory term that is sometimes used for Christians: "Dumb Sheep." And in many ways, that is a true assessment. We may not be the person we used to be, but we're still not the person we are going to be! How do we move forward? How do we improve in wisdom and in the practice of our faith? One way is to "LISTEN!" The more we learn to recognize God's voice, the more we grow in knowledge and wisdom.

I have been told, "True faith is not about emotion. You simply have to trust your faith in God." That is not entirely true! The Christian life is very emotional. It's one of the foundations of our faith. When the Holy Spirit moved into your heart, he began to produce fruit. Emotional fruit: "Love, joy, peace, patience, kindness, goodness, faithfulness, gentleness, and self-control." You will recognize his voice because he speaks with this fruit as a foundation. That is one ways you will know his voice! You learn to recognize it by experience. And how do you respond? "My sheep listen to my voice; I know them and they follow me."

THINK ABOUT IT!
Have you learned to recognize his voice?

DAY 286

I don't like Christians!" Sound familiar? We hear this all the time even from other Christians! Honestly, some have good reasons! If all your experiences with mechanics have been awful, you'll develop some prejudices against mechanics. Many people have been hurt by the church. Many have been unfairly judged by Christians. They have good reasons for refusing to listen to a self-proclaimed Christian.

1 Peter 3:15 says, "And if someone asks about your hope as a believer, always be ready to explain it." If they see your hope first, then there is something to chat about. The problem for many is that they haven't seen much hope in Christianity. Mostly judgement. The same may be the case with music. It's not that we should hide it, but sometimes it may just not come up naturally for a while.

If we want to reach people with music, then only playing on the Christian scene is not enough. We have to play on the metal scene—not just the "Christian metal scene." That's where the people are who need the message of our Savior. Don't limit yourself. A message of hope is always relevant wherever we go. We're called to live in the real world, but we are also called to show them the hope we have within!

THINK ABOUT IT!

Are people seeing your hope more than your judgment?

DAY 287

I think that young people still deal with suicide, they still deal with drug addiction—more now than ever
JIM LAVERDE (BARREN CROSS)

Don't you realize that you become the slave of whatever you choose to obey? You can be a slave to sin, which leads to death, or you can choose to obey God, which leads to righteous living.
ROMANS 6:16

Kicking addiction is extremely difficult! Your body has gotten used to certain cravings. When you don't provide them, your body will let you know! Many things are addictive. Porn, drugs, and alchohol are extremely addictive and therefore tremendously difficult to get rid of.

The best way to deal with addiction is to never get started. How many smokers would there be if nobody ever had their first cigarette? And how many times, when you pick up that pack of cigarettes, do you see the warning labels. Your health is at stake! When you watch pornography, you're not only hurting yourself and your (future) wife, but you're also supporting an industry that exploits women and makes money doing it!

If you are fighting addiction, you need to tell someone. Find someone you trust who can help. Find someone you can pray with, who will support you throughout your fight. It's so difficult fighting on you own. Prepare for the times you know you'll be tempted. Decide in advance what you'll do. Fight the battle before the battle. Start today!

THINK ABOUT IT!
Are you addicted?

DAY 288

*Regard as free not those whose status makes them outwardly free,
but those who are free in their character and conduct. For we should
not call men truly free when they are wicked and dissolute, since
they are slaves to worldly passions. Freedom and happiness of soul
consist in genuine purity and detachment from transitory things.*

ANTHONY THE GREAT

*So Christ has truly set us free. Now make sure that you stay
free, and don't get tied up again in slavery to the law.*

GALATIANS 5:1

Freedom doesn't come to you because you claim it, but only as you practice it. The freedom we were given as a result of Christ's death on the cross means nothing in itself. You must accept it as truth. Internalize it. Begin to practice it. Only then will it begin to transform your life. True freedom resides in the things that last forever, not in the things that pass away. Many people spend their lives chasing momentary pleasures. They brand themselves as free since they always do what they desire, but they don't experience true freedom. Momentary pleasures can never answer the deepest yearnings of the soul. Ecclesiastes taught us that thousands of years ago.

Would you rather live a meaningful life with periodic struggles and pain, or a life chasing pleasures that never fulfilled your deepest desires? That's the great joy in having God as our foundation. When the world and all it's momentary pleasures disappear, we still have eternal meaning, purpose, and joy!

THINK ABOUT IT!

*Would you rather have ultimate fulfillment
or chase momentary pleasures?*

DAY 289

*Obviously, within Christianity, there are many different doctrines
and things like that that not everybody agrees on. That's
why there are a gazillion denominations and churches.*
BRUCE FITZHUGH (LIVING SACRIFICE)

*I appeal to you, dear brothers and sisters, by the authority
of our Lord Jesus Christ, to live in harmony with each
other. Let there be no divisions in the church. Rather, be
of one mind, united in thought and purpose.*
1 CORINTHIANS 1:10

Harmony? United? We've messed this one up pretty badly. Christ called us to stand together as brothers and sisters. The church should be one, but we choose to focus on our differences instead of focusing on the most important thing we have in common: Jesus Christ! We have all been united with him. God has adopted all of us, and therefore we're brothers and sisters.

There are theological issues we don't agree upon: Bible-view, justification, the Eucharist, baptism, and so on. All of these are important issues, but compared to sharing life in Jesus Christ we shouldn't let them separate us. When we take our labels away, there is only one question that is important: "Have you accepted Jesus Christ as your Lord and Savior, and have you invited him into your heart?" We can discuss everything else! You'll spend an eternity with each other in God's presence. Don't let small things divide you, but rejoice when people from a different denomination reach others with the Gospel.

THINK ABOUT IT!

*Are you learning from your brothers and sisters who may
be part of a different denomination than yours?*

DAY 290

I n our fast-paced society, it's difficult to slow down long enough to put eternal things into perspective. Everyone has an opinion, and everyone has a theory. But in the face of eternity, your opinions and theories had better be correct! I'm always amazed at the sloppy job so many do when it comes to making this decision. Over the years, I have listened to many people explain to me why they don't believe in God. Usually not very well thought out, and generally full of holes and misinformation. Christianity is filled with very intelligent people who set out to disprove the existence of God and the fallibility of the Bible, only to become believers instead. Their study of the Word, and open heart to God, took them down a road they didn't expect.

Many times we come up with lame excuses on why we don't want to be a Christian, because we are concerned that God would make us become something we don't want to be. "Will he make me give up my music?" "Will he force me to wear a suit and tie, and go to church?" "Will he make me cut my hair?" It isn't about God ruining your life. Rather, it's about saving it! His desire is to set you free. If there's one thing I have heard over and over from new Christians, it's "I wish I would have done this a long time ago!"

THINK ABOUT IT!

Are your excuses keeping you away from God's plan for your life?

DAY 291

Maybe they had a loved one die or just anything
that they end up hating God for
TED KIRKPATRICK (TOURNIQUET)

O Lord, why do you stand so far away?
Why do you hide when I am in trouble?
PSALMS 10:1

How do you handle pain? Honestly, most of us have no idea what real pain feels like. There are some who have experienced pain so intense that it becomes difficult to believe that God is good and loving. For instance, take the pain of losing a child. I can't imagine anything as devastating. It changes your life completely. While we can argue the philosophical questions on how God can allow this, it really isn't what people in the middle of extreme pain need to hear. We need to shut up and listen. Some of their anger may be directed at God. But remember they are in pain. Sometimes people simply need to have the freedom to grieve and be mad at God.

Charles Darwin and his wife loved each other very much. They lived lives of extreme pain and sorrow having lost several of their children to disease. It brought Mrs. Darwin closer to God. She found comfort in the Lord. Charles, on the other hand, became angry that God could allow this. Difficult situations will either bring us closer to him or push us further away. Both usually begin with anger. Come to Jesus with it. Tell him your frustration. Allow him to comfort you. If you bury your emotions, it will lead you further away from him. Also, be patient with those going through the same things. Show them the love of Christ. And if necessary, use words.

THINK ABOUT IT!
How do you react during difficult times?

DAY 292

I don't know if it's "a calling" in the way that many people use the term. That is, I don't know that I've ever had a sort of epiphany type of moment where I "knew it was what God wanted me to do." I certainly used language like that earlier in my life, but I don't know how much weight it ever held.
JASON WISDOM (DEATH THERAPY)

Fight the good fight for the true faith. Hold tightly to the eternal life to which God has called you, which you have declared so well before many witnesses.
1 TIMOTHY 6:12

"God told me." I hear this statement a lot from some very well-meaning Christians. But honestly, I think it's a very dangerous statement to make. I have friends who use it, and then reuse it when things don't work out—as if God has changed his mind. There are very few times in my life when I have been able to say, "God told me." I have said, "I think he told me" or "I have strong desire that I believe is from the Lord," but I have always been careful about stating that I don't know the whole picture.

There have been many times in my life when I have followed what I thought was God's leading, and it has worked out great. Other times, things have flopped. That's why it's so important that we follow our passions with a lot of prayer. Not the kind of prayer where we tell God what to do, but rather, the kind of prayer where we ask God for his divine guidance and wisdom. The times I've been the most aware of God's calling in my life have usually been after I've been doing something for a while. After I am already doing what he as asked me to do it is apparent that it was his leading. Then I can say, with boldness, "God told me!"

THINK ABOUT IT!
Have you learned to handle your calling with prayer?

DAY 293

We just started an orphanage in India and more orphanages are on the way in different places around the world. God has really given me a burden in my heart for street children. We just have to save those children who sleep outside at night and scrape to survive.

BRIAN "HEAD" WELCH (KORN)

For I was hungry, and you fed me. I was thirsty, and you gave me a drink. I was a stranger, and you invited me into your home. I was naked, and you gave me clothing. I was sick, and you cared for me. I was in prison, and you visited me. Then these righteous ones will reply, 'Lord, when did we ever see you hungry and feed you? Or thirsty and give you something to drink? Or a stranger and show you hospitality? Or naked and give you clothing? When did we ever see you sick or in prison and visit you?' And the King will say, 'I tell you the truth, when you did it to one of the least of these my brothers and sisters, you were doing it to me!'

MATTHEW 25:35-40

Something quite fantastic happens when the Holy Spirit begins moving inside of you. The Bible describes his presence encouraging love, joy, peace, patience, kindness, goodness, faithfulness, gentleness, and self-control (Galatians 5:22-23). As this "fruit of the Spirit" begins to flow through your life, you begin to notice things you didn't see before. You begin to have concern for others that you didn't have before.

When Brian "Head" Welch talks about building orphanages in India, it is a result of the Holy Spirit in his life. God helps us see beyond ourselves, and we begin to realize our responsibilities and opportunities to help others. We become God's hands and feet. But especially, we become his heart!

THINK ABOUT IT!

Has God given you a burden for those he describes in Matthew 25 above?

DAY 294

*I think one of the biggest parts about being in an abusive relationship
is that you don't know that you're in one. People always say "Well,
why don't they just leave?" and it's like well, because they're
in love and they don't know what's going on around them.*
CORY BRANDAN (NORMA JEAN)

*Don't put your trust in mere humans. They are
as frail as breath. What good are they?*
ISAIAH 2:22

*Love is patient and kind. Love is not jealous or boastful or proud or
rude. It does not demand its own way. It is not irritable, and it keeps
no record of being wronged. It does not rejoice about injustice but
rejoices whenever the truth wins out. Love never gives up, never loses
faith, is always hopeful, and endures through every circumstance.*
1 CORINTHIANS 13:4-7

If you are alive and breathing, then you will struggle with trust issues. Yours. Mine. Others. I can't count the number of times I have been untrustworthy. I didn't set out to cause hurt. It simply happens in the course of human interaction. I tell my friend I'll call him, and then I forget. He thinks, "If Pastor Bob really cared about me, then he would have called." I agree to a magazine deadline and forget to write the article. They think, "Pastor Bob can't be trusted when it comes to deadlines."

What if the trust becomes an area of abuse? I didn't set out to hurt anyone, and yet people do get hurt because of my inabilities. We want to trust others we care about, and this makes it more difficult when they let us down. There's a good reason the Bible defines love. Otherwise, we wouldn't know what it looks like. The above scripture in 1 Corinthians 13 describes perfect love. Now, there isn't a person alive who is proficient in all of these qualities, but anyone who truly loves you should begin to display them!

THINK ABOUT IT!

*Do you understand that unconditional love doesn't
mean unconditional trust? Trust must be earned.*

DAY 295

You're just as much of a sinner. If you really read the scriptures and pay attention to what is being said, you are just as much of a sinner as the next person, so who are you to point the finger? You know, point the finger right back at yourself.
JESSE LEACH (KILLSWITCH ENGAGE)

This is a trustworthy saying, and everyone should accept it: "Christ Jesus came into the world to save sinners"—and I am the worst of them all. But God had mercy on me so that Christ Jesus could use me as a prime example of his great patience with even the worst sinners. Then others will realize that they, too, can believe in him and receive eternal life.
1 TIMOTHY 1:15-16

We get upset when people sin differently than we do. We have somehow gotten the idea that we are better and more spiritual than others around us. Nothing could be further from the truth. The Bible levels the playing field: "For everyone has sinned; we all fall short of God's glorious standard" (Romans 3:23). Everyone. You. Me. Those around us.

Christ died on the cross for all of us, since all of us needed redemption. So how could we possibly justify our superior attitude? The Apostle Paul said he was the "worst sinner." He wants to make sure that people understand that he is an example of God's power to transform our lives. His example should be our example. Your greatest example to others should never be one of condemnation, but rather, a testimony of God's amazing transformation of your life.

THINK ABOUT IT!

Are people able to see God's testimony in your life, or do they only see your judgment?

DAY 296

A lot has happened in my life since the Bloodgood days, not the least of which is pastoring.
MICHAEL BLOODGOOD (BLOODGOOD)

Take care and be on guard for yourselves and for the whole flock over which the Holy Spirit has appointed you as overseers, to shepherd (tend, feed, guide) the church of God which He bought with His own blood.
ACTS 20:28 (AMPLIFIED BIBLE)

But among you it will be different. Whoever wants to be a leader among you must be your servant.
MATTHEW 20:26

The Bible defines what a "Pastor" should be: a person who looks after the spiritual needs of the church, the believers in Jesus Christ. During these days of "Superstar Pastors," we can easily lose focus on what a true pastor is all about. We get spiritual gifts confused. Is a Pastor a CEO? No! That is the job of someone with the gift of Administration, or the gift of Finances (Giving). We place pastors in impossible situations these days, and then wonder why they get burned out and frustrated.

When a Pastor is free to nurture the believers, and to feed and guide them, then he is operating in his gifting. When he is able to serve the congregation, he is acting out what Christ asked him to do. He may not have the skills for other jobs in the church, but he isn't supposed to! We all have a position in the Body of Christ! What a wonderful calling. And what a great responsibility at the same time. Not everyone operating in the position of "pastor" has a true heart for it. When you look for someone to "pastor" you, make sure you find someone whom God has qualified by looking at their heart!

THINK ABOUT IT!

Does your pastor "nurture, feed and guide" you?

DAY 297

And we know that God causes everything to work together for the good of those who love God and are called according to his purpose for them.
ROMANS 8:28

As I write this, I have been working with the homeless here in Nashville. Tennessee for the past 12 years. I have gotten to know hundreds of them very well. There are some truly amazing people on the streets. One used to be a county commissioner. Another a lawyer. Several were school teachers. Many owned their own business. But now, they're on the streets without anything.

If there's a common thread that I have experienced with our homeless friends, it is "lack of purpose." They are simply trying to survive. Most of them no longer dare to dream about or even consider God's purpose for their lives. Most are simply thankful that we are feeding them, and they have one less thing to worry about for the day. That isn't living. It is simply existing. And you don't have to be homeless on the street to suffer from this mentality. God designed you with a specific purpose in mind. Your purpose will give you hope and direction. It will become your motivation in life. When you are living within your purpose, you won't feel like you have to work another day in your life! You begin to truly enjoy what you are doing, and have the motivation to do it!

THINK ABOUT IT!

What is your purpose in life?

DAY 298

*Once you put something out there as art, you're
opening yourself up to criticism.*
BRUCE FITZHUGH (LIVING SACRIFICE)

*Do everything without complaining and arguing, so that no one can
criticize you. Live clean, innocent lives as children of God, shining
like bright lights in a world full of crooked and perverse people.*
PHILIPPIANS 2:14-15

Nothing could ever stop Kiss. I've seen the band in down times where critics were like vultures circling overhead saying things like, 'Well, you know it's the end of your career'" (Paul Stanley). When you put yourself out there you become open to criticism. It doesn't matter what you do. When you are in the public eye, people will try to shoot you down. Even if you preach about loving unconditionally and helping people in need, you'll be criticized from legalistic Christians. Someone won't like the "tone" of your voice. Others will criticize the way you look. Others will put words in your mouth and assume you are saying things that you're not. Playing music that sounds a bit "different" will get you in trouble among certain groups. But we can't stop serving the Lord because someone may not like what we do. Ultimately, we're serving the Lord, not people's opinions.

The greatest things you will experience in life take courage. It involves putting yourself out there. Taking risks. Knowing this could break your heart. You may feel exposed and vulnerable. Criticism from others may have already taken a toll on your self-esteem and your willingness to take risks. But when people criticize you, you can rest in knowing that the only real judgement to fear is the judgement of Jesus Christ. And he has already paid that price! You don't have to fear temporary judgement from people, who don't even have the authority to judge. Only God can judge. And he has already pronounced you "Not Guilty!"

THINK ABOUT IT!

Are you held back in life by worrying about other people's judgement?

DAY 299

To define Tourniquet is to not define us
TED KIRKPATRICK (TOURNIQUET)

*"Once you had no identity as a people; now you are God's people.
Once you received no mercy; now you have received God's mercy."*
1 PETER 2:10

W ho are you, and what do you do? "My name is…I study at…
and I work as a…" Whatever your answer is, you reveal how
we view our own identity. One of the difficult things about
being unemployed is being forced to answer those questions! People
often let their jobs define them, which puts them into an existential crisis when they get fired. Other people live out their search for meaning
through their kids. This creates an enormous pressure on the children.
They have to not only find meaning themselves, but also carry the weight
of their parents' search for identity.

Of course our families, relationships, and jobs are a part of who we
are. They tell a lot about us. But when they become our whole identity
and the center of our world, we become extremely vulnerable. What
then is your identity? You are a child of God. He has created you in his
image. He has bought you at a great price. He has given you a purpose
and even death cannot separate you from him. Let this be your ultimate
identity. No one can take it away from you!

THINK ABOUT IT!
How do you identify yourself?

DAY 300

*Now, with having a kid, it makes me want to
be more genuine and more real.*
BROOK REEVES (IMPENDING DOOM)

*I could have no greater joy than to hear that
my children are following the truth.*
3 JOHN 4

I've listened while older fathers give soon-to-be fathers advice. "You have no idea how much it will change your life!" Every time I see the father-to-be shake his head. Even though he may appreciate the information, he can't fully understanding or even anticipate the total change of life that is coming. I have lived enough years now to hear those same new fathers giving the same advice to the soon-to-be's.

I have observed the transformation over and over again. Some of the people who were the most self-centered have become totally consumed with their children. You almost need to be a father to understand this verse when it says, "I could have no greater joy." But it doesn't just apply to our earthly father/son relationships. That is the heart of God for YOU as well!

THINK ABOUT IT!

*Do you really understand that God
celebrates his relationship with you?*

DAY 301

The measure of his kindness exceeds the measure of his discipline.
GREGORY OF NAZIANZUS

*So God can point to us in all future ages as examples of the
incredible wealth of his grace and kindness toward us, as shown
in all he has done for us who are united with Christ Jesus.*
GALATIANS 2:7

*For the Lord corrects those he loves, just as a
father corrects a child in whom he delights.*
PROVERBS 3:12

I sat trapped. It was an 8 hour flight to Copenhagen, and I was sitting in the window seat. In front of me was the most unruly 2 year old I have ever experienced. She kept looking at me, and then started making faces and hiding. If I didn't acknowledge her, she would throw something at me to get my attention. She was loud, fidgety, and consistent. I kept hoping she would take a nap at some point, but it lasted far into the trip. Out of desperation, I asked her mother to please keep her turned around in her seat since she was really annoying me. The mother basically told me that she had no control over her daughter and that I was stuck with her behavior. For 8 hours!

There are many children who desperately need the discipline of their parents. This wasn't about the temperament of the child; it was about the lack of discipline from the parent. God realizes that we need the same thing to grow into our spiritual maturity. For us to realize our full potential, and to become the best we can be, we need to be trained in righteousness. It's never pleasant. We usually complain. That's why Hebrews 12:11 says, "No discipline is enjoyable while it is happening—it's painful! But afterward there will be a peaceful harvest of right living for those who are trained in this way."

THINK ABOUT IT!

Have you allowed God to train you in righteousness?

DAY 302

*It's like with any art, "out of the overflow of the heart, the
mouth is going to speak." So, as far as Christianity, it's
who I am and it's who I've become. It's at the forefront and
the thought of what I'm doing and why I'm doing it.*
JOSH SCOGIN (NORMA JEAN, THE CHARIOT, 68)

*A good person produces good things from the treasury of a good
heart, and an evil person produces evil things from the treasury
of an evil heart. What you say flows from what is in your heart.*
LUKE 6:45

I continue to be amazed by what comes out of my heart and my mouth sometimes. I know myself very well, and there are times when I don't recognize me. Since the Holy Spirit has taken residence in my heart, the things that flow from there surprise me! I find myself loving beyond my own capacity. I find myself being patient more than my natural limits. I'm surprised by gentleness, when I know that my natural inclination is to speak harshly and let someone know they have rubbed me the wrong way!

Josh Scogin says, "It's who I am and it's who I've become." After being a Christian for so many years, I hardly remember the person I used to be. And I don't really want to. The person I am becoming is a huge blessing to me. It allows me to operate in HIS love and integrity. I don't always get it right, and I struggle sometimes to "let go and let God," but the change he has made in me is nothing short of a miracle. And, he isn't finished with me yet!!

THINK ABOUT IT!

In what ways has God changed you?

DAY 303

When suffering is all that you know, the pain is easy
LYRICS FROM "IGNOMINY" BY BROKEN FLESH

*We can rejoice, too, when we run into problems and trials, for
we know that they help us develop endurance. And endurance
develops strength of character, and character strengthens
our confident hope of salvation. And this hope will not lead to
disappointment. For we know how dearly God loves us, because
he has given us the Holy Spirit to fill our hearts with his love.*
ROMANS 5:3-5

None of us are immune from pain. Just today as I write this another
rock star has committed suicide. Tragic. And yet, all of us feel this
way from time to time. Some even get a bit used to their misery. They can't remember feeling any other way. As strange as it sounds,
depression has almost become a friend.

HOPE is the missing element. In my opinion, it is a lack of hope that
leads us to pain and depression in the first place. Becoming a Christian
isn't a cure-all. There will continue to be situations in life that wipe us out.
There will the be times when we lose hope. But this verse assures us that
God's "hope will not lead to disappointment." The Holy Spirit desires to
break through our hopelessness and "fill us with his love."

THINK ABOUT IT!

*Has pain become so familiar to you that it's
difficult to imagine moving on without it?*

DAY 304

And the more I knew God, the more I wanted to know about God.
PETE SANDOVAL (MORBID ANGEL)

God blesses those who hunger and thirst for
righteousness, for they will be satisfied.
MATTHEW 5:6

Becoming a Christian is the beginning of a wonderful life-long adventure! That doesn't mean that it is an easy road, but it is definitely the greatest adventure you can ever undertake! Pete Sandoval says that the more he traveled on this adventure, the more he had a desire to keep going! The more you learn about God and Christ's amazing sacrifice for us, the more you desire deeper and deeper intimacy with him.

People ask me to describe my relationship with God. That's a very difficult question to answer. Partly because it is difficult to put into words, but also because it is difficult to understand once you actually find the difficult words! It becomes very intimate and personal. When you realize it's a relationship and not just a belief system, your life truly becomes transformed. And, like anything that feels good to us, we desire it more and more!

THINK ABOUT IT!
Do you hunger and thirst for more of God?

DAY 305

I knew that if I were to become a Christian, then I would have to make some changes in my life...outwardly, I thought. I did not understand that it would be changes on the inside.

ULF CHRISTIANSSON (JERUSALEM)

Don't copy the behavior and customs of this world, but let God transform you into a new person by changing the way you think. Then you will learn to know God's will for you, which is good and pleasing and perfect.

ROMANS 12:2

Ulf learned that any changes that happen on the outside must first begin on the inside! If you and I were capable of changing ourselves, God would never have sent Jesus to die on the cross. He knew we would always struggle to live a godly life. You see, it isn't about your discipline! It is all about surrender. God knew if you were going to discipline yourself to make changes, that you would always mess up. You would always fall short. You would always feel defeated! But when you surrender to the Holy Spirit inside of you and allow him to guide, you will find more power and wisdom to live a Christian life.

I think many of us are as surprised as Ulf was to find that any change that happens begins inside of us. Until our inside is transformed, our outside will continue to struggle. As Romans 12:2 says, God needs to change the way we think! And that is only done by the power of his Spirit inside of us!

THINK ABOUT IT!

Are you still relying on your own discipline to change your life? Are you allowing his Holy Spirit inside of you to change you from the inside?

DAY 306

*This tale is to teach you the dangers that rests inside. A lust for the
power provided by fame This fame is a drug and the addicts our gods.*
LYRICS FROM "DEALERS OF FAME"
BY OH, SLEEPER [CHILDREN OF FIRE]

*As Peter entered his home, Cornelius fell at his feet
and worshiped him. But Peter pulled him up and
said, 'Stand up! I'm a human being just like you!'*
ACTS 10:25-26

As I pulled up to the gas pump, I was shocked to see Vestal Goodman pumping gas. I am sure that name doesn't mean anything to you. But when I was growing up, she was the Queen of Gospel Music. I don't get star-struck with music celebrities. I have worked with them for the last 45 years. But this was different. It was Vestal. My hand was shaking as I went up to her to shake her hand. She smiled and was gracious to me, and probably wondered why this rough-looking metalhead was nervous to greet her.

We all have those whom we admire. They will always be bigger-than-life to us. Both the performer and the fans need to be careful. There is a huge trap that is prevalent in the world of music that takes it to an unhealthy level. Performers begin to grab for power and fame. Fans use their music as a drug and worship them as gods. This is nothing new. I remember watching TV when I was young to see how the girls reacted to Elvis. And then I remember watching when the Beatles visited America for the first time. It was mayhem! It's okay to admire those performers who rock our world, but we have to be careful that it doesn't become worship.

THINK ABOUT IT!

What performers do you admire, and why do you admire them?

DAY 307

But if you refuse to serve the Lord, then choose today whom you will serve. Would you prefer the gods your ancestors served beyond the Euphrates? Or will it be the gods of the Amorites in whose land you now live? But as for me and my family, we will serve the Lord."
JOSHUA 24:14-15

Being a Christian is a decision you make. Just because your grandmother is a Christian, doesn't make you one as well. God doesn't have any grandchildren. Just because you attend a church, doesn't guarantee your entrance into Heaven. Billy Sunday said, "Going to church doesn't make you a Christian any more than going to a garage makes you an automobile." God looks at your heart, and waits for you to respond to his invitation to accept Jesus' death on the cross as your redemption.

John 3:16 says, "For this is how God loved the world: He gave his one and only Son, so that everyone who believes in him will not perish but have eternal life." This verse was written in Greek originally. The word "believe" actually means, "trust in, rely on, and cling to." You see, it's not like saying "I believe in UFO's." It's a belief that makes a commitment. It forms a relationship. It changes your life. It is YOU developing a relationship with HIM. And only you can do that. Your grandmother can pray for you, and your church can teach and encourage you, but in the end—it is what goes on in your heart, and your personal relationship with Jesus—that eternally matters!

THINK ABOUT IT!

Have you accepted Christ's death on the cross as forgiveness of your sins, and established a relationship with God?

DAY 308

"If I am not today all that I hope to be, yet I see Jesus, and that assures me that I shall one day be like Him."
CHARLES H. SPURGEON

Since we have been united with him in his death, we will also be raised to life as he was.
ROMANS 6:5

I'm not what I used to be, and I'm not what I'm going to be!" That is a phrase I have used for 50 years! It actually illustrates something that is simply too amazing to understand: will we someday stop fighting this battle with the flesh? When we get to Heaven, will our new minds put this war to rest? It's difficult to understand how God views us now. Justified. Without guilt. But, to imagine that we some day will be totally unaffected by sin seems too incredible to be true! But it is!

One day you'll live in holiness with Christ. There will never be another evil thought in your mind. You'll never do another selfish act. You'll be perfect in righteousness. Your love will be pure and unconditional for everyone around you. And everyone else will treat you the same way! You will be loved. No one will ever commit a selfish act against you. No one will think a single bad thought about you.

Heaven is just too amazing to understand. But, reflecting on it is helpful. It creates hope in our lives now and hope for our future. Our lives will change more than we can possibly imagine. For that, we can take no credit. It's all because of Jesus. He paved the way for evil people to be made holy. And that gives hope for you and I!

THINK ABOUT IT!

Can you imagine that someday you will actually be holy?

DAY 309

The law is for the self-righteous, to humble their pride:
the gospel is for the lost, to remove their despair.
CHARLES H. SPURGEON

What sorrow awaits you teachers of religious law and you Pharisees.
Hypocrites! For you are careful to tithe even the tiniest income from
your herb gardens, but you ignore the more important aspects of
the law—justice, mercy, and faith. You should tithe, yes, but do not
neglect the more important things. Blind guides! You strain your water
so you won't accidentally swallow a gnat, but you swallow a camel!
MATTHEW 23:23-24

For I am not ashamed of this Good News about Christ.
It is the power of God at work, saving everyone who
believes—the Jew first and also the Gentile.
ROMANS 1:16

There is a good reason why we don't call Christianity a "religion." It is so much more than that! It's a "relationship" with the God who made you! But there are still those today who are self-righteous and teach out of a heart of hypocrisy. Jesus warned us to avoid them. He called them Pharisees. Hypocrites. Blind guides. Their adherence to the law and their own self-righteous pride hinder the teachings of grace. And, in the end, no one is encouraged and no one is truly set free from the bondage of the law.

The real power of God is not at work through the law, but rather, through his grace. That is why it's called "Good News!" The Apostle Paul says it contains "…the power of God at work, saving everyone who believes…" As Charles Spurgeon said, the Gospel isn't for the self righteous to humble their pride, it is for the lost—to remove their despair! How wonderful to know that the very creator of the universe cares about YOU! His desire is to have a relationship with you—based on his love and grace!

THINK ABOUT IT!

Are you more motivated by the law or by His grace?

DAY 310

*The natural tendency of our sinful nature is to trust in our
own flesh and call on God only in times of emergency. We
want to encourage people to get back to a daily practice
of faith in God, through good times and bad.*

TED KIRKPATRICK (TOURNIQUET)

*Then he said to the crowd, "If any of you wants to be my follower, you
must give up your own way, take up your cross daily, and follow me."*

LUKE 9:23

G od, HELP!" For some, those are the only words they have spoken
to God. If you only turn to God in a time of great need, you'll get
a wrong impression of what it is to have a relationship with him.
For many, prayer becomes a long request of things we want from him.
It's like sitting on Santa Claus' lap at Christmas time and telling him
what you want for Christmas. God wants to be a part of your whole life.
He wants to hear from you no matter what mood you're in. He wants to
guide you in both good and bad times.

As in any intimate relationship, you should be able to laugh and cry
together. That's how you really get to know somebody! You experience
all sides of each other. A marriage needs honest contact every day. You
spend time together even when you don't have anything to say. We need
to spend time with the Lord every day to get to know him and develop a
better relationship with him. As you are consistent in this, you'll realize
you know him a little better, and that he has changed you in ways you
didn't expect. He's the one who is perfect, which makes his the greatest
relationship you'll experience in your lifetime. Don't miss out!

THINK ABOUT IT!
Do you seek the Lord every day?

DAY 311

Keep watch and pray, so that you will not give in to
temptation. For the spirit is willing, but the body is weak!
MATTHEW 26:41

When I was a young child, our family went to the drive-in movies to see Bambi, a Walt Disney movie. Since we had a pet deer at the time, the movie really impacted me. In church, our pastor did a sermon on prayer. He told us to pray and ask God for whatever you need. I needed a Bambi record. So I prayed I would get one for Christmas. I also let my request be known to my family, and my extended family. When Christmas came, I received 3 Bambi records! I was amazed at how well prayer worked! I couldn't wait to ask God for more records! Of course, I have learned a lot since then.

Prayer really isn't about asking God to give us stuff; it's more about asking him for direction and to supply our needs, both physically and spiritually. So how do you keep from falling into temptation? Two things: WATCH and PRAY. Don't just pray and then go on about your day as if you are not involved with God's provision. Watch. Be aware. Look for the ways in which God will move. We will always be weak, and in need of God's strength. Watch and Pray!

THINK ABOUT IT!
Have you learned to watch and pray?

DAY 312

The best thing and the most rewarding thing, is that we can be just five regular dudes with our own problems and histories. But when we write songs in a sweaty garage somewhere, or in a dungeon with a light in the middle of the room and no windows, someone we might never meet will be affected by that music.

CORY BRANDAN (NORMA JEAN)

You see, we don't go around preaching about ourselves. We preach that Jesus Christ is Lord, and we ourselves are your servants for Jesus' sake. For God, who said, "Let there be light in the darkness," has made this light shine in our hearts so we could know the glory of God that is seen in the face of Jesus Christ. We now have this light shining in our hearts, but we ourselves are like fragile clay jars containing this great treasure. This makes it clear that our great power is from God, not from ourselves.

2 CORINTHIANS 4:5-7

When I was in high school, I almost flunked speech class. I hated to get up in front of everyone and speak. My hands would shake, and I could hardly hold my note cards! I remember one speech in particular. The assignment was a 5 minute speech. I rehearsed it over and over again. I had it down. It took exactly 5 minutes in practice. But then, when I gave it, I finished in just under 4 minutes. I was so nervous, I spoke too quickly. The teacher said I needed to prepare a little better, and that my voice was a bit too monotone and uninteresting.

A lot has happened over the years. I probably feel more comfortable in front of huge crowds speaking than anything else. And these days, I make much of my living on doing voice-over work. People love my voice, and find it soothing and engaging. Who knew? I am sure my speech teacher would be shocked! It is always amazing how God can use us—in spite of ourselves. Little becomes much when you place it in the Master's hands!

THINK ABOUT IT!

How has God used you, in spite of your limitations?

DAY 313

I'm writing a book. I've got the page numbers done" (Steven Wright). There have been many times during the writing of METAL DEVO that I have felt this way. It has been a huge task, but a real labor of love. We should all aspire to be one of two types of people: "Writers" or "Doers." Benjamin Franklin said, "Either write something worth reading or do something worth writing about." Honestly, I enjoy doing both! A good writer is also a good teacher. And to be a good teacher, you have to be a good student. It is the experiences and emotions we gather in life that allow us to share our hearts on paper.

Realizing how much we don't know is a good way to get started as a student, teacher, or writer. Be happy when you're corrected and learn from it. How do you begin? Remember one thing: simple truths don't change! In ten years you'll be able to explain things in a better way, but you will still use those simple truths you learned as a foundation. But have the courage to get started. The simple truths of life are the most important ones and have the power to change lives.

THINK ABOUT IT!

Are you sharing what you've learned in life with others?

DAY 314

So long I've labored in vain. For a worthless prize and empty gain.
Father help me to see what I truly need. The pearl of Your kingdom
LYRICS FROM "PEARLS, THE FRAILTY OF MATTER"
BY THE BURIAL [LIGHTS AND PERFECTIONS]

When he discovered a pearl of great value, he
sold everything he owned and bought it!
MATTHEW 13:46

What are your eyes fixed upon? It's easy to get caught up in simply living an ordinary life, and forgetting that there is a bigger picture! It's easier to focus on momentary decisions that make you feel good today. Enjoying the moments of life really is a virtue. But as Christians, we're part of a bigger story. We have a pearl worth more than anything. We have the Kingdom of God!

Matthew 6:21 says, "Wherever your treasure is, there the desires of your heart will also be." It's important to realize what your treasures are. When we do, it affects the priorities and focus of our everyday life. Our struggles become easier since we know the pain will fade. Serving others becomes easier when you realize you have eternal joy in the Kingdom of God. Everything in life is given to us by God. We have nothing we can take credit for. Since everything good is given to us, we need to pass it forward to others.

THINK ABOUT IT!

Are you reflecting on the treasure you have in
heaven? A difficult day can become so much better
when you can focus on the bigger picture!

DAY 315

*I try to "press on," as the Apostle Paul put it, and
grow in my relationship with the Lord.*
MICHAEL BLOODGOOD (BLOODGOOD)

*I don't mean to say that I have already achieved these things
or that I have already reached perfection. But...I focus on this
one thing: Forgetting the past and looking forward to what lies
ahead, I press on to reach the end of the race and receive the
heavenly prize for which God, through Christ Jesus, is calling us.*
PHILIPPIANS 3:12-14

There you are. Sitting down in the middle of the road. Tired of running. Defeated. Depressed. You don't have the energy to walk, no less run a race! There are days when it doesn't take much to get wiped out. When you make one mistake, you automatically feel like slowing down and maybe even stopping completely. The same thing is true when it comes to our spiritual life. Things may be going really well. You suddenly make one mistake, and the guilt stops you from moving on. You were running a good race, but one mistake caused you to stop.

It's important to move on quickly in a situation like this. You know where to find forgiveness. Simply go to Jesus and ask. Honestly, he has already forgiven you. It's still important to get it off of your chest. Trust him when he says you're forgiven! Move on quickly. Don't let guilt bring you down. Finish the race. Others need to hear about the same forgiveness.

THINK ABOUT IT!

Has something made you stop running?

DAY 316

*I find it sad that many bands out there don't take any
responsibility for what they sing about or do on stage.*
STEVE WHITTAKER (BARREN CROSS)

*The heart of the godly thinks carefully before speaking;
the mouth of the wicked overflows with evil words.*
PROVERBS 15:28

It's been said, "Be wise today, and you won't cry tomorrow." Your life has consequences. Whether speaking or remaining silent, you will have consequences. This is simply the way it works! Many bands don't have any real content in their lyrics. Their writing doesn't reflect their lifestyle. To speak about nothing of meaning is a choice. Whatever platform you may have, you're responsible for using it wisely.

Technology makes it easy to say whatever you feel. That is the definition of social media! People say things on-line they would never say to someone's face. We're also responsible for wasting our time by filling it only with entertainment that doesn't really help anybody. Laughing is awesome, but when it's all we try to do life will soon feel empty. Everybody needs real content!

Some people are good at starting conversations. You know the type. They are awesome to be around. You leave them feeling encouraged, and uplifted. Be that person! Be someone who brings both depth and meaning to your conversations!

THINK ABOUT IT!

*Are you taking responsibility for both what
you say and what you don't say?*

DAY 317

We've tried to give it a positive spin and say that tomorrow is not guaranteed so we have to live "For Today." Make today count.
MATTIE MONTGOMERY (FOR TODAY)

So don't worry about tomorrow, for tomorrow will bring its own worries. Today's trouble is enough for today.
MATTHEW 6:34

Dreams without goals are just dreams! There's nothing wrong with thinking about the future. It's exciting to imagine things that could happen! If you have big dreams, it's important to begin preparing for them. It's an exciting focus, but it can't become your only focus. Some people spend so much time thinking about the future, they actually fail in their present life. They continuously focus on what's coming next, so they are never truly present in the moment.

It's important to have a large perspective on life. It's great to dream about the future and make plans for it. But, what about today? Tomorrow? Next week? Next Year? People need your attention in the meantime. We need to fully commit to what is happening around us today, as we prepare for tomorrow. Quality of life is very important!

Be present today with the people you're around. Plan for the future, but don't worry about it. Make sure those around you have your full attention, and have a quality relationship with you.

THINK ABOUT IT!
Are you present with your friends and family today?

DAY 318

It's the first time I've written a song that's sort of a constructive criticism of my own faith or religion in general, I would say. There's a bit of a departure, as far as my thought process, but my faith hasn't changed at all.
JESSE LEACH (KILLSWITCH ENGAGE)

Pay careful attention to your own work, for then you will get the satisfaction of a job well done, and you won't need to compare yourself to anyone else.
GALATIANS 6:4

Have you ever sat in a meeting listening to someone throwing criticism toward people who are failing at areas of their lives? As you scan the room, you wonder how many of those sinful people are guilty of these very things! It never occurs to you to critique yourself! Part of growing in character is honestly looking at yourself. When we hear someone voice what's wrong in the church or society, we immediately think it must be everybody else's fault. When we do that, we're guilty of self-righteousness. Luke 6:41 says, "why worry about a speck in your friend's eye when you have a log in your own?"

Don't be so quick to judge others. Look inside! The people on social media who are always writing about the flaws of others reveal this in their own lives. Their character looks for fault in everybody else, but not in themselves. Next time you meet a person whose opinion differs from yours, consider listening and learning. Maybe you have been blind in some areas of your life or your opinions. It truly is a blessing having others to engage in conversation with, since there's always so much to learn.

THINK ABOUT IT!

What is your attitude when you hear someone being critical?

DAY 319

So if the old way, which has been replaced, was glorious, how much more glorious is the new, which remains forever! Since this new way gives us such confidence, we can be very bold.
2 CORINTHIANS 3:11-12

Few of us are bold by nature. We have difficulty being bold about anything! It is usually those things that cut to our heart that we react to. But we have to be convinced first. When someone becomes a new Christian, and other Christian friends tell them to be "bold in their faith," they are asking for more than the new believer is usually capable of. They haven't experienced enough to have any kind of boldness yet.

The more we grow in our faith, and the more God works in our lives, the more our faith develops boldness. Michael Bloodgood hopes their music will inspire Christians to be bold in their faith. What a wonderful motivation for a band! As we stay strong together, and grow in the faith as a body of believers, the more boldness we will have.

THINK ABOUT IT!

Are you bold in your faith?

DAY 320

*For a time is coming when people will no longer listen to sound
and wholesome teaching. They will follow their own desires and
will look for teachers who will tell them whatever their itching ears
want to hear. They will reject the truth and chase after myths.*

2 TIMOTHY 4:3-4

Whenever I ask someone what kind of church they attend, they usually say, "We just teach the Bible." Many of them are actually from churches who abuse their congregations and teach things that are contrary to the Word of God. Why? We have gotten used to letting other people think for us! Church has become a "spectator sport" in much of the world today. You walk in the door and sit down. You respond as someone leads singing, and then you listen to someone speak. Your personal interaction is not necessary, or even wanted. Is this the New Testament teaching for what a "church" (the body of believers) should look like?

No! Not at all. I have no problem with this form of church as long as it is only part of the whole program. YOU are part of the program. God gave YOU spiritual gifts to use with others. No one in the church will be balanced without everyone using their spiritual gifts in harmony. God knew that it would be easy for pastors and teachers to get off track. That's why it is important that no one is elevated above the rest, and that we all have a voice in the process of finding truth together!

THINK ABOUT IT!

Do you attend a "balanced" church?

DAY 321

*I used to have everything that people usually strive to get. I really
had it all! But when you realize that you have to leave it all behind,
you'll be asking yourself what the point of it all really was.*

BRIAN "HEAD" WELCH (KORN)

*Store your treasures in heaven, where moths and rust cannot
destroy, and thieves do not break in and steal. Wherever your
treasure is, there the desires of your heart will also be.*

MATTHEW 6:20

We have become a world of consumers. We continue to buy more and more "stuff" we don't need. We purchase larger homes to hold our "stuff" and continue to collect more "stuff." I was one of those. I owned a 4,300 square foot home (400 square meters). I had a lot of "stuff."

One day, while I was trapped in the snow while staying in a chalet in Switzerland, the Lord spoke to me very plainly that it was time to downsize. He wanted me to get rid of most of my stuff. When I came back to the USA, I began selling everything. Today I live in 300 square feet. I gave all my clothes away to the homeless. I own 3 pairs of pants, and three shirts, and I feel so much better. I didn't need any of that. I feel much more "blessed" than I ever did with all the "stuff!" It isn't material possessions that make you happy. It is storing your treasure in Heaven that makes the difference!

THINK ABOUT IT!

Where is your treasure stored?

DAY 322

What else does anxiety about the future
bring you but sorrow upon sorrow?
THOMAS A KEMPIS

Look at the birds. They don't plant or harvest or store
food in barns, for your heavenly Father feeds them. And
aren't you far more valuable to him than they are? Can
all your worries add a single moment to your life?
MATTHEW 6:26-27

Worry does not empty tomorrow of its sorrow, it empties today of its strength" (Corrie ten Boom). It isn't difficult to find things to worry about. Money. Relationships. School. Shelter. Job. Transportation. Life is filled with concerns! Ask yourself, "When was the last time I benefitted from worrying?" Honestly, never! We all need to prepare for the future, but that isn't the same as worrying. It's simple common sense to prepare for what is ahead. If you have built your life on the right foundation, you'll be fine when unforeseen difficulties come around. Even if the thing you've worried about comes to pass, you'll be better prepared if you have laid those foundations ahead of time, instead of worrying about them!

Worrying is actually a lack of trust in God. If we trusted him completely, we wouldn't have to worry. But, as imperfect humans, we struggle with trust. Instead of worrying, realize that it's pointless. When worrying about things (that probably won't go wrong anyway), you need to tell yourself not to be pessimistic about it. Being positive literally has an effect on the way your brain is physically wired. By practicing these things for a long time, you'll become more positive and focus more on solutions. You'll be able to put the energy you used to spend worrying to good use.

THINK ABOUT IT!

Do you understand the difference between preparing and worrying?

DAY 323

*After I became a Christian it was more about trying to be
selfless and coming from a place of selflessness.*
BROOK REEVES (IMPENDING DOOM)

*Don't be selfish; don't try to impress others. Be humble, thinking
of others as better than yourselves. Don't look out only for
your own interests, but take an interest in others, too.*
PHILIPPIANS 2:3-4

Our natural tendency is to be selfish. We all look out for ourselves and make sure we have what we need. As I write this, we've been serving the homeless in Nashville, Tennessee for 12 years. These are people who basically have nothing, including a place to live. When they come through our food line, they want every option. Their plates are piled high. But later, as I watch them throw their plates away, I see them discarding a lot of uneaten food as well. Since they have nothing, it is difficult for them to turn anything down!

There is a difference between what we need and what we want. Most of us don't struggle for the things we need. And because we live in a more affluent society, we want to put our own interests first. It wasn't until I began serving the homeless of our city that I became less selfish. I realized how much I had that I didn't really need. Since then, I have downsized to less than 10% of what I originally owned when I started. I got rid of over 90% of my possessions. It was actually a huge burden lifted, and I have never regretted it!

THINK ABOUT IT!

Are there areas of your life where you could be more selfless?

DAY 324

What most of all hinders heavenly consolation is that
you are too slow in turning yourself to prayer.

THOMAS A KEMPIS

Understand this, my dear brothers and sisters: You must all
be quick to listen, slow to speak, and slow to get angry.

JAMES 1:19

When all else fails, then pray!" Good advice? NO! Rather, it should read, "So all else doesn't fail, pray!" Thomas a Kempis tells us that we are too slow in turning to prayer. That is the message from James as well. We could rephrase it and say, "Be quick to listen in prayer, and slow to speak back." Usually, during a difficult time, we come to God quickly with a lot to say. "Lord, get me out of this situation." "God, help me stand strong." Both prayers are good ones, but probably a bit late. Wouldn't it be a better idea to always be in an attitude of prayer?

Allow God to continue to speak to you and prepare you for what comes your way. I have had many people over the years who schedule a counseling appointment with me, and then never really give me a chance to speak. They come with their problems, they give me all the details, and then try to solve it themselves in front of me. Sometimes they leave having only heard their own bad advice, and I realize they are headed for problems. I am sure God feels the same way many times. He is the counselor, not you. He possesses the wisdom. You don't. Would it make more sense to simply be quiet and let him speak?

THINK ABOUT IT!

Are you quick to listen, or quick to speak?

DAY 325

Remember that the Lord Jesus came to take away sin in three ways; He came to remove the penalty of sin, the power of sin, and, at last, the presence of sin.

CHARLES H. SPURGEON

He has removed our sins as far from us as the east is from the west.

PSALM 103:12

And I will forgive their wickedness, and I will never again remember their sins.

HEBREWS 8:12

When [Jesus] died, he died once to break the power of sin. But now that he lives, he lives for the glory of God. So you also should consider yourselves to be dead to the power of sin and alive to God through Christ Jesus.

ROMANS 6:10-11

I'm amazed by the modern church's preoccupation with sin. We condemn others for their sins. We preach about it from the pulpit. And yet, we rarely talk about the true impact that Jesus' death on the cross made for sin once and for all! First, he removed your sin. It's gone. "…as far as the east is from the west." It cannot be found again.In fact, he also chooses to forget them. The Greek word used here means he "forgets that he forgets." They are removed.

That gives us a tremendous opportunity to pursue holiness. My sins are no longer held against me. For some reason, many well-meaning pastors are afraid if people are armed with this wonderful information, they will use it as a license to sin. I'm sure that many try that for a season. But, in reality, God is still the "Hound of Heaven." He always pursues us. And at some point we realize the Christian life isn't about trying to see how close we can get to the world without falling in, but rather, it is all about pursuing the depths of our relationship with God. Those who use this freedom to sin have a bigger misunderstanding than just sin. They've missed the whole point!

THINK ABOUT IT!

Do you feel free to pursue holiness?

DAY 326

*David also ordered the Levite leaders to appoint a choir of
Levites who were singers and musicians to sing joyful songs
to the accompaniment of harps, lyres, and cymbals.*
1 CHRONICLES 15:16

The Bible is full of examples of men going to war with their musicians playing. Not only is that true of the Bible, but it has been true of many battles since. Andrew Fletcher said, "Let me make the songs of a nation, and I care not who makes its laws." Many world leaders (and even dictators) have believed in the power of music. You may not be heading off to war, or have a need to inspire a whole nation with music. Maybe you simply want to be inspired personally! I usually choose my daily music with two things in mind: What is my current mood? What lyrical content will inspire me and motivate me? So many times people complain of depression and anxiety. When I ask what music they are listening to, it usually reflects that mood—and amplifies it. Doesn't it make more sense to choose something that will lift you out of your situation, instead of pushing you deeper into despair?

THINK ABOUT IT!

*Are you careful when choosing your music so that it uplifts
you, instead of amplifying a current situation?*

DAY 327

*There's no going back and changing it once it's out there, so
we have to make sure it's right. We have to put the time
and work into it to make sure it's the right thing.*

CORY BRANDAN (NORMA JEAN)

*"But Lord," exclaimed Ananias, "I've heard many people talk
about the terrible things this man has done to the believers in
Jerusalem! And he is authorized by the leading priests to arrest
everyone who calls upon your name."But the Lord said, "Go,
for Saul is my chosen instrument to take my message to the
Gentiles and to kings, as well as to the people of Israel.*

ACTS 9:13-15

Saul was busy killing Christians at the time when God called him. Wait what? This is not a guy I would have chosen to write most of the New Testament, and to be a leader of the Christian movement. It would almost have been like selecting Hitler to lead the Jews! Ananias was not thrilled when God told him Saul (who would later be renamed "Paul") was coming to his home. "But Lord!"

When God orchestrates something, it is usually more than we can imagine, and seems just slightly out of our grasp much of the time. But, with God's help and guidance, we can do things correctly from the beginning—especially when it impacts a lot of people. Cory Brandan says (above), "There's no going back and changing it once it's out there, so we have to make sure it's right." It is an amazing thing when God transforms us, breathes new life into us, and then uses us for his purpose here on earth!

THINK ABOUT IT!

How is God using you since he entered your life?

DAY 328

The whole is greater than its parts. And it is interesting, because when you take Barren Cross apart you have four guys, really average musicians, nothing spectacular but something special happens when we get together, play music, write music and when we hit the stage.

JIM LAVERDE (BARREN CROSS)

If one part suffers, all the parts suffer with it, and if one part is honored, all the parts are glad. All of you together are Christ's body, and each of you is a part of it.

1 CORINTHIANS 12:26-27

Have you ever experienced being with a group of people where you just click? It's a great feeling! It often happens with people who share similar interests. But sometimes it happens with some you have absolutely nothing in common with on paper. This is really exciting! There's so much to learn from people who are different than you. It's also a good balance for you to be around people like that. It helps you reflect on your own way of doing things, and it might inspire you to change a few of them.

This is especially true in church fellowships. When Christ is the center of a group of people, something exciting happens. You might be completely different people, but you then have the single most important thing in your lives in common: Jesus Christ as your Savior! Then all of a sudden, there's so much to share: struggles, testimony, encouragement, shortcomings, and hope.

If you're in a fellowship that clicks, you should consider doing something together. Reach out to others as a unit. Invite non-Christians into your fellowship. The love you have for each other will be an amazing testimony and help convince them of the love of Christ. Loneliness is a huge issue today. A group of people reaching out together has the potential to change someone's life!

THINK ABOUT IT!

Have you found a good fellowship?
If so, are you reaching out as a unit?

DAY 329

We see what we do as a privilege and a responsibility
TED KIRKPATRICK (TOURNIQUET)

"The master was full of praise. 'Well done, my good and faithful servant.
You have been faithful in handling this small amount, so now I will
give you many more responsibilities. Let's celebrate together!'
MATTHEW 25:21

We hear a lot these days about "random acts of kindness." You know, helping people out in random ways. Doing these random acts is a good character building exercise. However, there is a greater need for people to actually take responsibility. For example, helping the homeless on Easter and Christmas is fine, but what about the rest of the year? People need you to actually take responsibility. They need to know they can count on you more than just on holidays—when everyone else is also doing their "random acts."

Working for the Lord is an amazing privilege! You get to serve the Most High King and be called his child. But, we have to take responsibility as well. And this is the difficult part. Many people don't like committing to do something for a period of time. They assume someone else will do it. But without people taking responsibility, not much happens. Get involved in caring for people's needs around you. Be faithful in the small things, and the Lord will give you more to take care of. The Kingdom of God needs people to take responsibility to serve.

THINK ABOUT IT!

What responsibilities do you have to the Kingdom?

DAY 330

The way we do it [share our faith] has probably changed
a little bit, and we've learned a lot over the years
BRUCE FITZHUGH (LIVING SACRIFICE)

I have been sent out to tell others about the life he
has promised through faith in Christ Jesus.
2 TIMOTHY 1:1

How do you share your faith in God? There are some Christians who actually make their living by teaching you how to do it. Witnessing 101. Really? Some theologians have made it into a science. But actually, it's very simple. Sharing your faith may seem like a difficult thing that takes courage and training. The most important thing is to simply "live your life in front of people." Be yourself and let people see that Christ has turned your life around and given you hope. Seek the Lord. Let him change you. Give people a chance to see it. It's that simple.

People seek something real. It's important to be honest with them. Share your struggles as well as your successes. Let others see how you handle difficult situations. We often invite people to become vulnerable with us and share their deepest secrets, while we are not willing to do the same! We cannot expect them to do what we aren't willing to do so ourselves! We must be vulnerable with people. We need to show them that Christianity, though giving the opportunity for an awesome life, isn't a gateway to a life without struggle and pain. Be transparent. People all around you are seeking meaning and answers to life. Be the kind of person they feel comfortable sharing their questions with!

THINK ABOUT IT!

Are you sharing your doubts and
struggles with people outside the faith?

DAY 331

Our confidence in Christ does not make us lazy, negligent, or careless, but on the contrary it awakens us, urges us on, and makes us active in living righteous lives and doing good. There is no self-confidence to compare with this.

HULDRYCH ZWINGLI

So I have reason to be enthusiastic about all Christ Jesus has done through me in my service to God.

ROMANS 15:17

Who am I? Great question. The best way to answer it is by asking, "Who does God say I am?" You have been adopted into God's family through the sacrifice of Christ. This is your new identity:

- You're chosen of God, holy and dearly loved. (Col 3:12)
- You're a temple of God. His Spirit and His life dwells in you. (1Cor 3:16; 6:9)
- You're a new creation. (2Cor 5:17)
- You're a saint. (Eph 1:1; 1Cor 1:2; Phil 1:1; Col 1:2)
- You have been justified; completely forgiven and made righteous. (Rom 5:1)
- You're free from condemnation. (Rom 8:1)
- Christ Himself is in you. (Col 1:27)

Exciting, isn't it? These characteristics are true no matter how you feel about them. Remind yourself of these promises often. That will give you all the confidence in the world and help you grow spiritually. Christianity isn't just something we do – it's who we are!

THINK ABOUT IT!

Do you believe these things about yourself?

DAY 332

*The desire for possessions is dangerous and terrible, knowing no
satiety; it drives the soul which it controls to the heights of evil.*
ISIDORE OF PELUSIA (DESERT FATHERS)

*But people who long to be rich fall into temptation
and are trapped by many foolish and harmful desires
that plunge them into ruin and destruction.*
1 TIMOTHY 6:9

I have always loved sports cars. When people ask me if I have ever
been addicted to drugs or alcohol, I tell them that I haven't. But
I have been addicted to sports cars. Seriously! In the past, I have
owned too many cars that I couldn't afford. I am still far too attracted to
shiny new sports cars. Even though I have honestly enjoyed them (and
driven a bit too fast!), it wasn't the purchase that I enjoyed the most. It
was dreaming about the purchase and researching the car. By the time
I actually bought the car, I had worn out the brochure! And every year,
when the new cars came out, I began to "lust" all over again!

The desire for possessions is impossible to satisfy. If it's allowed to
grow and fester, it crowds out the important things in life. It distorts our
perspectives. And, in short, critically limits wise decisions and our spiritual growth. In the last few years, I have downsized a lot. I went from living in a 4,300 square foot home to living in 300 square feet. And I have
never been happier!

THINK ABOUT IT!

Do you have an unhealthy desire for possessions?

DAY 333

I'm blessed to recognize betrayal and move on
DAN SPITZ (ANTHRAX)

*Even those closest to you,—your parents, brothers, relatives,
and friends--will betray you. They will even kill some of you.*
LUKE 21:16

All of us have been betrayed in some way, from minor scrapes to major injuries. Others have experienced horrible betrayal: a parent leaving the family or a spouse having an affair. There have even been instances of innocent people ending up in jail for a crime they didn't commit. As you can imagine, these experiences leave a wound that is difficult to live with. Falling in love with someone who ends up hurting you may leave you fearful of falling in love again. Many feel that their parents have hurt them in some way, even though they have generally been good parents. The sobering fact is this: all of us have also betrayed another person. We have all caused pain in someone else's life.

Jesus tells us to forgive each another. This may seem like a difficult and impossible request if you have been wounded by another person. It may even take a long time to get to this place. But it is, nonetheless, a command from God. It helps to realize that no matter what has happened to us, Christ has experienced something far worse. We have hurt Jesus more than anybody could have hurt us. And he forgives us for all of it!

Forgiveness is not easy. When we choose not to forgive, we become hard-hearted. It actually keeps us in bondage. The secret? When we forgive, we start to receive healing ourselves. Forgiving someone else actually sets us free. You may have a really good reason for not forgiving someone in your life. Even though it is difficult, don't hesitate to do it. You need to be set free from your anger and begin to heal.

THINK ABOUT IT!

What is difficult for you to forgive? Have you done so anyways?

DAY 334

*I didn't grow up in a Christian household, so I don't want to push what
I believe onto other people because I don't know their journey.
I know where I used to be and where I was. And, I know there were
times when…I don't know for me…I like befriending people and
just being able to understand them and know them one-on-one.*
JOSH SCOGIN (NORMA JEAN, THE CHARIOT, 68)

If you judge people, you have no time to love them.
MOTHER TERESA

*Love each other with genuine affection,
and take delight in honoring each other.*
ROMANS 12:10

*So now I am giving you a new commandment: Love each
other. Just as I have loved you, you should love each other.*
JOHN 13:34

I enjoy talking to people. Everywhere and at any time. Standing in
line at the grocery store or sitting at the coffee shop, I always make it
a point to say hello to the people around me. 95% of the time they
talk back—even in those countries where I am told "no one talks to each
other." My theory is that it's not because they don't want to talk, it is just
that no one wants to start the conversation. So, I initiate it.

I constantly ask God to make me aware of the people around me. So
many of those conversations have resulted in ministry to the individual.
Many of the encounters have surprised me. The person who I ended up
having a conversation with is nothing like what I thought they would be. I
imagine Jesus did this: As he walked along, he looked people in the eyes, and
spoke into their lives and hearts. He touched them with his words in a nonjudgmental, non-threatening way. What a great example to follow. Give his
"agapé" love away! "Just as I have loved you, you should love one another."

THINK ABOUT IT!

*Have you learned to Agapé those around you? Do you
pray to be aware of people during an ordinary day?*

DAY 335

We are representing Almighty GOD here, be worthy to represent Him.
JAYSON SHERLOCK (MORTIFICATION, PARAMAECIUM AND HORDE)

I am in chains now, still preaching this message as God's ambassador.
So pray that I will keep on speaking boldly for him, as I should.
GALATIANS 6:20

As Christians, we are ambassadors of Christ! This applies to all of us, not only to the preacher in church or the musician on stage. In the late Middle Ages, a big part of the church had become very hierarchical. Martin Luther reminded Christians of what the Bible teaches about the royal priesthood of all believers. Every Christian is a "pastor"—not just the man in the pulpit.

This has enormous practical implications! Whatever job you may have, you are a "pastor" in that situation. You are representing Christ when you buy groceries, raise your children, or hang out with your friends. Living your life in front of people is actually one of the best ways to demonstrate your transformation through Christ. When you surrender to God, the Holy Spirit shines his light and hope through you. The people at your job and your friends will notice the difference. When you let people get close to you, they will see you have something different—something out of this world! And they will ask about the hope you have within you.

We really need to invest in the people around us. It's easy to simply surround yourself with Christians. But we have to share life with non-believers as well. Dare to be honest with them about the struggles of life. And when you do, you'll realize they have a lot to offer you as well.

THINK ABOUT IT!

Does your life represent Christ? And are you
investing in healthy relationships with people who
do not share your Christian worldview?

DAY 336

I am shocked that you are turning away so soon from God, who called you to himself through the loving mercy of Christ. You are following a different way that pretends to be the Good News but is not the Good News at all. You are being fooled by those who deliberately twist the truth concerning Christ.
GALATIANS 1:6-7

Many of us were brought up in the church. But not everyone was raised in a church that believed in and practiced grace. Even today, there are churches that teach grace + works = salvation. His grace. Your works. NOT TRUE! You didn't do anything to receive salvation. You didn't earn it. You would not have been able to earn it. He GAVE it to you. It is his free gift. And, like any gift, it is simply yours when you receive it. So the real equation looks like this: GRACE + NOTHING ELSE = SALVATION. Too good to be true? It sure seems like it, doesn't it? But it is true! You are saved by the loving mercy of Jesus Christ. He was hung on a cross for you. He died for you. He rose from the dead for you. And he forgave your sins—past, present, and future. That is his amazing gift for you!

THINK ABOUT IT!

Have you accepted his amazing grace to you?

DAY 337

*But we are looking forward to the new heavens and new earth
he has promised, a world filled with God's righteousness.*
2 PETER 3:13

In the beginning God showed his awesome powers by creating a vastly complex universe. In the end we'll experience that power again as he restores and makes everything new. The Kingdom of God will be complete and without any flaws. God's righteousness will reign. There will be nothing to bring us down, hurt us, or make us angry. Col 3:1 says, "...set your sights on the realities of heaven."

The most amazing thing will be to experience God's presence completely. We can feel God now. The Holy Spirit can bring us joy, if we allow him to work inside of us. This is a feeling you will learn to recognize by experiencing him. It truly is the greatest feeling. But, when we're united with the Father on the new earth, we'll experience it to the fullest! God's holy presence is a scary thing, if we're unrighteous. Hebrews 10:31 says, "It is a terrible thing to fall into the hands of the living God." But by accepting Jesus into our hearts we have the righteousness of Christ! We can stand righteous before our Creator without fear. Through Jesus, we have become family!

Being in perfect union with The Father, The Son, and The Holy Spirit is the greatest thing about being saved. There will be unlimited love, joy, peace, intimacy, beauty, and fellowship. And it'll be everlasting. How amazing and beautiful is the face of God the Father!

THINK ABOUT IT!

Are you looking forward to the righteousness of the Father?

DAY 338

I'm blessed to know adversity and plow through.
DAN SPITZ (ANTHRAX)

Remember those in prison, as if you were there yourself. Remember also those being mistreated, as if you felt their pain in your own bodies.
HEBREW 13:3

L ife can be painful. Sometimes you go through day after day with no hope, praying that things will get better. There are those periods in life when you feel so badly that you would rather die then suffer. And in the midst of these periods, it's difficult to imagine that your life will ever get better. Most of us have gone through at least one period like this.

It is these periods in life that have a tremendous effect on our character. It can take years to recover from the difficulties of our past. Those who have clung to Jesus and gone through these times would agree that they have grown immensely through them. They teach us so much about life and about ourselves. Our experience through times like this are of enormous value, and can be used for the rest of our lives.

If you're in the middle of some difficult times, it's hard to see the light at the end of the tunnel. But, it's important not to view yourself as a victim. Instead, reflect on what you have learned. Use the experience to benefit and counsel others. You will run into people on your journey who desperately need your guidance.

THINK ABOUT IT!
How have difficult times benefited you?

DAY 339

Don't copy the behavior and customs of this world, but let God transform you into a new person by changing the way you think. Then you will learn to know God's will for you, which is good and pleasing and perfect.
ROMANS 12:2

I s Christianity a label or a lifestyle for you? Maybe your parents were Christians, and you simply assume you're a Christian by heredity. Or maybe you call yourself a Christian, but you've never really experienced any actual change in your life. You're losing interest.

Christianity isn't a side-dish you add to the meal of life. Christ becomes your identity, and not just some set of values you find attractive. The Christian life isn't meaningful unless you jump in with both feet! You may not realize Christ is all you need, until he's all you have. Jesus speaks very radically about following him. There's a price for doing so, but the reward is incredible!

If you've accepted Jesus Christ into your life, he has accepted you as his child. Now, begin to understand more of what that means. Grow in your relationship with him. Realize that your whole life has to do with your identity in him. There's an exciting life to be lived as his follower. He will transform you into a new person. God's will for you is certainly good, pleasing, and perfect. Be as extreme in pursuing him as the music you listen to.

THINK ABOUT IT!

Are you a Christian by name, or have you chosen to follow him?

DAY 340

Crushed beneath the heel, fallen serpent your time is short
LYRICS FROM "BY HIS BLOOD" BY BROKEN FLESH

*Because God's children are human beings—made of flesh
and blood—the Son also became flesh and blood. For only
as a human being could he die, and only by dying could he
break the power of the devil, who had the power of death.*
HEBREWS 2:14

The devil made me do it!" That was a classic line from a popular comedian in the 1960's—Flip Wilson. It was his excuse every time he did something wrong. Sadly, it is our excuse too much of the time as well. We attribute a lot to Satan. In fact, I know Christians who probably spend more time thinking about how much Satan is attacking them then they do about how much God has blessed them.

I've got some really good news for you today: SATAN HAS BEEN DEFEATED. Past tense. Old news. It's finished. Satan was defeated at the cross. His only power in your life at this point is to lie. Since he is called "the father of lies," he is pretty good at it! It's his native tongue. The more you know the truth, the easier it is to see what is false. Just another great reason to read the Bible and get to know the heart of God!

THINK ABOUT IT!

*Have you been able to distinguish between
Satan's lies and God's truth?*

DAY 341

If we keep remembering the wrongs which men have done us, we destroy the power of the remembrance of God.
ABBA MACARIUS (DESERT FATHERS)

Make allowance for each other's faults, and forgive anyone who offends you. Remember, the Lord forgave you, so you must forgive others.
COLOSSIANS 3:13

Remember to forget. That is basically the advice of the Desert Fathers. When we focus on the abuse we have suffered in our past, it becomes very difficult to keep our eyes on Jesus. Hebrews 12:2 says, "We do this by keeping our eyes on Jesus, the champion who initiates and perfects our faith." Your faith begins with him and is sustained by him. It is impossible to wipe past events from your memory. In fact, we seem to have instant recollection when it comes to painful memories. It isn't about a simple fleeting memory, but instead playing it over and over in our heads. It's the difference between playing the trailer or the whole movie!

Philippians 4:8 says, "And now, dear brothers and sisters, one final thing. Fix your thoughts on what is true, and honorable, and right, and pure, and lovely, and admirable. Think about things that are excellent and worthy of praise." Great advice. And when you train yourself to think about these things, you limit the space your mind will use to remember that past.

THINK ABOUT IT!

Do you remember to forget?

DAY 342

The Lord gave this message to Jonah son of Amittai: "Get up and go to the great city of Nineveh. Announce my judgment against it because I have seen how wicked its people are."
JONAH 1:1-2

When God called Jonah to go to Nineveh, he fled in the opposite direction. He was trying to escape the Lord so he went on a boat towards Tarshish. A huge storm arose. The sailors found out that it was because of Jonah so they ended up praying to Yahweh, even though they worshipped other gods themselves. After being thrown overboard, swallowed by a big fish, and vomited up on the beach, Jonah finally obeyed the Lord and went to Nineveh. The people of Nineveh (including their king) received his message, and turned away from their wicked path. 120,000 men plus women and children were saved! Did Jonah celebrate? Hardly! He hated the people of Nineveh. He became very angry and complained to the Lord, "That is why I ran away to Tarshish! I knew that you are a merciful and compassionate God, slow to get angry and filled with unfailing love" (Jonah 4:2). He even asked God to kill him! His anger increased when the plant that provided his shade withered. He said, "Death is certainly better than living like this!" (Jonah 4:8).

Jonah was the worst missionary in the history of the world! But God still used him to do mighty things. God can use you no matter how awkward you feel, or whatever you might have done in the past. It may surprise you just how much he is able to use you!

THINK ABOUT IT!

Have you convinced yourself that you don't have what it takes for God to use you?

DAY 343

Expect temptation to your last breath.
ANTHONY THE GREAT

As he was speaking, the teachers of religious law and the Pharisees brought a woman who had been caught in the act of adultery. They put her in front of the crowd, but Jesus stooped down and wrote in the dust with his finger.
JOHN 8:3-9

Have you ever wondered why Jesus bowed his head and wrote in the dust? The Bible doesn't record what he wrote, as it is insignificant to the story. There's probably a very simple explanation. First and foremost, the woman was probably wearing few if any clothes since she was "caught in the act." We are told that Jesus was tempted as we are, so he probably kept himself occupied so as not to be tempted with her nakedness. Then, when everyone had left and the woman had a chance to get dressed, he spoke to her.

When it comes to temptation, we usually have more confidence in ourselves than we should. "Others may not be able to handle it, but I'll be fine. I will just look for a moment, and then I will look away." So, how well is that working for you? This is just one of the lies we tell ourselves. We are not an exception. Jesus didn't even consider himself an exception! In The Lord's Prayer he says, "Pray that you will not give in to temptation" (Luke 22:40). When we look at the temptation, we will certainly fail. When we keep our eyes on Jesus, we will not fall in sin.

THINK ABOUT IT!

Do you consider yourself strong enough to play with temptation without failing?

DAY 344

I wanna tell people that God can really change our lives and he can show us his path of life in abundance, his way of victory.
PETE SANDOVAL (MORBID ANGEL)

The thief's purpose is to steal and kill and destroy.
My purpose is to give them a rich and satisfying life.
JOHN 10:10

Many times over the years I have looked heavenward and asked God why he was making my life so difficult. It seemed like things were spinning out of control, and he didn't seem to be taking things in the direction that I had hoped for. Every one of those times have been a misunderstanding on my part. I have lived enough years to see his handprint on every area of my past. Looking back on things that I actually prayed for, I'm so happy he knew better than I what was actually needed.

This verse in John tells us Satan's purpose: Steal. Kill. Destroy. I am sure you are already aware of that. When Satan pulls his tricks on me, I usually think I have the answers to what will correct the situation. But I don't. God is dedicated to giving you a rich and satisfying life. No one knows better how to correct your situation than he does! As Pete Sandoval says, it's "his way of victory!"

THINK ABOUT IT!

Have you given God permission to direct your life?

DAY 345

We have to pray with our eyes on God, not on the difficulties.
OSWALD CHAMBERS

*"For I know the plans I have for you," says the Lord. "They are plans
for good and not for disaster, to give you a future and a hope."*
JEREMIAH 29:11

Whenever I buy a new (used) car, I begin saving for the next one. It is my goal to save $1,000.00 per year in my car fund. It had been 12 years since I purchased my last car. At the beginning of the year, I needed to take half of the money to use for the homeless ministry. I thought, "My car will just have to last longer!" But it didn't. The repair would have cost thousands of dollars. The value of the car was only $500.00 at that point. So I began to look around. I didn't see anything that would give me the kind of stability I needed. At that price point, there would surely be more problems!

A friend heard about my situation and asked the manager of a car lot to do me a favor. To make a long story short, I drove away with a $14,000.00 car for $6,000.00. I am always surprised when God pulls this kind of stuff off! But I shouldn't be. He has done it my whole life! When I focus on the problems, I only see problems. But when my eyes are on him, and my focus is on the opportunities ahead of me, I SEE the opportunities. It makes all the difference!

THINK ABOUT IT!

Do you focus on the problems or the opportunities in your life?

DAY 346

*All the head knowledge made its way to my
heart and made a big difference.*
JAYSON SHERLOCK
(MORTIFICATION, PARAMAECIUM AND HORDE)

*The purpose of my instruction is that all believers
would be filled with love that comes from a pure
heart, a clear conscience, and genuine faith.*
1 TIMOTHY 1:5

Knowledge is awesome. Learning is an enjoyable activity for many. Wisdom, however, is better! Wisdom takes knowledge and applies it. It goes from the head to the heart. It becomes experience that can be used in a variety of situations in your life. It will be your guide, and will help in guiding others.

Wisdom is the main theme in the book of Proverbs. Wisdom starts with a healthy respect for the Lord. Wisdom is more valuable than gold. A wise person is happy to have someone correct him, instead of becoming angry. Wisdom has a lot to do with character, gentleness, and patience. Does your character reflects this?

How do we get started? James 1:5 says we should ask God for wisdom, who will give it generously. We need to surrender our lives to Him and let Him work in us. The Holy Spirit will give us patience and a tender heart. He will guide us so we can move our knowledge of him from our head to our hearts—from knowledge to wisdom. This is the character we desire. When somebody criticizes you, you'll be able to respond with a tender heart. You'll begin to be excited for the opportunity to grow. Start the process of becoming a person who is wise in whatever situation you might face.

THINK ABOUT IT!

*Are you able to not just know what's right, but also apply
what you know differently under different circumstances?*

DAY 347

*But now you are free from the power of sin and have
become slaves of God. Now you do those things
that lead to holiness and result in eternal life.*
ROMANS 6:22

"Christianity is a relationship, and not a religion." That may seem like a cliché. It is, however, profoundly true! We often forget the consequences of it. When Jesus came to earth, he taught a lot about living a moral life. The Bible teaches us how to live life, how to live in fellowship with each other, and how to take care of those less fortunate than we are. All of this is very important. But don't forget the reason he died on the cross for us.

What makes Christianity a relationship rather than a religion? It's that God looks at us and says, "I don't want your pious worship, your money, or your good deeds. I want YOU!" He desires to spend eternity with you. The mighty Creator of this universe has His eye on you. Now, this doesn't mean that good deeds and a good moral life aren't important. It would be a giant disappointment if the all-knowing Creator didn't give us some helpful guidelines to live by. But we must not lose focus on our relationship with God. This relationship is the core of our faith.

THINK ABOUT IT!

*If you look away from your moral lifestyle and just look
at your relationship with Him, do you really know
Him? Today is a good day to enjoy being His child
and spending time with your Heavenly Father!*

DAY 348

All our own reasoning will only keep us in uncertainty, not security.
ULF CHRISTIANSSON (JERUSALEM)

For God has not given us a spirit of fear and timidity,
but of power, love, and self-discipline.
2 TIMOTHY 1:7

There are no absolutes. Faith is whatever you want it to be. You simply have to create your own destiny." Wisdom? Not at all! How hopeless! The older you get, the more you'll realize how silly it is to actually think you can create your own destiny. Mankind longs for absolutes. We want something that we can believe in. We want to be able to count on someone—especially in a higher power than ourselves. We desire security! How exciting to know that God has given us that security! POWER. LOVE. SELF-DISCIPLINE. Isn't that what we are all looking for?

While the world around us is drowning in uncertainty, God gives us his security! It's a relief to know that I am not in charge of my own destiny. I already realize I need help! I need to know there are absolutes, otherwise I feel aimless and out of control. I also need something to place my faith in. It's not enough to have "faith in my faith." The object of your faith is Jesus Christ. Now THAT'S security!

THINK ABOUT IT!

Are you still trying to create your own absolutes, faith and destiny?

DAY 349

*I know as a teenager that was very young in my faith, having
music that I could relate to and that glorified God was really
important and made me feel like I was not alone in my faith.*
BRUCE FITZHUGH (LIVING SACRIFICE)

*Paul stayed in Corinth for some time after that, then said good-
bye to the brothers and sisters and went to nearby Cenchrea...
Then he set sail for Syria, taking Priscilla and Aquila with him.*
ACTS 18:18

I live in the "belt buckle of the Bible belt." Here in Nashville, Tennessee faith in God is important to most of us. But in many parts of the world, that isn't true. It's harder to realize how many brothers and sisters in Christ are actually out there. You may find yourself being the only Christian in your school or at work. In fact, you might not even know very many Christians, or Christian metalheads for that matter! It's easy feeling pretty much alone following Christ since many are used to being a minority.

It can be an encouragement to see how many Christians there really are in other parts of the world. Enormous awakenings are going on in places like China and the Middle East. If you look around, you will find revival happening all over the world. Christianity is by far the largest in the world. These are exciting times to be alive!

Do you sometimes get bummed out being one of the few Christians in your location? When you consider the larger picture, you are far from being alone! You have brothers and sisters in Christ everywhere around the world. And remember: in the beginning of Acts there were only a very few Christians, and they ended up changing the world!

THINK ABOUT IT!

*Are you aware that there are millions of Christians
around the world worshipping Jesus?*

DAY 350

*We are mirrors whose brightness is wholly derived
from the sun that shines upon us*
C S LEWIS

*For God, who said, "Let there be light in the darkness," has
made this light shine in our hearts so we could know the
glory of God that is seen in the face of Jesus Christ.*
2 CORINTHIANS 4:6

The moon shines enough to bring light to the earth. But the moon has no light on its own. It simply reflects the light of the sun. Still, it shines brightly and beautifully. The same is true for Christians. We cannot shine for the world on our own. We're totally depended on the light of Christ! He's the one who shines through us. And only by letting him shine are we able to be lights for the world.

As the light of the world, Christ stepped down into the darkness of a sick and sinful earth. Now, because of his work here on earth, our citizenship is in Heaven. The Bible tells us that we have already passed from death to life! Now, he calls us to bring light to the world as he did. We're united with Christ, and he'll shine through us as we go in to all the corners of the earth. By growing in our relationship with him, we'll become a stronger flame. We'll be more dependent on him, and therefore he'll be able to shine brighter through us.

Surrender is important. We need to do it every day. By surrendering we give up our own agenda and let go of our negative emotions. We allow the Holy Spirit to do whatever he wants to do inside of us. Christ is now in charge of our identity. Allow him to do as he pleases, and he'll shine brightly through you. The world desperately needs light. Let him shine through you!

THINK ABOUT IT!

Do you believe Christ can shine brightly through your life?

DAY 351

D o you enjoy listening to yourself speak? Maybe it's time to zip it! It's great spending time with people you can learn from. You find yourself looking forward to seeing them again. But, what about those people who enjoy hearing themselves speak? You know the type. They continue to interrupt you with their own stories and experiences. Their attitude is so frustrating you can't wait to leave, hoping to never encounter them again!

Concentrate more on listening than speaking. It's a great joy to teach, but it's an even greater joy to learn! If you feel like you have something to offer in a conversation, start by listening carefully so you'll understand the tone of the conversation. It's a great joy for others to have someone who is sincerely interested in what they have to say. When you do this, others will often listen with the same desire to your words. You must not consider your own voice more important than others. If you think you have wiser things to say than others do, you are being unwise, since the wise listen.

THINK ABOUT IT!

Do you spend more energy listening than talking?

DAY 352

I'm always there for people if they need prayer and definitely have been approached several times by people who are like "Hey, I don't believe what you believe, but there's some crazy stuff going on right now." So, I like that, when it's very natural rather than trying to sell something."

JOSH SCOGIN (NORMA JEAN, THE CHARIOT, 68)

Instead, you must worship Christ as Lord of your life. And if someone asks about your hope as a believer, always be ready to explain it. But do this in a gentle and respectful way.

1 PETER 3:15-16

Sad. Worthless. Hopeless. The National Center for Health Statistics, a federal government agency, publishes an annual survey. The last one that was made public was done in 2012. People were asked: "Do you feel 'sadness' all of the time or some of the time? 10.1 percent of the random sample answered affirmatively. That's one in ten people who are sad more or less frequently. In other words, in a concert with a hundred people, ten of them will be sad. They also asked: "Do you experience 'hopelessness?'" 6.1 percent said they did. "How about 'worthlessness?'" 5.1 percent affirmed that they felt worthless.

There are many people out there who really need what you have. Slow down. Live your life in front of people. Allow them to ask you questions about the hope you have within you. Genuinely care about them and respond, "…in a gentle and respectful way." We know the way to constant joy, worth, and hope during even the toughest circumstances of life. That needs to be shared!

THINK ABOUT IT!

Are you ready to explain to anyone who asks about the hope you have within you?

DAY 353

Faithless is he that says farewell when the road darkens.
J. R. R. TOLKIEN

*He gives power to the weak and strength to the powerless.
Even youths will become weak and tired, and young men
will fall in exhaustion. But those who trust in the Lord will find
new strength. They will soar high on wings like eagles. They
will run and not grow weary. They will walk and not faint.*
ISAIAH 40:29-31

Where God guides, he provides. This simple saying is also the biggest test! Do we trust the Lord or ourselves? It's easy to trust yourself when you are trying to achieve financial security. What do you do, though, when God calls you into seemingly insecure places? Those are the times it gets more difficult to trust him. And actually, it's kind of silly when you think about it. We find it easier to trust ourselves rather than trusting the almighty God.

We need to learn to listen to God's voice. It's important that you do not misunderstand where God is calling you to, since God only promises to provide where he guides. Listen carefully. Not only is a mistake in this area discouraging to you, it's also discouraging for others. If we say God called us to something, we need to demonstrate to ourselves and to others his power to provide.

When he actually calls, don't hesitate. He has everything under control even though he may only reveal part of the journey to you. It also doesn't mean that everything will go smoothly and the road will be easy. On the contrary; your faith will probably be stretched. You'll have to step out of your comfort-zone. Just remember: God never panics. He will take care of you. Even when the goal may seem far away, he has you in his hands.

THINK ABOUT IT!

Do you believe "where God guides, he provides?"

DAY 354

*Sure, I go through trials every day, but God helps
me and speaks to me in many different ways.*
BRIAN "HEAD" WELCH (KORN)

*Dear brothers and sisters, when troubles of any kind come
your way, consider it an opportunity for great joy. For you
know that when your faith is tested, your endurance has a
chance to grow. So let it grow, for when your endurance is fully
developed, you will be perfect and complete, needing nothing.*

JAMES 1:2-4

Becoming a Christian means that you no longer struggle with sin or temptation, right? You wish! The Bible actually promises trials. In the verse above it doesn't say "IF" troubles come it says "WHEN" they come. Expect it! Trials are just a part of life. But this is actually where it gets exciting! Those trials are actually "an opportunity for great joy." Wait what?

The end result of a trial is being "perfect, complete, and needing nothing." God is right there every step of the way. Guiding us. Coaching us. Bringing us to that point where we have learned and grown from the trial. None of us enjoy the process. In fact, most of the time I look to Heaven and ask God why he would allow such horrible things to happen to me! But when I look back later, I realize that he did just as he promised he would do—and I am a stronger person and a more thankful Christian as a result.

THINK ABOUT IT!

*Have you considered your trials an opportunity for great
joy since you know the outcome will be your maturity?*

DAY 355

If there were no God, there would be no atheists.

G K CHESTERTON

When I look at the night sky and see the work of your fingers— the moon and the stars you set in place— what are mere mortals that you should think about them, human beings that you should care for them?

PSALMS 8:3-4

Modern astronomy reveals some truly amazing things about the improbability of the universe and the existence of life. The improbabilities are so extreme that some estimate it to be less than 1 in 10282 (282 zeros in a row!). Mathematically, there's simply no chance that life could occur without some extremely intelligent designer behind it.

When facing the scientific facts, it's almost impossible to deny a creator. When you take the question of how it all started into account, a creator seems even more obvious. Nothing comes out of nothing. There must have been something or someone that caused it all. In atheism, there's no cause for the universe to come into existence. And even if there was, it would be so extremely improbable that it would lead to intelligent life. It barely counts as a serious worldview. As Christians, we can have great confidence in the existence of our Creator. The Biblical description fits right on the money with what modern science reveals to us. The best part is this: God created all of this for you! The foundation of his handiwork was to bless you, and give you an amazing place to live. Again, God's desire is to have a relationship with you. He has gone a long way to make it happen!

THINK ABOUT IT!

Have you considered how amazing it is that life even exists?

DAY 356

Follow my advice, my son; always treasure my commands.
Obey my commands and live! Guard my instructions
as you guard your own eyes. Tie them on your fingers
as a reminder. Write them deep within your heart.
PROVERBS 7:1-3

Becoming a good student of theology doesn't matter...unless you get to know God whom theology is all about. Knowing the commandments without knowing God makes them seem boring and lifeless. When we know God, that changes everything! We understand he wants the best for us. We understand how his commandments help us truly live. It is because he cares for us that he gives us guidelines on living a successful life. Any good parent knows that love is the motivation for setting limits for their children. The unloving parent lets their child do things that will end up harming them.

Your goal should always be to know God better every day. As you grow in your relationship with him you'll find yourself getting to know him more intimately. The burdens on his heart will become your burdens as well. You will find yourself becoming more like Christ, who obeyed God in everything. And, as a result, our eternity was forever changed!

THINK ABOUT IT!

How does knowing your Creator change
your view on his commandments?

DAY 357

*But really, this is what I do! It's the music that I love and
it's what I believe and that's just how it comes out.*
MATT SMITH (THEOCRACY)

*A good person produces good things from the treasury of a good
heart, and an evil person produces evil things from the treasury
of an evil heart. What you say flows from what is in your heart.*
LUKE 6:45

Create in me a clean heart, O God. Renew a loyal spirit within me.
PSALM 51:10

I have friends who are experts at sarcasm. They are constantly making very cutting remarks, followed by "just kidding!" It gets old. And it makes me wonder just how many times they are really "just kidding?" When our minds automatically go to negative, belittling remarks, it speaks to where our hearts are at. The Bible tells us to pay attention to how we conduct ourselves. Not just because people are watching, but because it reflects the depths of our relationship with God.

God wants to renew your mind and your spirit. He knows when that happens your heart and your mouth will reflect the change. How do we make it happen? You don't have the power to change your heart. But the Holy Spirit does. That is why Jesus promised he would send the Holy Spirit (John 7:37-39), and he would create the change we all needed. Are you tired of what is coming out of your mouth? Ask God to make you aware of it, and then invite the Holy Spirit to instigate a change. As you allow him to work, you'll be amazed at what comes out!

THINK ABOUT IT!
What is coming out of your mouth?

DAY 358

*Human fellowship can go to great lengths, but not all
the way. Fellowship with God can go to all lengths.*
OSWALD CHAMBERS

*Dear friend, you are being faithful to God when you care for the
traveling teachers who pass through, even though they are strangers
to you. They have told the church here of your loving friendship.*
3 JOHN 5-6

Friendships can be simple, or messy and complex. When dealing with your closest friends it's important for both to agree on the nature of the friendship. We all need those special friends who we're accountable to. Friends who we can share intimate and painful details of our lives with. People who have taken the time to get to know and have earned our trust. These relationships are worth their weight in gold!

A friendship will never be perfect since people are involved. But a solid and close friendship goes a long way in life. Support and encouragement from a good friend can help in good and bad times. Sharing spiritual matters can help in your walk with the Lord. During a time of frustration towards God, a friend can remind us of the times the Lord has come through for us. Make sure you have at least one of these kinds of friends that you can count on. Real friendship shares the good, the bad, and the ugly. Real friendship builds each other up and carries each other's burdens.

THINK ABOUT IT!

*How do you and your friends benefit from
each other spiritually and in life?*

DAY 359

Isaac Newton was one of the greatest scientists the world has ever known. When commenting about his work he said, "If I have seen further than others, it is by standing upon the shoulders of giants." The same is true for us today. We have this opinion that people were less intelligent 3,000 years ago. This is absolutely not true. Some of the wisest writings have come from that era. Today, we simply have more information available.

This should humble us. Whatever knowledge we have obtained was gained from someone else. We have the privilege of discussing theology today. In the past, that may have resulted in death. The Christian metal community is frustrated from time to time with the way the church has treated us, and rightly so. But we forget that it has also helped bring our life saving faith to us! They may have made some mistakes, but they taught us about Jesus. It may be time to both forgive them and thank them!

Let someone who's had a great influence on your walk with the Lord know how grateful you are. Send them a text or say it to their face today. It'll be encouraging for them to hear.

THINK ABOUT IT!

*Do you respect your elders, even though they
may have made mistakes that hurt you?*

DAY 360

We usually know what we can do, but temptation shows us who we are.
THOMAS A KEMPIS

The temptations in your life are no different from what others experience. And God is faithful. He will not allow the temptation to be more than you can stand. When you are tempted, he will show you a way out so that you can endure.
1 CORINTHIANS 10:13

And remember, when you are being tempted, do not say, "God is tempting me." God is never tempted to do wrong, and he never tempts anyone else. Temptation comes from our own desires, which entice us and drag us away. These desires give birth to sinful actions. And when sin is allowed to grow, it gives birth to death.
JAMES 1:13-15

We are all tempted to do things that we shouldn't do. Many people fall under the weight of it. But God promises you that "...he will show you a way out so that you can endure." You see, none of us can use the excuse that the temptation was just too much for us. Some temptations are powerful, and our knees may get weak while we try to stand, but God asks us to persevere. And if we fail, he asks us to try again next time.

Just remember the process here in James 1:13-15. The temptation begins with our own desires. Don't be surprised by them. When you entertain them, you are dragged away and enticed by them. At this point, it give birth to a sinful action. Remember to "fight the battle before the battle." Be prepared for the temptation before it happens. You know yourself and your desires. They are not a surprise! If you prepare yourself for the next time, and rehearse what you will do at the moment it happens, you are in a much better position to fight it off!

THINK ABOUT IT!

How can you "fight the battle before the battle" in the areas you are tempted in?

DAY 361

*Philip ran over and heard the man reading from the prophet Isaiah.
Philip asked, "Do you understand what you are reading?" The
man replied, "How can I, unless someone instructs me?" And
he urged Philip to come up into the carriage and sit with him.*
ACTS 8:30-31

Discussing theology can be an awesome thing. There certainly have been many extremely important debates throughout the history of the church. You can learn a lot from discussions with a person who comes from a different tradition than you. But unfortunately there are many people who just want to argue for the sake of arguing. These kind of debates aren't healthy, especially on social media. We often feel like other people just aren't as smart as we are, and that we are superior in our abilities to reason.

We need to check our own character. Are you willing to learn? Are you willing to change your position when faced with a better position? If we are honest with ourselves, this is actually difficult. We have to get rid of our ego because it's important to acquiring a teachable spirit of learning. If we want to teach others, we have to become students ourselves. We don't have all the answers. The more we learn, the more we realize how many questions we yet have to answer!

Are you the kind of person who creates fruitful conversations? Do you make sure that each of you benefits from the discussion? Do you also have input in your life from people who are older and more experienced than you? Titus 2:4-6 talks about the importance of the young being taught by the old. Instead of getting into a heated argument with someone, try learning from them as well. Help to create conversations that will be beneficial for the person you are chatting with, but also for yourself as well.

THINK ABOUT IT!

*When debating, do both you and the other
person leave feeling happy and enriched?*

DAY 362

We will not be influenced when people try to trick us with lies so clever they sound like the truth. Instead, we will speak the truth in love.

GALATIANS 4:14-15

Are you wise in your own eyes? It's difficult to be humble when you are always right, isn't it? None of us are perfect. But there are times when we actually have something wise to share with others. When we deal with friends who have other opinions, we need to use wisdom when facing ethical dilemmas. We can't hate the sin, love the sinner in practice. We can't draw a sharp line as most people see their actions as part of their identity. If we want to influence their lives, we must not antagonize them. If they ask for our views, we can answer them in a nonjudgmental way. But we cannot correct them to their face unprovoked and expect them to listen to us.

To have influence, we need to invest time with people. As they get to know you, they'll also get to know your ethical opinions. When this happens, there's no need to correct them when they do something you disagree with. It's not your job to act as moral police.

The bottom line is this: we need to care more about people! God cares deeply for every soul. If we are to reflect his image, we need to do the same. Earning the right to speak into someone's life takes investing in them: doing what they enjoy, sharing about your own struggles, and being brutally honest. They are people, not projects. We must care for them and love them deeply and fully!

THINK ABOUT IT!

Have you earned the right to influence someone?

DAY 363

What do I want to achieve with Theocracy? Whatever God will allow. I don't dare try to predict the future. I just want to continue to give my very best and pray that God blesses it.
MATT SMITH (THEOCRACY)

Work willingly at whatever you do, as though you were working for the Lord rather than for people. Remember that the Lord will give you an inheritance as your reward, and that the Master you are serving is Christ.
COLOSSIANS 3:23-24

I ts been said, "Choose a job you love, and you will never have to work a day in your life." That has certainly been true for me! Although there are aspects of what I do that I certainly don't enjoy, I have really loved working with Christian Rock and Heavy Metal all these years! When you feel passionate about what you are doing, your enthusiasm and energy level is different. I believe this is a foundation for happiness in life.

Find out what God has given you a passion and a calling to do. It is some of the most important information you can attain in life. Matt Smith loves his music. Besides being a good friend, I have watched him many times in concert. He makes you "feel" his music. His passion for it oozes from the performance, and the crowd is electrified. You may not be a great singer armed with a microphone on a Metal stage, but you can have an electrifying impact simply doing what you are passionate about.

THINK ABOUT IT!
Have you discovered what you are passionate about?

DAY 364

My life is dedicated to follow Christ.
ALICE COOPER

At this point many of his disciples turned away and deserted him.
JOHN 6:66

People loved it when Jesus did "tricks" in front of them. In this Scripture, we encounter a group of people who have witnessed some truly amazing things: the feeding of the five thousand. Besides that, they had also heard about Jesus walking on the water. But after Jesus had told them of the consequences of following him, things just started getting a bit too difficult, which resulted in some people turning away—verse 666 (6:66).

The sacrifices we make as Christians look very different around the world. Some of us may have it fairly easy. We might get teased a bit in school. Or maybe criticized for giving money to the poor or the church. Still others might find it odd that we may not party as hard as they do. Some of this criticism may even come from other Christians. We may look a bit different, or listen to a different style of music. Throughout the history of the church, there have been many who have sacrificed their lives for their beliefs. Many are still doing it today. What an admirable faith!

In the two following verses, Jesus turns to the twelve disciples and asks if they're also going to leave. On behalf of the disciples, Peter answers, "Lord, to whom would we go? You have the words that give eternal life." Even though it might become difficult for them, they had no one else to follow. They were already in the presence of the one who could offer them real, everlasting life. And they understood that this was much more valuable than anything else. Even though they went through sufferings in their earthly life, they wouldn't change it for anything else. They knew, in the end, they would inherit the Kingdom of God.

THINK ABOUT IT!

Do you know someone who has stopped following Jesus? They may need a gentle reminder from you that Jesus loves them and his Kingdom awaits!

DAY 365

Hear me declare with boldness. I am a Christian.
POLYCARP

For God has not given us a spirit of fear and timidity,
but of power, love, and self-discipline.
2 TIMOTHY 1:7

I was 16 years old. It was before Christian bumper stickers were popular. I made a sign for the back window of my car that read, "JESUS LOVES YOU!" It was a bold statement in those days. People in my town were not very open about their faith. As I was standing in line at the local fast food restaurant, a young guy came up to me and said, "Is that your car with the religious sign in the window?" I replied proudly, "Yes, it is!" "Here's what I think about that," he replied as he punched me in the nose.

I knew my nose was broken so I drove myself to the hospital to have it put back in place. The procedure was quite painful. I kept reminding myself that I had been a martyr for my faith. A few years went by, and I was invited by a friend to his birthday party. When I walked in the door, I recognized the guy who had broken my nose. He came over and introduced himself. I informed him that we had met before. "You actually broke my nose a few years ago because of the sign in my back window."

A huge smile came across his face. "I have prayed that I would meet you one day. I was running from God, and he was trying to get my attention. I told him to leave me alone, and then I saw the sign on your car. It made me so angry that I took it out on you. But your words are what turned me around." Words? I didn't remember saying anything to him! "You said, 'Jesus loves you, man' and then you drove off." You never know how God is going to use you. Be bold!

THINK ABOUT IT!

Have you asked God to give you boldness in your faith?

BIBLIOGRAPHY

Day 1: Duncan, Ryan. "20 Wise Quotes from G.K. Chesterton." *Crosswalk.com*. Salem Web Network, 05 June 2015.

Day 2: Grayson, and Adrian. "Josh Scogin of '68 Interview 5.5.2014." *SkullyServes.com*, 25 May 2014.

Day 3: Calvin, John. "Calvin Quotes." *Calvinquotes.com*.

Day 5: Metal Bible, Page 4. Comp. Jonsson, Johannes. *Bible for the Nations*.

Day 6: Chambers, Oswald. "18 Powerful Quotes from Oswald Chambers." *ChristianQuotes.info*.

Day 7: Wycliffe, John. "Top 19 quotes by John Wycliffe." *A-Z Quotes.com*.

Day 8: Case, James "Uncle NecRo." "Interview: BLOODGOOD." *Confessions Of A Christian Freak. Wordpress*, 29 Oct. 2013.

Day 9: Metal Bible, Page 7. Comp. Jonsson, Johannes. *Bible for the Nations*.

Day 10: Aquinas, Thomas. "Thomas Aquinas quotes." *A-Z Quotes.com*.

Day 11: Of Assisi, Francis. "Francis of Assisi Quotes." *BrainyQuote.com*.

Day 12: Saint Augustine. "50 Powerful Quotes by Saint Augustine." *Quote Sigma.com*, 27 Feb. 2015.

Day 13: Knox, John. "13 John Knox Quotes." *ChristianQuotes.info*.

Day 14: Metal Bible, Page 18.

Day 16: Metal Bible, Page 29

Day 17: Arvizu, Reginald "FIEDLY." "KORN's FIELDY Says His Encounter With Jesus Christ Made Him Easier To Get Along With." *blabbermouth.net*, 16 Sept. 2016.

Day 18: Mabee, Justin. "Impending Doom." *HM Magazine.com*, 6 Nov. 2013.

Day 19: Metal Bible, Page 34. Comp. Jonsson, Johannes. *Bible for the Nations*.

Day 21: Sandoval, Pedro "Pete." "Former MORBID ANGEL Drummer PETE SANDOVAL: How 'I Fell In Love With God'." *Blabbermouth.net*. Ed. Andrew Haug., 26 Mar. 2015.

Day 22: Metal Bible, Page 23. Comp. Jonsson, Johannes. *Bible for the Nations*.

Day 23: Downey, Ryan J. "We Need People to Step up and Take Personal Responsibility." *Altpress.com*, 13 Feb. 2014.

Day 24: Scogin, Josh. "Interview with The Chariot." *TheChronicle.com.au.*, 22 Apr. 2011.

Day 25: Duncan, Ryan. "20 Wise Quotes from G.K. Chesterton." *Crosswalk.com*. Salem Web Network, 05 June 2015.

Day 27: Lewis, C. S. "C. S. Lewis Quotes." *A-Z Quotes.com*.

Day 31: ArttieTHE1manparty. "TALKIN' TRASH WITH....Rex Carroll of Whitecross / King James!" *Glitter2Gutter.blogspot.se*, 23 Jun 2015.

Day 32: Case, James "Uncle NecRo." "Interview: BLOODGOOD." *Confessions Of A Christian Freak. Wordpress*, 29 Oct. 2013.

Day 33: Downey, Ryan J. "We Need People to Step up and Take Personal Responsibility." *Altpress.com*, 13 Feb. 2014.

Day 34: Metal Bible, Page 27. Comp. Jonsson, Johannes. *Bible for the Nations.*

Day 35: Arvizu, Reginald "FIEDLY." "KORN's FIELDY Says His Encounter With Jesus Christ Made Him Easier To Get Along With." *blabbermouth.net*, 16 Sept. 2016.

Day 36: Calvin, John. "Calvin Quotes." *Calvinquotes.com*. Page 2

Day 38: Rosén, Simon "Pilgrim." "Interview, Crimson Moonlight." *666metal.com*, 24 Feb. 2006

Day 39: Lewis, C. S. "C. S. Lewis Quotes." *A-Z Quotes.com.*

Day 41: Aquinas, Thomas. "56 Powerful Quotes by Thomas Aquinas." *Quote Sigma.com*, 13 Mar. 2015.

Day 42: Metal Bible, Page 37. Comp. Jonsson, Johannes. *Bible for the Nations.*

Day 43: Knox, John. "13 John Knox Quotes." *ChristianQuotes.info.*

Day 44: Saint Augustine. "50 Powerful Quotes by Saint Augustine." *Quote Sigma.com*, 27 Feb. 2015.

Day 46: Mabee, Justin. "Impending Doom." *HM Magazine.com*, 6 Nov. 2013.

Day 47: Downey, Ryan J. "We Need People to Step up and Take Personal Responsibility." *Altpress.com*, 13 Feb. 2014.

Day 48: Sandoval, Pedro "Pete." "Former MORBID ANGEL Drummer PETE SANDOVAL: How 'I Fell In Love With God'." *Blabbermouth.net*. Ed. Andrew Haug., 26 Mar. 2015.

Day 49: Branson, Tim. "Korn Bassist Fieldy on the Christian Life." *CBN.com—The Christian Broadcasting Network*, 700 Club producer, 17 Sept. 2013.

Day 50: Arvizu, Reginald "FIEDLY." "KORN's FIELDY Says His Encounter With Jesus Christ Made Him Easier To Get Along With." *blabbermouth.net*, 16 Sept. 2016.

Day 51: Christian Metal Fellowship. "Interview with Jayson Sherlock. " *Christianmetalfellowship. blogspot.se*, 15 Oct. 2009.

Day 52: Metal Bible, Page 4. Comp. Jonsson, Johannes. *Bible for the Nations.*

Day 53: Ultimate Metal. "Crimson Moonlight—At Their Most Brutal." *Ultimate Metal—Heavy Metal Forum and Community*, 15 May 2005.

Day 54: Case, James "Uncle NecRo." "Interview: BLOODGOOD." *Confessions Of A Christian Freak. Wordpress*, 29 Oct. 2013.

Day 55: Sandoval, Pedro "Pete." "Former MORBID ANGEL Drummer PETE SANDOVAL: How 'I Fell In Love With God'." *Blabbermouth.net*. Ed. Andrew Haug., 26 Mar. 2015.

Day 56: Metal Bible, Page 19. Comp. Jonsson, Johannes. *Bible for the Nations.*

Day 57: Mabee, Justin. "Impending Doom." *HM Magazine.com*, 6 Nov. 2013.

Day 58: Luther, Martin. "18 Martin Luther Quotes That Still Ring True." *RELEVANT Magazine. com*, 31 Oct. 2017.

Day 59: Richardson, James. "Quotes from the Early Church Fathers: On the Trinity." *Apostles Creed.org*, 18 Mar. 2015.

Day 60: Coles, Mike. "Interview with Eric Clayton of Saviour Machine." *Adkoi.com/theoutcast*, 28 Dec. 1998.

Day 63: Ramanand, Liz. "W.A.S.P. Frontman Blackie Lawless Delves Deep Into His Faith + New Album 'Golgotha'." *Ultimate Classic Rock.com*, 26 Sept. 2015.

Day 67: Metal Bible, Page 29. Comp. Jonsson, Johannes. *Bible for the Nations*.

Day 71: Downey, Ryan J. "We Need People to Step up and Take Personal Responsibility." *Altpress.com*, 13 Feb. 2014.

Day 72: Metal Bible, Page 39. Comp. Jonsson, Johannes. *Bible for the Nations*.

Day 75: Carlsen, Les. "Frontman, Lead vocals—Biography." Bloodgoodband.com.

Day 76: Arvizu, Reginald "FIEDLY." "KORN's FIEDLY Says His Encounter With Jesus Christ Made Him Easier To Get Along With." *blabbermouth.net*, 16 Sept. 2016.

Day 77: Metal Bible, Page 7. Comp. Jonsson, Johannes. *Bible for the Nations*.

Day 78: Costes, Judea. "INTERVIEW WITH RYAN CLARK OF DEMON HUNTER." *Rock Edition.com*, 13 Apr. 2012.

Day 79: Aquinas, Thomas. "56 Powerful Quotes by Thomas Aquinas." *Quote Sigma.com*, 13 Mar. 2015.

Day 80: Narciso, Isaiah. "American Rock Star Legend Alice Cooper Opens Up about His Christian Faith." *The Gospel Herald.com*, 01 Jan. 2015.

Day 81: Ramanand, Liz. "W.A.S.P. Frontman Blackie Lawless Delves Deep Into His Faith + New Album 'Golgotha'." *Ultimate Classic Rock.com*, 26 Sept. 2015.

Day 82: Sandoval, Pedro "Pete." "Former MORBID ANGEL Drummer PETE SANDOVAL: How 'I Fell In Love With God'." *Blabbermouth.net*. Ed. Andrew Haug., 26 Mar. 2015.

Day 85: Calvin, John. "Calvin Quotes." *Calvinquotes.com*.

Day 86: Luther, Martin. "18 Martin Luther Quotes That Still Ring True." *RELEVANT Magazine. com*, 31 Oct. 2017.

Day 87: Bonhoeffer, Dietrich. "37 Dietrich Bonhoeffer Quotes." *ChristianQuotes.info*.

Day 88: Metal Bible, Page 25. Comp. Jonsson, Johannes. *Bible for the Nations*.

Day 89: Mabee, Justin. "Impending Doom." *HM Magazine.com*, 6 Nov. 2013.

Day 92: Coles, Mike. "Interview with Eric Clayton of Saviour Machine." *Adkoi.com/theoutcast*, 28 Dec. 1998.

Day 93: Metal Bible, Page 27. Comp. Jonsson, Johannes. *Bible for the Nations*.

Day 95: Good Reads. "Quotes about Denominations." *Goodreads.com*.

Day 96: D., Jonni. "The Big Über Rock Interview: Ryan Clark (Demon Hunter)." *Uberrock. co.uk*, 30 Apr. 2017.

Day 98: Swindoll, Charles R. "Top 10 Charles R. Swindoll quotes." *Brainyquote.com*.

Day 99: Downey, Ryan J. "We Need People to Step up and Take Personal Responsibility." *Altpress.com*, 13 Feb. 2014.

Day 100: Bonhoeffer, Dietrich. "37 Dietrich Bonhoeffer Quotes." *ChristianQuotes.info.*

Day 101: Metal Bible, Pages 4 and 5. Comp. Jonsson, Johannes. *Bible for the Nations.*

Day 102: Spurgeon, Charles. "100 of the Best Charles Spurgeon Quotes." *Leadership Resources. org*, 22 Aug. 2014.

Day 103: Sandoval, Pedro "Pete." "Former MORBID ANGEL Drummer PETE SANDOVAL: How 'I Fell In Love With God'." *Blabbermouth.net.* Ed. Andrew Haug., 26 Mar. 2015.

Day 104: Carlsen, Les. "Frontman, Lead vocals—Biography." Bloodgoodband.com.

Day 105: Welch, Brian "Head." "With my eyes wide open: miracles and mistakes on my way back to KoRn." Publisher: Thomas Nelson, Ref. Page 202, 31 Oct. 2015.

Day 107: Metal Bible, Page 39. Comp. Jonsson, Johannes. *Bible for the Nations.*

Day 108: Metal Bible, Page 19. Comp. Jonsson, Johannes. *Bible for the Nations.*

Day 111: Franciscan Friars Of The Renewal. "Saint Quote of the Day Archive." *Cfr-newmexico. com*—San Juan Diego Friary., 5 Nov. 2010.

Day 112: Metal Bible, Page 7. Comp. Jonsson, Johannes. *Bible for the Nations.*

Day 114: Metal Bible, Page 39. Comp. Jonsson, Johannes. *Bible for the Nations.*

Day 118: Coles, Mike. "Interview with Eric Clayton of Saviour Machine." *Adkoi.com/theoutcast*, 28 Dec. 1998.

Day 123: Darlington, Tracy. "Disciple Interview: Kevin Young." *Titletrakk.com.*

Day 124: Coles, Mike. "Interview with Tourniquet." *Adkoi.com/theoutcast*, 25 Jul. 1998.

Day 127: Sandoval, Pedro "Pete." "Former MORBID ANGEL Drummer PETE SANDOVAL: How 'I Fell In Love With God'." *Blabbermouth.net.* Ed. Andrew Haug., 26 Mar. 2015.

Day 128: Aquinas, Thomas. "56 Powerful Quotes by Thomas Aquinas." *Quote Sigma.com*, 13 Mar. 2015.

Day 129: Lewis, C. S. "C. S. Lewis Quotes." *A-Z Quotes.com.*

Day 130: Darlington, Tracy. "Disciple Interview: Kevin Young." *Titletrakk.com.*

Day 131: Bonhoeffer, Dietrich. "37 Dietrich Bonhoeffer Quotes." *ChristianQuotes.info.*

Day 132: Spurgeon, Charles. "100 of the Best Charles Spurgeon Quotes." *Leadership Resources. org*, 22 Aug. 2014.

Day 133: Metal Bible, Page 85. Comp. Jonsson, Johannes. *Bible for the Nations.*

Day 134: Ambrose. "Ambrose Quotes." *A-Z Quotes.com.*

Day 135: A Kempis, Thomas. "Thomas a Kempis Quotes." *Brainyquote.com.*

Day 136: Swindoll, Charles R. "Top 10 Charles R. Swindoll quotes." *Brainyquote.com.*

Day 137: Barth, Karl. "Karl Barth Quotes." *Brainyquote.com.*

Day 138: Kierkegaard, Soren. "Soren Kierkegaard Quotes." *Brainyquote.com.*

Day 141: Sandoval, Pedro "Pete." "Former MORBID ANGEL Drummer PETE SANDOVAL: How 'I Fell In Love With God'." *Blabbermouth.net*. Ed. Andrew Haug., 26 Mar. 2015.

Day 142: Coles, Mike. "Interview with Tourniquet." *Adkoi.com/theoutcast*, 25 Jul. 1998.

Day 143: Branson, Tim. "Korn Bassist Fieldy on the Christian Life." *CBN.com—The Christian Broadcasting Network*, 700 Club producer, 17 Sept. 2013.

Day 144: Metal Bible, Page 97. Comp. Jonsson, Johannes. *Bible for the Nations*.

Day 145: Tahmasian, Michael. "Interview: Becoming The Archetype." *Mind Equals Blown.net*, 19 Sept. 2012.

Day 152: Bonhoeffer, Dietrich. "37 Dietrich Bonhoeffer Quotes." *ChristianQuotes.info*.

Day 153: Spurgeon, Charles. "100 of the Best Charles Spurgeon Quotes." *Leadership Resources. org*, 22 Aug. 2014.

Day 154: Coles, Mike. "Interview with Eric Clayton of Saviour Machine." *Adkoi.com/theoutcast*, 28 Dec. 1998.

Day 155: A Kempis, Thomas. "Thomas a Kempis Quotes." *Brainyquote.com*.

Day 156: Metal Bible, Page 39. Comp. Jonsson, Johannes. *Bible for the Nations*.

Day 157: Metal Bible, Page 31. Comp. Jonsson, Johannes. *Bible for the Nations*.

Day 158: Kierkegaard, Soren. "Soren Kierkegaard Quotes." *Brainyquote.com*.

Day 159: Ambrose. "Ambrose Quotes." *A-Z Quotes.com*.

Day 160: Of Nassy, Gregory. "Gregory of Nassy Quotes." *A-Z Quotes.com*.

Day 161: Anthony the Great. "Anthony the Great Quotes." *A-Z Quotes.com*.

Day 162: Kierkegaard, Soren. "Soren Kierkegaard Quotes." *Brainyquote.com*.

Day 163: McCarthy, Michael. "Exclusive Interview: Michael Sweet Of Stryper." *Love Is Pop.com*, 2015.

Day 164: Bonhoeffer, Dietrich. "37 Dietrich Bonhoeffer Quotes." *ChristianQuotes.info*.

Day 166: Branson, Tim. "Korn Bassist Fieldy on the Christian Life." *CBN.com—The Christian Broadcasting Network*, 700 Club producer, 17 Sept. 2013.

Day 167: Swindoll, Charles R. "Top 10 Charles R. Swindoll quotes." *Brainyquote.com*.

Day 168: Narciso, Isaiah. "American Rock Star Legend Alice Cooper Opens Up about His Christian Faith." *The Gospel Herald.com*, 01 Jan. 2015.

Day 170: Tolkien, J.R.R. "The Letters of J.R.R. Tolkien Quotes." *Good Reads.com*.

Day 172: Kierkegaard, Soren. "Soren Kierkegaard Quotes." *Brainyquote.com*.

Day 173: Coles, Mike. "Interview with Tourniquet." *Adkoi.com/theoutcast*, 25 Jul. 1998.

Day 174: McCarthy, Michael. "Exclusive Interview: Michael Sweet Of Stryper." *Love Is Pop.com*, 2015.

Day 175: Metal Bible, Page 42. Comp. Jonsson, Johannes. *Bible for the Nations*.

Day 176: Mabee, Justin. "Impending Doom." *HM Magazine.com*, 6 Nov. 2013.

Day 177: Young, Kevin. "Forging Ahead: A Conversation With Disciple's Kevin Young, Part 2." *New Release Today.com*. Ed. Mary Nikkel.

Day 179: Narciso, Isaiah. "American Rock Star Legend Alice Cooper Opens Up about His Christian Faith." *The Gospel Herald.com*, 01 Jan. 2015.

Day 183: Metal Bible, Page 5. Comp. Jonsson, Johannes. *Bible for the Nations*.

Day 184: Metal Bible, Page 98. Comp. Jonsson, Johannes. *Bible for the Nations*.

Day 186: Coles, Mike. "Interview with Eric Clayton of Saviour Machine." *Adkoi.com/theoutcast*, 28 Dec. 1998.

Day 187: Spurgeon, Charles. "100 of the Best Charles Spurgeon Quotes." *Leadership Resources. org*, 22 Aug. 2014.

Day 189: Bonhoeffer, Dietrich. "37 Dietrich Bonhoeffer Quotes." *ChristianQuotes.info*.

Day 190: Metal Bible, Page 110. Comp. Jonsson, Johannes. *Bible for the Nations*.

Day 192: Metal Bible, Page 118. Comp. Jonsson, Johannes. *Bible for the Nations*.

Day 193: Metal Bible, Page 9. Comp. Jonsson, Johannes. *Bible for the Nations*.

Day 195: Ambrose. "Ambrose Quotes." *A-Z Quotes.com*.

Day 196: Costes, Judea. "INTERVIEW WITH RYAN CLARK OF DEMON HUNTER." *Rock Edition.com*, 13 Apr. 2012.

Day 197: Of Nassy, Gregory. "Gregory of Nassy Quotes." *A-Z Quotes.com*.

Day 199: Metal Bible, Page 43. Comp. Jonsson, Johannes. *Bible for the Nations*.

Day 200: Metal Bible, Pages 54 and 55. Comp. Jonsson, Johannes. *Bible for the Nations*.

Day 201: Montgomery, Mattie. "Interview: Mattie Montgomery of For Today." *The Moshville Times.co.uk*. Ed. MOSH, 22 Sept. 2015.

Day 202: Spurgeon, Charles. "100 of the Best Charles Spurgeon Quotes." *Leadership Resources. org*, 22 Aug. 2014.

Day 203: A Kempis, Thomas. "Thomas a Kempis Quotes." *Brainyquote.com*.

Day 204: Coles, Mike. "Interview with Eric Clayton of Saviour Machine." *Adkoi.com/theoutcast*, 28 Dec. 1998.

Day 205: Metal Bible, Page 55. Comp. Jonsson, Johannes. *Bible for the Nations*.

Day 206: Anthony the Great. "Anthony the Great Quotes." *A-Z Quotes.com*.

Day 207: Saint Ignatius. "Saint Ignatius Quotes." *Brainyquote.com*.

Day 208: Martyr, Justin. "Justin Martyr Quotes. "*A-Z Quotes.com*.

Day 209: Spurgeon, Charles. "100 of the Best Charles Spurgeon Quotes." *Leadership Resources. org*, 22 Aug. 2014.

Day 210: Coles, Mike. "Interview with Tourniquet." *Adkoi.com/theoutcast*, 25 Jul. 1998.

Day 211: James, Gary. "Robert Sweet Interview (Stryper)." *Famous Interview.ca*

Day 212: Metal Bible, Page 5. Comp. Jonsson, Johannes. *Bible for the Nations*.

Day 213: Metal Bible, Page 119. Comp. Jonsson, Johannes. *Bible for the Nations.*

Day 214: Martyr, Justin. "Justin Martyr Quotes. "*A-Z Quotes.com.*

Day 217: Narciso, Isaiah. "American Rock Star Legend Alice Cooper Opens Up about His Christian Faith." *The Gospel Herald.com*, 01 Jan. 2015.

Day 218: Ramanand, Liz. "W.A.S.P. Frontman Blackie Lawless Delves Deep Into His Faith + New Album 'Golgotha'." *Ultimate Classic Rock.com*, 26 Sept. 2015.

Day 220: Metal Bible, Page 98. Comp. Jonsson, Johannes. *Bible for the Nations.*

Day 222: Kosloski, Philip. "10 Inspiring Quotes from St. Athanasius." *Aleteia—Catholic Spirituality, Lifestyle, World News, and Culture.* Aleteia, 02 May 2016.

Day 224: Metal Bible, Page 32. Comp. Jonsson, Johannes. *Bible for the Nations.*

Day 226: Montgomery, Mattie. "Interview: Mattie Montgomery of For Today." *The Moshville Times.co.uk.* Ed. MOSH, 22 Sept. 2015.

Day 228: Spurgeon, Charles. "100 of the Best Charles Spurgeon Quotes." *Leadership Resources. org*, 22 Aug. 2014.

Day 229: Kosloski, Philip. "10 Inspiring Quotes from St. Athanasius." *Aleteia—Catholic Spirituality, Lifestyle, World News, and Culture.* Aleteia, 02 May 2016.

Day 230: Narciso, Isaiah. "American Rock Star Legend Alice Cooper Opens Up about His Christian Faith." *The Gospel Herald.com*, 01 Jan. 2015.

Day 231: Kierkegaard, Soren. "Soren Kierkegaard Quotes." *Brainyquote.com.*

Day 232: Spitz, Dan. "Former ANTHRAX Guitarist DAN SPITZ: 'Jesus Is The Reason I Still Breathe'." *blabbermouth.net.* Ed. Blabbermouth. , 02 Jan. 2013

Day 233: Bowen, Lincoln, and Steve Rowe. "An Interview With…Mortification." *Art for the Ears.nl.* Ed. MPO. 30 Jun. 1999.

Day 235: Branson, Tim. "Korn Bassist Fieldy on the Christian Life." *CBN.com—The Christian Broadcasting Network*, 700 Club producer, 17 Sept. 2013.

Day 236: Costes, Judea. "INTERVIEW WITH RYAN CLARK OF DEMON HUNTER." *Rock Edition.com*, 13 Apr. 2012.

Day 239: Sandoval, Pedro "Pete." "Former MORBID ANGEL Drummer PETE SANDOVAL: How 'I Fell In Love With God'." *Blabbermouth.net.* Ed. Andrew Haug., 26 Mar. 2015.

Day 240: M., Stephen. "Interview : Bruce Fitzhugh (Living Sacrifice)." *Indie Vision Music.com*, 08 Aug. 2009.

Day 242: Mabee, Justin. "Impending Doom." *HM Magazine.com*, 6 Nov. 2013.

Day 244: Ramanand, Liz. "W.A.S.P. Frontman Blackie Lawless Delves Deep Into His Faith + New Album 'Golgotha'." *Ultimate Classic Rock.com*, 26 Sept. 2015.

Day 245: Saint Ignatius. "Saint Ignatius Quotes." *Brainyquote.com.*

Day 246: Sweet, Robert. "Robert Sweet / Stryper." *Art for the Ears.nl.* Ed. MPO. 4 Sep. 2000.

Day 249: Montgomery, Mattie. "Interview: Mattie Montgomery of For Today." *The Moshville Times.co.uk.* Ed. MOSH, 22 Sept. 2015.

Day 253: Saint Basil. "Saint Basil Quotes*"A-Z Quotes.com*

Day 254: Metal Bible, Page 25. Comp. Jonsson, Johannes. *Bible for the Nations.*

Day 255: Bowen, Lincoln, and Steve Rowe. "An Interview With…Mortification." *Art for the Ears.nl.* Ed. MPO. 30 Jun. 1999.

Day 258: Leach, Jessie. "KILLSWITCH ENGAGE Singer JESSE LEACH Says 'Divine Intervention' Helped Him Beat Depression." *Blabbermouth.net,* Ed. Blabbermouth, 4 Nov. 2014.

Day 260: Metal Bible, Page 119. Comp. Jonsson, Johannes. *Bible for the Nations.*

Day 261: Kierkegaard, Soren. "Soren Kierkegaard Quotes." *Brainyquote.com.*

Day 262: Tragedy, Jeff. "Interview with Steve Whittaker, Drummer of Barren Cross." *Adkoi.com/ theoutcast.*, 22 Jan. 2008

Day 263: M., Stephen. "Interview : Bruce Fitzhugh (Living Sacrifice)." *Indie Vision Music.com*, 08 Aug. 2009.

Day 264: Metal Bible, Pages 32 and 33. Comp. Jonsson, Johannes. *Bible for the Nations.*

Day 265: Coles, Mike. "Interview with Tourniquet." *Adkoi.com/theoutcast*, 25 Jul. 1998.

Day 266: Of Nassy, Gregory. "Gregory of Nassy Quotes." *A-Z Quotes.com.*

Day 267: Branson, Tim. "Korn Bassist Fieldy on the Christian Life." *CBN.com—The Christian Broadcasting Network*, 700 Club producer, 17 Sept. 2013.

Day 268: Anthony the Great. "Anthony the Great Quotes." *A-Z Quotes.com.*

Day 270: Spurgeon, Charles. "100 of the Best Charles Spurgeon Quotes." *Leadership Resources. org*, 22 Aug. 2014.

Day 271: Ramanand, Liz. "W.A.S.P. Frontman Blackie Lawless Delves Deep Into His Faith + New Album 'Golgotha'." *Ultimate Classic Rock.com*, 26 Sept. 2015.

Day 272: Spitz, Dan. "Former ANTHRAX Guitarist DAN SPITZ: 'Jesus Is The Reason I Still Breathe'." *blabbermouth.net*. Ed. Blabbermouth. , 02 Jan. 2013

Day 275: A Kempis, Thomas. "Thomas a Kempis Quotes." *Brainyquote.com.*

Day 276: Van Pelt, Doug. "The Van Halen of Metal: Killswitch Engage Welcomes Back Jesse Leach. Now, They're New All over Again." *HM magazine.com*, 1 Apr. 2013.

Day 279: Of Nassy, Gregory. "Gregory of Nassy Quotes." *A-Z Quotes.com.*

Day 280: Koch, Simeon. "ELUVEITIE Parts Ways With Guitarist, Announces Replacement." *Blabbermouth.net.* Ed. Blabbermouth, 6 Sept. 2012.

Day 281: Kierkegaard, Soren. "Soren Kierkegaard Quotes." *Brainyquote.com.*

Day 282: Troyan, Greg. "Thomas Winkler of Gloryhammer Interview." *Sleaze Roxx.com*, 16 Oct. 2015

Day 283: Coles, Mike. "Interview with Tourniquet." *Adkoi.com/theoutcast*, 25 Jul. 1998.

Day 284: Beresford, Leah. „Interview: NORMA JEAN." *Blare Magazine.com*, 31 Aug. 2016.

Day 286: McCarthy, Michael. "Exclusive Interview: Michael Sweet Of Stryper." *Love Is Pop.com*, 2015.

Day 287: Vosseler, Andreas, and Daniel Frick. "Barren Cross Concert Review and Interview." *Eskapismus Konzertberichte—Wordpress*, 28 Mar. 2012.

Day 288: Anthony the Great. "Anthony the Great Quotes." *A-Z Quotes.com.*

Day 289: Smith, Mike. "Interview Frontman Bruce Fitzhugh Of Living Sacrifice Discusses New Album "Ghost Thief," Reflects On Past." *Metalunderground.com*, 11 Nov. 2013.

Day 291: Coles, Mike. "Interview with Tourniquet." *Adkoi.com/theoutcast*, 25 Jul. 1998.

Day 292: Hecox, Seth. "Interview : Seth Hecox (BTA) Interviews Jason Wisdom (Death Therapy)." *Indie Vision Music.com*, 14 Feb. 2017.

Day 293: Metal Bible, Page 33. Comp. Jonsson, Johannes. *Bible for the Nations.*

Day 294: Beresford, Leah. „Interview: NORMA JEAN." *Blare Magazine.com*, 31 Aug. 2016.

Day 295: Van Pelt, Doug. "The Van Halen of Metal: Killswitch Engage Welcomes Back Jesse Leach. Now, They're New All over Again." *HM magazine.com*, 1 Apr. 2013.

Day 296: Case, James "Uncle NecRo." "Interview: BLOODGOOD." *Confessions Of A Christian Freak. Wordpress*, 29 Oct. 2013.

Day 297: Tragedy, Jeff. "Interview with Steve Whittaker, Drummer of Barren Cross." *Adkoi.com/ theoutcast.*, 22 Jan. 2008

Day 298: Smith, Mike. "Interview Frontman Bruce Fitzhugh Of Living Sacrifice Discusses New Album "Ghost Thief," Reflects On Past." *Metalunderground.com*, 11 Nov. 2013.

Day 299: Coles, Mike. "Interview with Tourniquet." *Adkoi.com/theoutcast*, 25 Jul. 1998.

Day 300: Reeves, Brook. "Interview: Brook Reeves of Impending Doom." *Metalriot.com*. Ed. Longhairedpoet, 21 Oct. 2013.

Day 301: Of Nazianzus, Gregory. "Gregory of Nazianzus Quotes and Sayings." *inspiringquotes. us*. Page 3

Day 302: Grayson, and Adrian. "Josh Scogin of '68 Interview 5.5.2014." *SkullyServes.com*, 25 May 2014.

Day 304: Sandoval, Pedro "Pete." "Former MORBID ANGEL Drummer PETE SANDOVAL: How 'I Fell In Love With God'." *Blabbermouth.net*. Ed. Andrew Haug., 26 Mar. 2015.

Day 305: Metal Bible, Page 10. Comp. Jonsson, Johannes. *Bible for the Nations.*

Day 308: Spurgeon, Charles. "100 of the Best Charles Spurgeon Quotes." *Leadership Resources. org*, 22 Aug. 2014.

Day 309: Spurgeon, Charles. "100 of the Best Charles Spurgeon Quotes." *Leadership Resources. org*, 22 Aug. 2014.

Day 310: Coles, Mike. "Interview with Tourniquet." *Adkoi.com/theoutcast*, 25 Jul. 1998.

Day 312: Beresford, Leah. „Interview: NORMA JEAN." *Blare Magazine.com*, 31 Aug. 2016.

Day 313: Smith, Mike. "Interview Frontman Bruce Fitzhugh Of Living Sacrifice Discusses New Album "Ghost Thief," Reflects On Past." *Metalunderground.com*, 11 Nov. 2013.

Day 315: Case, James "Uncle NecRo." "Interview: BLOODGOOD." *Confessions Of A Christian Freak. Wordpress*, 29 Oct. 2013.

Day 316: Tragedy, Jeff. "Interview with Steve Whittaker, Drummer of Barren Cross." *Adkoi.com/theoutcast.*, 22 Jan. 2008

Day 317: Montgomery, Mattie. "Interview: Mattie Montgomery of For Today." *The Moshville Times.co.uk.* Ed. MOSH, 22 Sept. 2015.

Day 318: Van Pelt, Doug. "The Van Halen of Metal: Killswitch Engage Welcomes Back Jesse Leach. Now, They're New All over Again." *HM magazine.com,* 1 Apr. 2013.

Day 319: Case, James "Uncle NecRo." "Interview: BLOODGOOD." *Confessions Of A Christian Freak. Wordpress,* 29 Oct. 2013.

Day 321: Metal Bible, Page 34. Comp. Jonsson, Johannes. *Bible for the Nations.*

Day 322: A Kempis, Thomas. "Thomas a Kempis Quotes." *Brainyquote.com.*

Day 323: Reeves, Brook. "Interview: Brook Reeves of Impending Doom." *Metalriot.com.* Ed. Longhairedpoet, 21 Oct. 2013.

Day 324: A Kempis, Thomas. "Thomas a Kempis Quotes." *Brainyquote.com.*

Day 325: Spurgeon, Charles. "100 of the Best Charles Spurgeon Quotes." *Leadership Resources. org,* 22 Aug. 2014.

Day 327: Beresford, Leah. „Interview: NORMA JEAN." *Blare Magazine.com,* 31 Aug. 2016.

Day 328: Vosseler, Andreas, and Daniel Frick. "Barren Cross Concert Review and Interview." *Eskapismus Konzertberichte—Wordpress,* 28 Mar. 2012.

Day 329: Coles, Mike. "Interview with Tourniquet." *Adkoi.com/theoutcast,* 25 Jul. 1998.

Day 330: Smith, Mike. "Interview Frontman Bruce Fitzhugh Of Living Sacrifice Discusses New Album "Ghost Thief," Reflects On Past." *Metalunderground.com,* 11 Nov. 2013.

Day 331: Zwingli, Huldrych. "Huldrych Zwingli Quote: Our confidence in Christ does not…" *A-Z Quotes.com*

Day 333: Spitz, Dan. "Former ANTHRAX Guitarist DAN SPITZ: 'Jesus Is The Reason I Still Breathe'." *blabbermouth.net.* Ed. Blabbermouth. , 02 Jan. 2013

Day 334: Grayson, and Adrian. "Josh Scogin of '68 Interview 5.5.2014." *SkullyServes.com,* 25 May 2014.

Day 335: Christian Metal Fellowship. "Interview with Jayson Sherlock. " *Christianmetalfellowship.blogspot.se,* 15 Oct. 2009.

Day 337: Lewis, C.S. "Top 100 C.S. Lewis Quotes." *Deseretnews.com,* 27 Jan. 2012.

Day 338: Spitz, Dan. "Former ANTHRAX Guitarist DAN SPITZ: 'Jesus Is The Reason I Still Breathe'." *blabbermouth.net.* Ed. Blabbermouth. , 02 Jan. 2013

Day 339: Saint Ignatius. "Saint Ignatius Quotes." *Brainyquote.com.*

Day 342: Servant Life. "Missions Quotes." Servantlife.com.

Day 343: Anthony the Great. "Anthony the Great Quotes." *A-Z Quotes.com.*

Day 344: Sandoval, Pedro "Pete." "Former MORBID ANGEL Drummer PETE SANDOVAL: How 'I Fell In Love With God'." *Blabbermouth.net.* Ed. Andrew Haug., 26 Mar. 2015.

Day 346: Christian Metal Fellowship. "Interview with Jayson Sherlock. " *Christianmetalfellowship.blogspot.se*, 15 Oct. 2009.

Day 347: Hartmann, Graham. "Megadeth's Dave Mustaine: "I Have a Personnal Relationship with Christ but I Don't Believe in Religion."" *Loudwire.com*, 14 Sept. 2013.

Day 348: Metal Bible, Page 11. Comp. Jonsson, Johannes. *Bible for the Nations*.

Day 349: M., Stephen. "Interview : Bruce Fitzhugh (Living Sacrifice)." *Indie Vision Music.com*, 08 Aug. 2009.

Day 350: Lewis, C.S. "Top 100 C.S. Lewis Quotes." *Deseretnews.com*, 27 Jan. 2012.

Day 351: Saint Ignatius. "Saint Ignatius Quotes." *Brainyquote.com.*

Day 352: Grayson, and Adrian. "Josh Scogin of '68 Interview 5.5.2014." *SkullyServes.com*, 25 May 2014.

Day 353: Tolkien, J:R:R. "J :R :R : Tolkien Quotes." *Brainyquote.com.*

Day 354: Metal Bible, Page 34. Comp. Jonsson, Johannes. *Bible for the Nations*.

Day 355: Duncan, Ryan. "20 Wise Quotes from G.K. Chesterton." *Crosswalk.com*. Salem Web Network, 05 June 2015.

Day 356: Saint Ignatius. "Saint Ignatius Quotes." *Brainyquote.com.*

Day 357: Grassman, Jennifer. "THEOCRACY Vocalist Matt Smith—"We Definitely Share A Lot Of Fans With Bands Like BLIND GUARDIAN…"" *Bravewords.com*, 7 Dec. 2011.

Day 358: Chambers, Oswald. "18 Powerful Quotes from Oswald Chambers." *ChristianQuotes. info.*

Day 359: Aquinas, Thomas. "Thomas Aquinas quotes." *A-Z Quotes.com.*

Day 360: A Kempis, Thomas. "Thomas a Kempis Quotes." *Brainyquote.com.*

Day 361: Hartmann, Graham. "Megadeth's Dave Mustaine: "I Have a Personnal Relationship with Christ but I Don't Believe in Religion."" *Loudwire.com*, 14 Sept. 2013.

Day 362: Knox, John. "13 John Knox Quotes." *ChristianQuotes.info.*

Day 363: Jonsson, Johannes. "Theocracy: interview with the band's founder Matt Smith." *Metal for Jesus.org*

Day 364: Narciso, Isaiah. "American Rock Star Legend Alice Cooper Opens Up about His Christian Faith." *The Gospel Herald.com*, 01 Jan. 2015.

TOPICAL INDEX

Identity in Christ

Saved: 11, 16, 25, 29, 30, 36, 38, 49, 61, 67, 84, 90, 93, 101, 118, 137, 139, 141, 152, 165, 220, 259, 267, 271, 274, 277, 308, 331, 336, 340, 350

Welcoming Him into your life: 50, 114, 212, 295, 307, 339, 364

Growing as a Christian: 10, 14, 19, 26, 31, 34, 55, 76, 79, 109, 125, 128, 145, 149, 154, 167, 200, 227, 230, 235, 244, 245, 256, 260, 264, 282, 302, 319, 327, 347, 354, 358, 365

Joy: 24, 104, 129, 175, 282

Judging others: 38, 99, 146, 155, 190, 204, 222, 237, 264, 276, 286, 318, 362

Mission: 1, 7, 21, 23, 68, 71, 96, 103, 104, 111, 113, 150, 157, 162, 177, 187, 190, 191, 217, 226, 232, 243, 244, 263, 264, 265, 270, 278, 293, 313, 330, 334, 335, 342, 352, 362

Money, stuff, and giving: 33, 44, 46, 58, 102, 147, 159, 203, 205, 321, 323, 332, 345

Passion: 21, 51, 72, 92, 105, 108, 158, 210, 236, 240, 248, 281, 297, 304, 357

Peace: 73, 89, 180, 208, 211, 272, 293

Perseverance: 2, 8, 31, 162, 279, 293, 315, 344, 354

Prayer: 19, 43, 64, 69, 87, 91, 120, 123, 144, 181, 192, 269, 310, 311, 324

Pride: 22, 26, 41, 146, 151, 182, 221, 309

Rest: 62, 79, 126, 209

Sex: 45, 343

Sin: 25, 28, 31, 35, 45, 49, 50, 53, 54, 90, 134, 146, 151, 152, 179, 198, 201, 229, 242, 253, 287, 306, 323, 325, 336, 343, 360

Struggles: 18, 54, 89, 132, 168, 184, 199, 250, 260, 267, 330, 354

Suicide: 132, 169, 249, 303

Thankfulness: 159, 173, 186, 203, 268

Trust: 142, 210, 294

Unconditional love: 13, 17, 29, 37, 76, 97, 99, 124, 148, 163, 166, 204, 222, 266, 276, 294, 334

Wisdom: 64, 79, 102, 161, 167, 195, 220, 248, 346, 351, 361, 362

PASTOR BOB
ONLINE

HOME PAGE:
PastorBobBeeman.com

EMAIL:
PastorBobBeeman@gmail.com

INSTAGRAM:
instagram.com/PastorBobBeeman

YOUTUBE:
youtube.com/SanctuaryInternationalMatrix

FACEBOOK:
www.facebook.com/PastorBob

TWITTER:
twitter.com/PastorBobBeeman

SPOTIFY:
PastorBobBeeman

MERCHANDISE:
WeAreMetalWeAreFamily.com

HOMELESS MINISTRY:
SanctuaryHomelessRefuge.com

PAYPAL:
www.paypal.me/PastorBob

INTENSE RADIO:
IntenseRadio.com

70272128R00216